THE LONG RETREAT

The Calamitous American Defense of New Jersey 1776

The sick and half naked veterans
of the long retreat streamed past.
—Attributed to Charles Willson Peale, watching the
American retreat across the Delaware River, 1776

I shall not now attempt to give all the particulars
of our retreat to the Delaware; suffice it for the present
to say, that both officers and men, though greatly harassed
and fatigued, frequently without rest, covering, or provision,
the inevitable consequences of a long retreat,
bore it with a manly and a martial spirit.
—Thomas Paine, *The American Crisis—Number One*

D1221729

THE LONG RETREAT

The Calamitous American Defense of New Jersey 1776

ARTHUR S. LEFKOWITZ

Rutgers University Press
New Brunswick, New Jersey, and London

First published by The Upland Press,
Metuchen, New Jersey, 1998

Reprinted by Rutgers University Press,
New Brunswick, New Jersey, 1999

Library of Congress Cataloging-in-Publication Data
Lefkowitz, Arthur S.
The long retreat : the calamitous American defense of New Jersey,
1776 / Arthur S. Lefkowitz.
  p.   cm.
Originally published: Metuchen, N.J. : Upland Press, 1998.
Includes bibliographical references (p.   ) and index.
ISBN 0-8135-2759-7 (alk. paper)
1. New Jersey—History—Revolution, 1775–1783—Campaigns.
2. United States—History—Revolution, 1775–1783—Campaigns.
3. Washington, George, —1732–1799—Military leadership.   I. Title.
E263.N5L44   1999
973.3'32'09749—dc21   99-29035

Manufactured in the United States of America

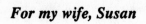

For my wife, Susan

CONTENTS

PREFACE

General Washington's whole army followed that night, and made a grand but dreadful appearance. All the shores where lighted up with large fires. The Boats continually passing and repassing full of men, Horses, artilery, and camp Equipage. The Hollowing of hundreds of men in their difficulties . . . made it rather the appearance of Hell than any earthly scene.[1]

--Charles Willson Peale on the escape of the rebel army
across the Delaware River, December 1776

"These are the times that try men's souls." That opening line of Thomas Paine's initial essay of *The Crisis* is one of the most famous in American literature. "The Summer soldier and the sunshine patriot," Paine went on, "will, in this crisis, shrink from the service of their country: but he that stands it now, deserves the love and thanks of man and woman."[2] When he conceived the words, Paine was trudging along the muddy roads of New Jersey with George Washington's bedraggled army. He began to write the essay when the retreating force stopped briefly at Newark, and tradition has it that a drum head served as his desk. It was a gloomy November 1776, and the pursuing British seemed within reach of overtaking Washington and crushing the Revolution in its infancy.

---

[1]Charles Willson Peale, "Autobiography," undated entry, manuscript volume, American Philosophical Society, Philadelphia.

[2]Thomas Paine, "The American Crisis # 1 [1776]," *Collected Writings* (New York: Library of America, 1995), 91-99.

Paine's ringing call to duty helped awaken the rebel consciousness and galvanize popular support for the faltering rebellion. But if the words were legendary, their source of inspiration has been less understood. The retreat of Washington's army through New Jersey, while clearly a significant episode, has remained relatively obscure, hidden under the smoke and thunder of the Revolution's more storied events.

In fact, the three-week retreat of the American army across New Jersey was a remarkable saga, an event marked by blunders and bravery, politics and treachery, desperation and resourcefulness. It began when the British invaded New Jersey on the night of November 19th, 1776 and continued until Washington escaped with his battered command across the Delaware River into Pennsylvania on December 4th. The troops involved never forgot those traumatic days. Years later, artist Charles Willson Peale, then on active duty, vividly recalled watching as "the sick and half naked veterans of the long retreat streamed past."[1] The retreat marked the military low point of the war; it was arguably the closest the British came to winning the eight-year conflict.

Yet for all of its importance, historians have devoted scant attention to the 1776 retreat. The classic general history of New Jersey in the Revolution is Leonard Lundin's *Cockpit of the American Revolution* (1940), which offers the most comprehensive view of military operations during the eventful weeks of November and December. Beyond Lundin's book, however, there are only a handful of studies dealing with the retreat in any detail.[2]

Thus, the present book is the first to focus exclusively on the retreat across New Jersey and to trace the story of the rebel ordeal in all of its dramatic detail. Relating the story in a single narrative is an important task in itself, for the tale has never had a full telling. A comprehensive view of the retreat certainly adds another dimension to our understanding of what happened prior to the critical Battles of Trenton and Princeton. In fact, as I

---

[1] This quote has long been attributed to Peale, although it does not appear in any of his published or unpublished works. Yet the sentiments are similar to Peale's other observations on the retreat found in his unpublished "Autobiography."

[2] Leonard Lundin, *Cockpit of the Revolution* (Princeton: Princeton University Press, 1940). There also are accounts of the retreat in William Stryker's's *The Battles of Trenton and Princeton* (Boston: Riverside Press, 1898); Samuel Smith's *The Battle of Trenton* (Monmouth Beach, NJ: Philip Freneau Press, 1965); *The Battle of Princeton* (Monmouth Beach, NJ: Philip Freneau Press, 1967); and William Dwyer's *The Day is Ours!* (New York: Viking Press, 1983).

will argue, the bitter retreat is best interpreted as an integral part of the events that saw the fortunes of war swing back toward the Americans in the stunning campaign of late 1776 and early 1777. To see this clearly, however, we need to concentrate on the course and nature of the retreat itself.

This view is at some variance with most accounts of the patriot crisis of late 1776. Most studies, and even many contemporary accounts, have depicted an American army on the verge of final defeat, and an exhausted Washington reduced to indecisiveness. Yet less than three weeks after fleeing across the Delaware, this same rebel army and general rebounded to sting the British at Trenton and Princeton; with a stroke, the ragged army restored flagging patriot morale. It was one of the most stunning feats in the history of American arms.

But was it really the story of a beaten army rising from the near-dead? In reality, this traditional view, however satisfying, is probably inconsistent with the facts. There were no dramatic circumstances or events which changed the American situation between the time Washington was chased out of New Jersey and his Christmas night counterattack at Trenton. If anything, Washington's situation had deteriorated after he reached Pennsylvania and he certainly had no chance to take a rest from the war.

In fact, historians have tended to overdramatize aspects of the New Jersey retreat. Intentionally or not, the effect has been to make accounts of Washington's Trenton-Princeton campaign more electrifying. In turn, this has obscured our ability to see in the retreat itself anything of the nature of the army and its operations, of Washington's maturing as a commander, or of other significant aspects of the patriot war effort. This account seeks a fuller and more balanced perspective on those three turbulent weeks in late 1776, and thus a better view of why the war ultimately developed as it did.

Over the years, balancing perspectives on the 1776 retreat has not been easy. The early American accounts tended to idolize the participants, emphasizing their tribulations and sacrifices. Almost uniformly, patriotic accounts told of stalwart soldiers, resolute in the face of redcoat bayonets and eager to follow Washington to the front. Only time tempered such views. With few exceptions, serious studies of the American Revolution emerged only in this century. It took 150 years for the participants and their direct descendants to die-off and for emotions to calm down enough for authors to look at the Revolution at least a bit more dispassionately.

My conclusion is that the era of the American Revolution, and especially those days of the retreat across New Jersey, was very much like our own. As today, we saw the full spectrum of human behavior, from dedication and sacrifice to avarice and deceit. In this account, I have tried to present a balanced narrative of men serving under terrible stress, with some rising to the occasion and others sinking beneath its weight. And, admittedly, something of the old aura of respect for the rebels remains. It is justified: readers will find much here to make them proud of those who marched west with General Washington in late 1776.

Researching the retreat, like any other major event in the American Revolution, presented special challenges. One problem lay in the fact that only a relative handful of common soldier's diaries have survived from the Revolutionary era.[1] Such diaries and journals have offered some of the most telling perspectives on everyday military life and great battles. Unfortunately, many common soldiers were illiterate, and often it was just too much trouble for a soldier to carry a journal. In any case, first-hand accounts of the "long retreat" as seen from the ranks are rare.

Troop strength presented another problem. The issue is critical to understanding the events of November and December 1776, but records are confusing, making it difficult to evaluate the most alarming accounts of the state of the rebel army as the retreat gathered momentum. In fact, things were probably as bad as many contemporary stories indicated, a conclusion I have drawn from the troop returns tabulated in Charles H. Lesser's *The Sinews of Independence* (1976). Lesser has gathered all of the known returns of the army, shedding a great deal of light on the size and composition of the American forces for each month of the Revolution. Based on a review of Lesser's data, my account presents the rebels as a quite debilitated force. Yet however badly off, the patriot military was still a force to reckon with, a fact the British forgot at their peril.

Then there was the problem of General Charles Lee. Lee was an eccentric former British officer and Washington's senior lieutenant during the New Jersey retreat. Understanding Lee is crucial to understanding the events of late 1776. He died before the end of the Revolution and never wrote an autobiography. A biography of him appeared in London as early as 1792 and the New York Historical Society published his correspondence from 1871 to 1874. The *Lee Papers* are the foundation of our knowledge about the man. In 1951, John Aden wrote the only modern biography of this complex general,

---

[1]For a listing of extant published diaries and similar accounts by enlisted men, see Howard Peckham, ed., *Memoirs of the Life of John Adlum in the Revolutionary War* (Chicago: The Caxton Club, 1968).

Charles Lee, Traitor or Patriot? Aden was a good historian, but Lee was such a complicated person that Aden was unsure what to make of him. Certainly he was not a traitor, although some historians (albeit not most professional historians) have claimed as much. But without finding him disloyal, my research has led me to think worse of Lee's conduct and character than have Alden and many other writers. Indeed, I believe his actions during the New Jersey retreat flirted with outright mutiny.

In addition to many other revealing accounts of the action in New Jersey, I was able to take advantage of a number of sources unavailable to previous historians of the retreat. Perhaps most helpful in this regard was the diary of Hessian Captain Johann Ewald, who served in America from 1776 to 1783. Ewald was in New Jersey in late 1776 and an active participant in the British efforts to catch-up with Washington's army.

Historians knew a little about Ewald's diary and snippets of it had been published during the nineteenth century. However, no one knew that Ewald's diary was intact until a German nobleman, ruined by World War II, offered to sell it to Major Joseph Tustin, a U.S. Air Force historian stationed in Germany at the end of the Second World War. Tustin, who was fluent in German, recognized the significance of the Ewald diary and purchased it. He spent the next twenty years tracking down a missing volume and translating and annotating the complete diary for publication. Ewald's *Diary of the American War* was published in 1979 by Yale University Press; it proved an essential source in the writing of *The Long Retreat*.

In quoting from portions of the Ewald diary, as well as other primary sources, I have followed modern convention and retained original grammar and spelling. In addition, I have extensively footnoted my text. The narrative is written so that anyone with a basic understanding of the American Revolution can follow the story; the footnotes are designed to give technical information and make my sources available to more serious students of the War for Independence.

A number of historians contributed their expertise and time to help me write this book. Several people were especially helpful and I am pleased to acknowledge their generous assistance. First is Lieutenant Colonel Donald Londahl-Smidt, a retired U.S. Air Force officer and expert on the role of the Hessians in the Revolution. Donald has me almost convinced that the Hessians who fought in America were British allies and not hired mercenaries. George Woodbridge, another outstanding historian and valued friend helped me with information about uniforms, flags and the military organization of the Revolutionary War armies. George did the cover art for this book, which is an example of his fine artistic and historical skills. Todd Braisted, who may know more about the Loyalists than anyone since Governor William Franklin, is another researcher who generously shared his knowledge with me. Finally, I want to give special thanks to Bergen County historian John Spring. John generously shared with me his considerable knowledge about the British army's entry into and march through Bergen County, and especially the legend of Polly Wyckoff.

I also want to acknowledge and thank William McMillen from Richmondtown Restoration, Staten Island. Bill helped me understand the road and ferry system in New York and New Jersey during the colonial period. John Muller, curator of the Fort Lee Museum, provided invaluable information about the British invasion of New Jersey; Kevin Wright, curator of the Stueben House in Bergen County, shared his knowledge of the Crown forces' assault on New Bridge; and Richard L. Porter, a cultural resource specialist with The RBA Group (a firm of engineers, architects and planners), generously briefed me on the events associated with Raritan Landing. John Mills, curator of the Thomas Clarke House at Princeton Battlefield State Park, shared his keen understanding of the campaigning in late 1776 and early 1777.

Another valued contributor was Charles Cummings, Assistant Director of the Newark Public Library and the official historian of Newark, New Jersey. I also wish to acknowledge help from Eric Olsen, chief historian at Morristown National Historic Park; William E. Davidson, Commanding Officer of a Revolutionary War reenactment group portraying Captain Alexander Hamilton's New York Artillery Company; John Rees, whose interests are the Revolutionary War exploits of General William Maxwell and Colonel Israel Shreve; Edward Ayres, historian at the Yorktown Victory Center in Yorktown, Virginia, who helped with information about Virginia troops in New Jersey in 1776. Mark Thompson, from the University of North Carolina, corresponded with me concerning Colonel Henry Knox. Also free with their valuable time and advice were Philander Chase, senior associate editor of the Revolutionary War Series of *The Papers of George Washington*; Harry Kels Swann, at Washington Crossing State Historic Park, New Jersey; Revolutionary War scholar Kemble Widmer; and the late Mrs. Chaire Tholl, a great lady and a fine Bergen County historian.

Research for this book was done at several libraries and I want to acknowledge their help and the wonderful service of their librarians: the Rutgers University Library Rare Book Collection; the Firestone Library at Princeton University; David Flowler and the David Library of the American Revolution at Washington Crossing, Pennsylvania; Ms. Joni Rowe, museum specialist at Morristown National Historical Park; Don Wilcox and David Bosse from the William L. Clements Library at the University of Michigan; Ms. Mariam Touba at the New York Historical Society; and, finally, the Library Company of Philadelphia, a grand institution for people like myself who suffer from bibliomania.

I am especially grateful to my wife, Susan, who patiently read chapter drafts and made valuable suggestions, and to whom I have dedicated this book.

Arthur S. Lefkowitz
Piscataway, New Jersey, 1998

ILLUSTRATIONS

Illustrations appear as a group following page 68.

INTRODUCTION

The 1776 campaign was every bit the perilous enterprise rooted in popular legend. Even the most scholarly accounts characterize the month between late November and late December 1776 as one of the most chaotic and desperate periods of the War for Independence. The shock of the debacle at Fort Washington was still fresh when Cornwallis struck on the New Jersey side of the Hudson River. The tactical surprise at Fort Lee, a near disaster in itself with major losses in stores, arms and equipment, threw the rebels almost completely off balance. Disorganized and unsure of the extent of the British thrust, and certainly unaware of its intentions, Washington's units had no alternative but to fall back into the interior of the state. The "long retreat," as soldier-artist Charles Willson Peale reportedly called it, was underway, and the fate of the Revolution itself was in the balance. The army traveled roads that led from Fort Lee and, finally, across the Delaware River near Trenton on December 7. Every step of the way, patriots in ranks, in Congress, and in state and local government worked frantically to keep Washington's army alive. Seldom, if ever, has the survival of the republic depended so directly on the fortunes of war and on the outcome of a single campaign.

If the story of the retreat was grim, however, it was also interesting. *In The Long Retreat,* Arthur Lefkowitz has offered a fresh and richly detailed new narrative of the rebel plight in all of its confusion and drama. But in looking below the familiar story of patriot despair and British prowess, Lefkowitz has made some telling new observations and added a number of helpful and novel perspectives on the winter campaign of late 1776. What emerges from the pages of *The Long Retreat* is an American war effort that, if no less battered and desperate than previous historians have had it, was arguably more resilient and resourceful than most earlier scholarship has allowed. As bad as things were, the rebel army always remained operational.

Perspective is the key to this book. Surprisingly, it is the first major study devoted solely to the 1776 retreat, and telling the story whole presents certain advantages. Among these were chances to set the record straight on a number of points, some of them basic. Matters such as American and British troop movements, for example, have been contentious issues for as long as historians have written about the retreat, and here receive a fresh and thorough review. Questions of which units went where, by exactly which routes, when, and why, are critical to understanding the campaign. Lefkowitz has sorted through the available evidence, much of it conflicting, and it appears that he has come as close as we will ever get to establishing a definitive itinerary for both armies over the months of November and December. This alone is a valuable contribution.

Troop movements, however, concerned more than just the comings and goings of the armies. The details were revealing. For example, in tracking the routes of Washington's men and the pursuing columns under Lord Cornwallis, Lefkowitz finally dispels any lingering questions over the pace of the retreat. It was no race to the Delaware. After the tactical surprise at Fort Lee, Washington was able to regroup and fall back in a more-or-less organized fashion. Cornwallis came after him, but only deliberately. The only *coup de main* came at For Lee itself, an operation that fully demonstrated the British capability to strike hard and fast when they wanted to. In fact, there was no repetition, or even an attempted repetition, of the dramatic opening blow at Hackensack, Newark, New Brunswick, or anywhere else along the route to Trenton. Why not? Why, and how, did the retreating patriot forces not only get away, but how did they do so in such a condition that they were able to counterattack within weeks after having abandoned New Jersey?

The heart of *The Long Retreat* is the author's attempt to answer these and similar questions.

Many of the explanations lay with operations of the British army. Indeed, Lefkowitz strenuously faults the British for allowing Washington to escape. He is at pains to note that Howe's initial plan did not envision a knock-out blow at Fort Lee, or even in its immediate aftermath somewhere in the New Jersey interior. The British general had wanted simply to fully secure the Hudson River; and if this limited objective was short on imagination, it was perhaps justified by Howe's scant knowledge of the situation west of the Hudson. But Howe showed little dash even after patriot distress became clear. When Cornwallis and other more aggressive officers urged a bolder course, the royal Commander-in-Chief finally agreed to push further into the state. Still, however, he warned his subordinates to avoid any unnecessary risks. There is no doubt that had Howe ordered it, Cornwallis could have caught Washington somewhere along the line of retreat. But the general, fully appraised of Washington's difficulties, never gave the order.

Nor did Howe bring his entire force to bear. Rather, in December he sent a major expedition against Rhode Island to secure Newport as a naval base. Some of his senior officers, including Henry Clinton, who commanded the six-thousand-man Newport operation, thought the move ill-advised. That many men, they pointed out, might have struck another blow through central New Jersey and linked up with Cornwallis in the interior. A move with any celerity at all could well have trapped Washington somewhere in the New Brunswick area. But Howe was not interested. He no longer saw the ragtag patriot army as a serious threat. Instead, he was content to let Cornwallis push the rebels toward the Delaware while he sought to encourage loyalist activity in the growing zone of British occupation. As a decisive military solution to the rebellion, the New Jersey campaign was an opportunity lost.

Subsequent events would reveal the folly of not making the destruction of Washington's army the primary objective in New Jersey. But British errors explained only part of the campaign. If Howe and other senior British commanders made mistakes, the same was true of the Americans. In fact, patriots frequently hurt themselves badly. Lefkowitz makes it clear that Washington and other patriot officers were guilty of miscues serious enough to invite their own destruction.

Like many previous authors, for example, Lefkowitz is highly critical of Washington's decisions regarding the defense of Fort Washington. After the loss of New York City, any post on the east bank of the Hudson was of dubious value to the rebel army. Washington could not readily support it from New Jersey, and its garrison, while still relatively large and well equipped, was not strong enough to pose an offensive threat to the British. It was only an inviting target, clearly at risk, and the rebels should have pulled out when they had the chance. Instead, at Washington's orders, they stayed.

In one of the better narratives of the affair, Lefkowitz carefully traces the Commander-in-Chief's efforts to deal with events leading up to the climactic action at Fort Washington on November 16. There is a cogent explanation of the initial decision to hang onto the tenuous fortification and then, at last, when it was too late, to evacuate the embattled garrison. Indeed, the description of the final debacle, as seen from Fort Lee on the New Jersey side of the Hudson River, is quite poignant. The author gives due notice to the often poor advice Washington received from other officers over the days leading up to the fiasco, but finds it impossible to acquit the general of virtually full responsibility for the result. It is a familiar story, but Lefkowitz's account, and his judgment, is stinging and very convincing.

The Fort Washington affair was in every sense a monumental blunder. The loss of over twenty-eight hundred troops and all of their weapons and equipment was grievous; the men and material would have come in handy in New Jersey. In addition, the defeat was a shattering blow to patriot morale, and planning for operations in New Jersey, from the very start, labored beneath an ominous and unpromising cloud. Crisis permeated the counsels of the rebel command. The door to Fort Lee and the interior of the state was open, and Washington seemed at a genuine loss as to how to respond. The crushing defeat on the east bank of the Hudson had bequeathed a problematic beginning to the defense of the west side of the river.

Fort Washington was not the Commander-in-Chief's only failure. Lefkowitz is equally critical of the general's handling of his principal subordinate, Major General Charles Lee. The author is honestly exasperated by Washington's Hamlet-like relationship with his second-in-command. The Commander-in-Chief had placed high hopes on Lee's ability to react promptly and forcefully in the event of a British invasion of New Jersey. This faith may have been misplaced. Any of Washington's initial expectations that Lee would quickly stem or substantially slow the invasion were unrealistic. Even so, Lee showed little inclination to move against Cornwallis or to join forces with his chief in the crucial first few days after the American debacle at Fort Lee. Granting allowances for prudence after the British assault, Lee still showed little subsequent inclination to join forces with the main rebel army under Washington. In Lefkowitz's view this dilatory conduct became increasingly questionable. Yet if Lee was balky, Washington was equally remiss in dealing with him.

The Commander-in-Chief never effectively asserted his control over Lee. Desperate for reinforcements, and wanting to consolidate his remaining forces, Washington was anxious for Lee to link up with the Grand Army as it moved toward Pennsylvania. He repeatedly sent couriers to Lee's column, imploring Lee to hasten his march. In return, he received evasive answers and excuses. The recalcitrant general evidently believed that he could do more for the rebel cause with an independent command, and perhaps find an opening against the British rear as they moved farther into the New Jersey interior. Or perhaps he wanted as little as possible to do with a commander whose abilities he now questioned and whose fortunes seemed to be in eclipse. At some point, however, it should have become clear that, whatever his motives, Lee was not about to comply with pleas to join the rest of the army with any degree of energy or approval. Still, Washington never issued a preemptory order to force the issue; nor, apparently, did he ever consider relieving Lee in favor of a more obedient officer.

It is impossible to fully explain the situation. Lefkowitz has done as much as anyone to review the available evidence, and ends up wondering whether the Commander-in-Chief remained, in spite of everything, a bit awed by Lee's experience and reputation as a soldier. Perhaps. An alternative view might hold that Washington simply had problems enough just holding his army together; forcing the issue with Lee, and certainly relieving him, would have brought additional turmoil to the patriot command at the worst conceivable time. Whatever the source of his hesitancy, however, the daring British capture of Lee took Washington off the hook. John Sullivan, who succeeded to Lee's command, moved quickly to join the main army, and an embarrassing and possibly dangerous situation became moot. Even so, it reflected poorly on Washington's performance as a commander.

It also spoke poorly of Lee. While never raising the hoary old questions about treachery or Lee's actual loyalty to Washington or the Revolution, Lefkowitz has little patience with the man. He concedes that Lee was an extraordinary fellow. Brave, intelligent, energetic, experienced, and undeniably talented, he served the rebel cause well in the early months of the war. Yet he was also possessed of a high opinion of himself and a penchant for intrigue and sarcasm, and these character flaws ultimately limited his value as a senior officer. In the crisis of 1776, the human element mattered; to function effectively in adversity, the rebel commanding officers needed to see eye-to-eye. Yet relations between the two senior patriot officers frayed badly, and Lefkowitz lays the blame squarely on General Lee. The author clearly implies that his capture was no loss to the rebels (even if many of them saw things differently at the time); and, harsh as it may be, it is a reasonable assessment of the Lee affair.

Other patriot failings were not the fault of the Commander-in-Chief, but they were nevertheless important and had a grave impact on the rebel war effort. The lack of experienced staff officers, for example, told heavily on the Americans. The details of moving an army made extended marches demanding exercises under the best of circumstances, and the 1776 retreat was anything but that: there were ammunition to distribute, reinforcements to rally, wagons and horses to arrange, food and forage to bring to the troops and their draft animals, and all manner of supplies to secure. Washington and his senior subordinates generally did the work themselves, and they kept the army supplied and moving. Yet they could not match the logistical skills of their British counterparts, and, at least in Washington's case, performed these functions only at the expense of operational concerns. The retreat was a grim test of the ingenuity and staying power of the young army; and in the pinch, frantic improvisation substituted for professional skills. But the very ability of the rebel army to get by in such fashion was a constant reminder of its amateur military status.

The Long Retreat, however, is at its best when looking beyond the mistakes of generals, British or American, or the shortcomings of Washington's young army. The rebels survived the campaign, and were in a position to counterattack, Lefkowitz argues, not only because of British blunders, but also because of steps taken on their own behalf. More than most other writers, the author credits patriots with orchestrating their own revival as 1776 drew to a close.

The first point to make in this regard was the state of the rebel army during the New Jersey campaign. It was in sorry condition: enlistments were running out, desertions increased, equipment losses were serious, and the enemy had the initiative. Yet the patriot ranks never broke. Washington and others called on every available resource, and in the end, they did so effectively. There was always just enough transport, ammunition, food, forage, and weapons; there remained an effective artillery arm; and, after the initial shock of invasion had worn off, a small but steady stream of reinforcements moved toward the retreating column. Units remained intact, even if thin. In short, patriot efforts kept their battered force operational. It was a retreating army, not a fleeing mob.

Washington also kept in touch with events beyond his immediate front. Even as he struggled to keep the main army alive, for instance, he acted prudently and decisively in providing command arrangements for patriot forces in Morris County (which would pay huge dividends in early 1777). He also maintained communications with Congress, state political leaders, and local officials, which gave him a fairly realistic view of popular opinion, militia activities, and intelligence on areas from which he could draw logistical support and reinforcements. With the exception of Lee, he worked reasonably well with his senior officers in efforts to concentrate scattered rebel troop formations and to rebuild the semblance of an effective Grand Army. In all of this, the Commander-in-Chief drove himself and his subordinates hard, but he produced results.

Significantly, Washington's aim was not purely defensive. Lefkowitz makes clear the general's desire to stabilize his own forces, and then find an opening for a counterattack. Certainly by the time he reached New Brunswick (November 29) he was looking for a chance to hit back, if only in some limited way. A success, no matter how small, would buy time for patriot forces to resupply and reinforce, keep Howe and Cornwallis off balance, and restore rebel morale. Still in retreat, Washington would fight if he could.

For those who looked carefully, there were signs that the battered rebels still had some fight left in them. At New Brunswick, Alexander Hamilton's artillery duelled gamely with the British across the Raritan River. Shortly thereafter, having marched through Princeton and on to Trenton, the Commander-in-Chief secured the safety of his baggage on the west bank of the Delaware and received encouraging word of reinforcements mobilizing in Pennsylvania. It was enough to tempt him to turn and fight. On December 6, he marched back to Princeton with some twelve hundred men, hoping to find an opportunity. He returned to Trenton and crossed to Pennsylvania only after learning that Cornwallis was moving from New Brunswick with a superior force. Frustrated for the moment, and understanding the seriousness of his army's condition, Washington's outlook nevertheless was not that of a beaten man.

When it came, the patriot counterattack at Trenton was a direct extension of the same impulse to strike back. The army that fought the Trenton-Princeton campaign, as Lefkowitz is at pains to point out, was not appreciably stronger than the force that had retreated across the Delaware. Bruised and staggered, it still had survived its ordeal in such condition as to allow a quick recovery. The period of rest, reinforcement, and reorganization in Pennsylvania was enough to allow Washington to seize the initiative; he struck the limited but telling blow he had sought to deliver at least since his brief stay in New Brunswick.

The results were all he could have wanted: Howe was profoundly embarrassed and the illusion of his army's invincibility shattered; subsequent British winter deployments returned most of central New Jersey to rebel hands; and the impact on patriot morale was electric. Really no more than minor fights--Trenton was a raid and Princeton a meeting engagement--the affrays of late 1776 and early 1777 yielded truly strategic rewards.

The author's assessment of the entire business seems sensible indeed. The retreat had been a rout only briefly. Washington's successful efforts to restore order and get his army across New Jersey spoke well of his ability to function under extreme pressure and to get the most out of his depleted resources. In the end, it is difficult to argue with Lefkowitz's conclusion that Washington did better with the men and material available to him than General

Howe did with his vastly superior resources.   Howe also made the mistake of complacency, reflected so clearly in his faulty winter quarters deployments. Whatever mistakes Washington made, complacency was not among them, and throughout the retreat, carelessness never contributed to the woes of his army.

There was a final lesson in *The Long Retreat*: The wise general will ruthlessly finish off even the most seemingly enfeebled enemy. Given a respite, competent leadership, and at least a minimal resource base, even a grievously wounded army can rise and fight again. Washington understood the point and redeemed a campaign and a revolution; Howe missed it and lost a war and much of an empire.

Mark Edward Lender
Kean University, 1998

CHAPTER ONE

Prelude to Invasion

To place any dependance upon Militia, is, assuredly, resting upon a broken staff.
—George Washington to John Hancock,
September 24, 1776

In March 1776, patriot fortunes in the War for American Independence were at high tide. After sustaining a siege of almost a year, the British army hastily abandoned the city of Boston. On March 17, they boarded warships and transports in Boston harbor and set sail for the Royal Navy base at Halifax, Nova Scotia. The evacuation was a galling retreat for the King's troops, and the news sent patriots cheering into the streets of the rebellious Thirteen Colonies while British sympathizers drew their curtains and waited.

The amateur army under George Washington had effectively besieged Boston. Washington's adversary, General William Howe, fully understood that offensive operations against the well-entrenched rebels would be costly, if even possible, and that New England was a hot-bed of patriot support. If he was to regain the initiative, he needed to regroup and reinforce his army, and then resume the offensive and crush the upstart Americans on ground of his own choosing.

General Howe's departure from Boston left the colonies completely in rebel hands, and patriot optimists, some of whom had stayed on the lines since the fighting at Lexington and Concord the year before, could be excused for thinking that the War for Independence was in its final stages.

George Washington's assessment was more sober. He had reason enough to be pleased with the successful operations at Boston, but he fully understood that the British had retreated only to reorganize, await reinforcements, and counterattack on a new front. The patriot commander was even sure he knew where they would strike. It would be to the South, at New York City.

A British initiative at New York made solid military sense. With a population of 22,000, New York was the second largest city in America; only Philadelphia, with 34,000, was larger. The city had a history as a British military base by the outbreak of the American Revolution. The British used it as their headquarters during the French and Indian War, and it had remained so until the shift to Boston shortly before the start of the Revolution. New York had an excellent harbor, which was free of ice in the winter, and had ample docks, ship repair facilities, warehouses and buildings which could be commandeered for the use of the military if necessary. The city also had a strategic location. Its position on the Hudson River was the key to communications and trade with New England and Canada; land routes to the interior lay across the river in New Jersey; and shipping from New York had relatively easy routes to the south. In addition, New York was a pleasant, tolerant city. It offered many diversions and a lively social life for officers and soldiers alike. Certainly the occupation of New York would offer the British better prospects than any attempt to recapture Boston.

The importance of New York City to the British was obvious to Washington even before Howe's evacuation of Boston. Thus, as he fenced with the redcoats in Massachusetts, his thoughts turned south and to how he might keep the great port on the Hudson in rebel hands. Unable to leave the Boston front himself, Washington ordered the army's most experienced officer, Major General Charles Lee, to go to New York and to take a look at the situation. Lee faced an arduous task, but he was the best man for the job, and he would play a major role in the subsequent events of 1776. His mission was one of the first key American steps in preparing for what both sides saw as the crucial showdown of the war. The army that emerged victorious at New York could well claim the final victory.

The man of the hour was Major General Charles Lee. In fact, Lee was one of the most extraordinary officers in the American army. Born in England in 1732, he was the son of a British colonel. He was the youngest of seven children, but only he and a sister, to whom he remained closely attached, survived to adulthood. Commissioned into his father's regiment as early as eleven years old, he was carried on the army roster while attending school. His education was extensive for the day. He studied in Switzerland and probably in France, and he emerged a well-read young man fluent in French and conversant in German, Italian, and Latin. Books were his constant companion throughout his life, and he enjoyed lacing his witty and often engaging letters and conversations with quotations from the classics. By any measure, he was one of the best educated and most intellectually accomplished men in Washington's army.

He was also a considerable soldier. By 1750, when his father died, and when he was eighteen, Lee began his active-duty career. In 1755, he came to America when fighting broke out between Britain and France, and he served on the ill-fated Braddock Expedition. During the march into western Pennsylvania, Lee met George Washington, then a colonel of Virginia militia. Like Washington, he survived the disaster, which saw the French and their Indian allies decimate the British column in the vicinity of what is now Pittsburgh. He served with distinction through the rest of the French and Indian War, including some hard fighting in northern New York, and in 1760 returned, as a captain, to England. Promoted to major the following year, he fought with great credit in Portugal, where he served until the war ended in 1763. He then went on half-pay when his regiment disbanded. By that time, Major Lee was a hardened veteran.

Without prospects for further glory or advancement with the British, Lee became a soldier of fortune in the Polish army. Poland was dominated by Russia, and Empress Catherine the Great had installed her Polish lover, Stanislaus Poniatowski, as King of Poland. Lee became an intimate of the puppet king and eventually rose to major general. His adventures included accompanying a Turkish army to Constantinople in 1766, during which his health suffered, several years recovering while roaming through Europe, fighting duels, and serving with the Russian army. In 1770, Lee returned to England, and although promoted to lieutenant colonel in 1772, the small peacetime British army offered him little hope for further advancement. Bored, he devoted himself to horses, politics, and land speculation in America.

In fact, politics became a serious interest, as Lee had developed some radical sympathies. He had come to hate monarchies. Perhaps he had seen the common people of eastern Europe suffering at the hands of tyrannical kings. But Lee especially came to despise George III, who had failed to fulfill promises to advance his career. As early as 1766, when the American colonies resisted the Stamp Act, Lee's anger was evident. "May God prosper the Americans in their resolutions," he wrote to his sister from Constantinople, "that there may be one Asylum at least on the earth for men, who prefer their natural rights to the fantastical prerogative of a foolish, perverted head because it wears a Crown."[1]

The growing political unrest in America suited Charles Lee's restless temperament and radical politics perfectly. In 1773, Lee returned to America after an absence of twelve years. Although his stated intention was to advance his land speculations, he promptly leaped into colonial politics, and his broad knowledge and military reputation gained him introduction to the most powerful men in America. Many of them, including his fellow survivor from the Braddock Expedition of 1755, Colonel George Washington, were spellbound by Lee's stories of his military adventures. Lee had lived the dashing military life that Washington had dreamed of as a boy. Citing the example of the Polish partisans, who waged *"la petite guerre"* against conventional European armies, Lee endlessly argued that the American colonists could defeat British regulars.[2] He became known in America as a military expert and a true friend of liberty.

Lee's first years back in America, from 1773 to 1775, were probably the happiest years of his life. Well regarded by a wide circle of acquaintances, reactions to him varied. At forty-three years old, few thought he was much to look at, for Lee was tall and skinny, with a large nose and small hands and feet. He was unmarried, although he had taken a Mohawk mistress during the

---

[1]Lee to Sidney Lee, March 1, 1766, *The Lee Papers* (New York: The New York Historical Society, 1871), I: 42-43.

[2]Guerrilla warfare was not an eighteenth-century term; irregular operations were called *"partisan warfare"* or *"petite-guerre"* at the time of the American Revolution. A military dictionary published in London in 1779 defined the terms: "Petite-Guerre, is carried on by a light party, commanded by an expert partisan, and which should be from 1000 to 2000 men; separated from the army, to secure the camp or a march; to reconnoitre the enemy or the country, to seize their posts, convoys, and escorts; to plant ambuscades, and to put in practice every stratagem for surprising or disturbing the enemy." George Smith, *An Universal Military Dictionary* (London: J. Milian, 1779), 202, reprint by Museum Restoration Service (Ottawa, Canada, 1969). Smith defined a partisan as "a person dexterous in commanding a party, who, knowing the country well, is employed in getting intelligence, or surprising the enemy's convoy, &c. The word also means an officer sent out upon a party, with the command of a body of light troops, generally under the appellation of the partisan's corps" (*An Universal Military Dictionary*, 199). Call it guerrilla warfare, petite-guerre or partisan warfare, it existed during the colonial wars and during the War for American Independence, with Lee as one of its exponents.

French & Indian War, with whom he had twin boys. Lee left her when his regiment moved on and he never saw her or his children again. He seemed incapable of a sustained romance with any woman, although some later thought him a libertine, and there are some hints in his correspondence that he may have been homosexual.[1] He had a moderate income from inheritances and was a man of modest tastes. Over the years his manners deteriorated, and although he could be a perfect gentlemen when he wanted, he was more commonly vulgar, sloppy and rude. He developed a strange passion for dogs and a troop of them followed him everywhere; Lee once quipped that he preferred the company of dogs to that of men. He was an egotist, a man of extreme moods and tempers. His new intimate in America, Colonel George Washington, politely called him "fickle," although others were less diplomatic. The powerful William Schuyler of New York thought Lee a sloppy and unwashed eccentric. John Adams, with no small ego himself, thought Lee the only man in America who knew more than he did about military affairs. He described him privately as "a queer creature. But you must love his dogs if you love him and forgive a thousand whims for the sake of the soldier and the scholar."[2] The perceptive Mercy Otis Warren, one of the most acute observers of the American scene, found Lee "plain in his person even to ugliness, and careless in his manners to a degree of rudeness. He possessed a bold genius and an unconquerable spirit: his voice was rough, his garb ordinary, his deportment morose. . .he was frequently agreeable in narration, and judicious and entertaining in observation."[3] Yet however they found him, Americans

---

[1]John W. Shy, "Charles Lee: The Soldier as Radical," in George Billias, ed., *George Washington's Generals* (New York: William Morrow and Company, 1964), 23.

[2]Billias, ed., *George Washington's Generals*, 23; James Flexner, *George Washington in the American Revolution* (New York: Little, Brown & Co., 1967), 23; Adams quoted in John Alden, *General Charles Lee* (Baton Rouge: Louisiana State University Press, 1955), 77.

[3]Mercy Otis Warren, *The History of the Rise, Progress and Termination of the American Revolution* (Boston, 1805), I: 292. Warren was the wife of the Governor of Massachusetts during the war; her history of the American Revolution was one of the first books to be authored by an American woman. Even earlier, however, another woman, Hannah Adams, dealt with the Revolution in her *A Summary History of New England. . .Comprehending a General Sketch of the American War* (Dedham, MA: H. Mann and J.H. Adams, 1799). Clergyman and historian Jeremy Belknap also left a vivid description of Charles Lee. Belknap found Lee, "a perfect original, a good scholar and soldier, and an odd genius; full of fire and passion, and but little good manners; a great sloven, wretchedly profane, and a great admirer of dogs." Quoted in Richard Ketchum, *The Winter Soldiers* (Garden City, NY:

thought more of Charles Lee than the British ever did. Certainly the more radical members of the Continental Congress, including John Adams and Benjamin Rush, admired him immensely.

At the outbreak of the Revolution, Lee's reputation was such that some Americans seriously considered him for Commander-in-Chief of the rebel army. But his English birth and the need to make political appointments precluded any chance he had for the top spot. The command went to Washington, the well-known and distinguished Virginian, while Artemus Ward of Massachusetts became second in command. Ward was elderly for a soldier, and few had much confidence in his military skills, but he was popular with patriots in New England and his appointment gave the army a necessary political balance. Lee, with the rank of major general, became the third highest ranking officer in the rebel army; it was a post of real significance, and as one of the few American officers with extensive military experience, patriots expected much of him.

Following his appointment to the Continental Army, Lee resigned his commission in the British army. He also insisted on a large compensation from the rebel Congress for the inevitable confiscation of his property in England where he would be declared a traitor. He then accompanied General Washington from Philadelphia to the seige at Boston. Washington was happy to have his eccentric but brilliant English friend at his side; as the war progressed, the commanding general was confirmed in his belief that Lee was an exceptional officer.

Ordered by Washington to prepare a defense of New York City, Lee left Boston in mid-January 1776. He arrived on February 14, bringing with him some zealous Connecticut militia recruited en route to help deal with New York Loyalists. Lee realized that the area around the city, with its waterways and islands, offered an almost endless combination of sea approaches and landing places. "What to do with the city puzzles me," he quickly wrote to Washington. "It is so encircled with deep navigable water that whoever commands the sea must command the town."[1] Lee expected a powerful Royal naval squadron to support any British invasion; but the Americans had no navy and faced the dangerous prospect of having to mount a static defense against an enemy which enjoyed every advantage. Yet Washington's determination to defend New York City was fixed; it was as much a political

---

Doubleday & Co., 1973), 200.

[1]*Lee Papers*, I: 309.

as a military decision. The Continental Congress wanted the city held and Washington felt obliged to carry out the wishes of his fellow delegates.

Lee began fortifying New York in late February, but within a few weeks he received a new assignment. The Continental Congress ordered him to go to South Carolina to help organize the defense of Charleston. Because of its milder winters, Charleston was under more immediate threat of attack than New York. Lee would do yeoman work in the South—in fact, he was instrumental in turning back a strong British assault in the spring of 1776—and his influence left its mark on New York's defenses. Soon after the British evacuated Boston, Washington started for New York with the rebel army. He arrived with the vanguard on April 13 and quickly put his soldiers to work on Lee's defensive plan. Lee's scheme called for extensive fortifications on the western tip of Long Island (modern Brooklyn) and Manhattan plus a gun battery on the New Jersey side of the Hudson River at Paulus Hook (today's Jersey City). Work went forward quickly, and the patriots had acted not a moment too soon.

In the midst of American preparations, the first British warships appeared in the waters off New York on June 25. Additional men-of-war and transports arrived and anchored off Staten Island in such numbers that, to some American defenders, their masts looked like a floating forest. On July 2, General William Howe landed his army unopposed on Staten Island.

The appearance of 25,000 British and Hessian troops among a Staten Island civilian population of 3,000 fueled Loyalists sentiments. On July 6, Howe gathered the local population to sign an oath of allegiance to the crown. A few days later, the Staten Island militia assembled at Richmondtown and were reviewed by Howe. They were estimated at 200 men and commanded by Colonel Christopher Billop, the island's largest landowner. The militia offered their services to General Howe who gratefully accepted. Throughout the summer of 1776, Howe continued to assemble his army on Staten Island. He proved to be a cautious and meticulous planner, and the unexpected lull was a blessing for the rebels, giving them additional time to prepare their defenses.[1]

---

[1] "Loyalist" or "Tory" were the terms used during the Revolution to describe Americans who remained loyal to England. Washington denounced them as "Unhappy wretches! Deluded mortals!" The Loyalists were as patriotic as the rebels, they just happened to be on the losing side. A popular rebel definition of a Loyalist (Tory) was "a thing whose head is in England, and its body in America, and its neck ought to be stretched." The Loyalist movement was widespread, and their numbers may have been up to one-third of the 2.2 million

In fact, Washington needed all of the time he could get. By the end of July, he had assembled an army of 12,333 officers and men to defend New York City and Brooklyn. An additional 3,677 rebel troops were stationed nearby in New Jersey under the command of General Hugh Mercer.[1] The number looked impressive, but the Army of the United Colonies consisted of untested Continentals and short term militia.[2] They were poorly armed and equipped, lacked cavalry, had no naval support, and were led by officers still learning their business.

Fortunately, some of the rebel officers displayed exceptional talent. In addition to Lee, there was Colonel Henry Knox, the talented and self-taught chief of artillery, as well as General Nathanael Greene. Only thirty-four when the war began, Greene was the son of a prominent Rhode Island family. Ambitious and headstrong, he was heavily built with graying hair and walked with a limp caused by a stiff right knee. Without previous military experience,

---

population of America, making the American Revolution as much a civil war as it was a war for independence. Probably some 50,000 Americans bore arms for the King during the Revolution as Loyalist militia, Provincials, or in the regular British army and navy.

[1]Charles H. Lesser, ed., *The Sinews of Independence, Monthly Strength Reports of the Continental Army* (Chicago, The University of Chicago Press: 1976), 26-28. The figures used are the "Present Fit for Duty & On Duty" and exclude the "Rank and File Sick, On Forlough, etc." There were other American forces in addition to those in and around New York City. There were 3,155 officers and men in South Carolina and 8,071 at Fort Ticonderoga and Skenesborough (present Whitehall), New York. The troops in upstate New York, "The Northern Department," were commanded at the time by General Horatio Gates.

[2]The term "American Army" at the time of the Revolution is a term of convenience. In reality, the rebels fought with a force composed of Continentals, State Troops, or militia. In June 1775, the Continental Congress authorized 60 regiments to be raised at the expense of the states. These regiments were known as the Continental Army (or Continental Line), which became the backbone of the rebel forces. Troops of the Continental Line initially agreed to serve for one year. The Continentals were under Washington's command, but from time to time, either Washington or the Congress ordered Continental regiments to support other American operations beyond Washington's direct control. In addition to raising Continental regiments, each state could enlist State Troops or "State Regiments." Such troops were under the control of the state governments and were generally raised for three to six months and used for home defense. They were often recruited from the militia, but were legally distinct. The militia were composed, in principle, of all eligible able-bodied men who were organized into local companies for emergency or limited service. The troops under General Washington's immediate command, be they Continentals, State Troops, or militia (and there was usually a combination of forces) were sometimes identified as "the Grand Army."

Greene nevertheless was a splendid organizer whose talents soon brought him to Washington's attention. By August 1776, the Rhode Islander was a major general and one of the Commander-in-Chief's closest advisors. But a few capable men could not substitute for a veteran staff or competent support services, a fact that bitter experience would soon drive home.[1]

Just how unready the Americans were quickly became apparent. On August 21, the patriot *Constitutional Gazette* of New York reported that "for some days past, the British army on Staten Island, have been embarking on board the transports; so that we expect their whole force before this city every tide. We hope to give them a reception, worthy of the free born sons of America, and may every freeman of America make this his Toast, That New York is now an asylum for American Liberty." It was not to be.

The following day British troops landed unopposed on the western tip of Long Island (modern Brooklyn), and a few days later Howe ordered a column of Hessians down the Flatbush Road to probe the American defenses. The move was only a feint. While the Hessians occupied the Americans at the Flatbush Road, a second column composed of British troops marched undetected further onto Long Island during the night of August 26-27 and outflanked the American defenses. Washington had no cavalry to patrol his exposed right, and British flanking troops got behind the American defenders in Brooklyn. Upon hearing the sound of gunfire to their right, the Hessians at the Flatbush Pass pressed their attack. The ensuing Battle of Long Island was

---

[1]Washington had no cavalry at this stage of the Revolution. Historians have pointed out that a company of horsemen from Connecticut arrived in the American camp during the spring of 1776, but Washington turned them away. Some historians claim that Washington refused the services of cavalry because he had no experience in how to use them. But Washington actually turned the horsemen away because they were more trouble than they were worth. According to Alexander Graydon, who witnessed the incident, the Commander-in-Chief had no real choice in the matter. "Among the military phenomena of this campaign," he recalled, "the Connecticut light horse ought not to be forgotten. These consisted of a considerable number of old fashioned men, probably farmers and heads of families, as they were generally middle aged, and many of them apparently beyond the meridian of life. They were truly irregulars; and whether their clothing, their equipments or caparisons were regarded, it would have been difficult to have discovered any circumstance of uniformity....Instead of carbines and sabers, they generally carried fowling pieces ; some of them very long, and such as in Pennsylvania, are used for shooting ducks. Here and there, one, 'his youthful garments, well saved,' appeared in a dingy regimental of scarlet, with a triangular, tarnished, laced hat." Graydon says that one of these horsemen was captured by the British, and "on being asked, what had been his duty in the rebel army, he answered, that it was to flank a little and carry tidings." John Stockton Littell, ed., *Memoirs of His Own Time...by Alexander Graydon* (Philadelphia: Lindsay & Blakiston, 1846, orig. 1811), 155-156.

a disaster for Washington, who was lucky to get his beaten command across the East River to Manhattan Island.

New York City was in chaos as frightened civilians fled the city in the midst of frantic military activity to defend the place. An English traveler who arrived in New York in the turmoil left a vivid account of conditions there: "Landed in New York about nine o'clock," he recalled, "when one Collins, an Irish merchant, and myself rambled about the town till three in the afternoon before we could get anything for breakfast." They finally got "a little Dutch tippling house" to serve them an almost unpalatable stew, but in general there was "nothing to be got here. All the inhabitants are moved out. The town is full of soldiers."[1]

The British were elated with their victory on Long Island, and many of them wanted to strike again quickly before Washington could regain his balance. But Howe waited almost a month following the battle before taking further offensive action against the rebels, probably hoping to bring them to terms without further combat. The general and his older brother, Admiral Lord Richard Howe, had been empowered as peace commissioners by the British government, with the authority to offer the colonists most of what they wanted short of independence.[2] The Howes were sympathetic towards the colonists and may have hoped to end the war through negotiation and return to England as heroes. Congress was willing to talk, but negotiations ultimately broke down in mid-September over the issue of independence.

Meanwhile, the unexpected but welcomed lull in the fighting gave George Washington valuable time to reorganize and decide what to do next. Realizing that any further defense of New York City was doomed, the rebel chief used the time to move his sick and wounded out of harm's way, along with some of the army's baggage, in preparation for abandoning the city. But until they could get everything away, Washington had to continue to defend New York City and the rest of Manhattan Island. Consequently, he divided his army into three parts. He ordered General William Heath with 9,000 men to Harlem Heights, on the rugged northern end of the island, to dig fortifications; these would serve as a fall-back position should the rest of the

---

[1]*The Journal of Nicholas Cresswell* (New York: Dial Press, 1924), 158.

[2]In addition to his role as a peace commissioner, and his tactical command in and around New York, Howe commanded all forces in the British colonies lying along the Atlantic Ocean from Nova Scotia to East Florida, with the exception of Crown forces in Quebec.

army have to evacuate positions further south. General Israel Putnam was posted with 5,000 men to defend the city itself. Between Putnam's and Heath's corps, Washington placed General Nathanael Greene with 5,000 men to protect the center of the island. The result was an American army of three isolated corps, strewn over a 13-mile area: a situation fraught with risk.

The extent of the risk soon became all too clear. On September 15, Howe made his move to capture New York. From his new bases on Long Island, the British commander bypassed Putnam's relatively strong defenses on lower Manhattan and launched an amphibious attack against Greene. Howe picked Kip's Bay Cove on the East River (presently East 34th Street) for his landing. The location was ideal for an amphibious assault: a somewhat rocky shore behind which lay a long flat meadow with few natural defenses. The attack was textbook perfect. The inexperienced militia defending Kip's Bay were quickly routed by bayonet-wielding infantry. Other American troops soon joined the terrified militia in their flight, all running as fast as they could towards the safety of Heath's fortifications at Harlem Heights. The enemy were close behind, mockingly sounding horns and bugles as if on a fox chase. As the British army pushed across Manhattan Island, Putnam's troops in New York City narrowly escaped capture by retreating up the Greenwich Road, on the Hudson River side of the island, to the safety of Heath's lines. For the Americans, the Kip's Bay affair was a fiasco.

Washington arrived in mid-Manhattan in the midst of the turmoil. He was shocked and furious as he watched the panic-stricken defenders of Kip's Bay throwing away their muskets and running and shoving their way towards the safety of Harlem Heights. The general rode among the frightened militia, screaming at them to form behind nearby farm fences and stone walls, but he was unable to stop them. According to one American officer who witnessed the scene, Washington became so angry that he flew into an uncontrollable rage and began striking the militiamen with his riding crop. "The General was so exasperated that he struck several officers in their flight, three times dashed his hatt on the ground, and at last exclaimed, 'Good God, have I got such troops as those!' It was with difficulty his friends could get him to quit the field, so great was his emotions."[1]

---

[1] Henry Steele Commager and Richard B. Morris, eds., *The Spirit of Seventy-Six* (New York: Harper & Row, 1976), 467. The letter quoted was written on September 20 by General George Weedon to John Page, President of the Virginia Council. Washington wrote his own account of what happened in a letter to his brother, John Augustine Washington, dated September 22: "I rode with all possible expedition towards the place of Landing, and

Appalled at the conduct of the militia at Kip's Bay, Washington wrote a lengthy letter to John Hancock, the President of the Continental Congress. He renewed his appeal for a "new model army" of professional soldiers instead of continued dependence on one-year enlistments and militia. "To place any dependance upon Militia," he told Hancock, "is assuredly, resting upon a broken staff. Men just dragged from the tender Scenes of domestick life, unaccustomed to the din of Arms; totally unacquainted with every kind of Military skill, which being followed by a want of confidence in themselves, when opposed to Troops regularly trained, disciplined, and appointed, superior in knowledge, and superior in Arms, make them timid, and ready to fly from their own Shadows." Aware of Congressional fears of a professional army, the Commander-in-Chief insisted that "the Jealousies of a standing Army, and the Evils to be apprehended from one, are remote; and in my judgment, situated and circumstanced as we are, not at all to be dreaded; but the consequence of wanting one, according to my Ideas, formed from the present view of things, is certain, and inevitable Ruin; for if I was called upon to declare upon Oath, whether the Militia have been most serviceable or hurtful upon the whole, I should subscribe to the latter."[1]

Ironically, the Continental Congress had already voted to raise eighty-eight regiments of Continentals in a series of resolutions in mid-September. Hancock wrote Washington from Philadelphia on September 24, giving the Commander-in-Chief the news. Hancock explained that Congress agreed to "engage the Troops to serve during the Continuance of the War." In addition, they voted to offer bounties of money and land to induce men to enlist in the army. The Congress also adopted new Articles of War to tighten discipline.[2] Washington was given a blueprint for his "respectable army," but

---

where Breast Works had been thrown up to secure our Men, & found the Troops that had been posted there to my great surprise & Mortification, and those ordered to their Support (consisting of Eight Regiments) notwithstanding the exertions of their Generals to form them, running away in the most Shameful and disgraceful manner." Dorothy Twohig, ed., *The Papers of George Washington* (Charlottesville and London: University Press of Virginia, 1994), Revolutionary War Series, VI: 373.

[1]*Ibid.*, 393-400. This letter was written on September 25, 1776 from "Colo. Morris's" (still standing today and known as the Morris-Jumel Mansion) in Harlem.

[2]The death of General Richard Montgomery was one reason the Continental Congress agreed to heed Washington's advice and raise an army for the duration of the war. Richard Montgomery was a popular and able former British army officer who remained in America following the French and Indian War. Commanding the American troops besieging

the reorganization was months away. Meanwhile, he had to struggle on until the end of the year dependent upon his one-year Continentals and militia.

Following the Battle of Kip's Bay, the war fell silent again.[1] Washington commanded a force of 20,435, most of whom were manning the defensive lines at Harlem Heights.[2] The Americans had built two forts on the Hudson River during the spring and summer of 1776 to prevent the British from sailing their warships up the Hudson. Fort Washington stood perched on one of the highest points on Manhattan Island. Almost directly across the Hudson River from Fort Washington was its sister fortification, Fort Lee. Fort Lee stood atop the Hudson Palisades.[3] The seemingly powerful Fort Washington-Fort Lee defensive line, with its big guns, was a comfort to the jittery American army in their makeshift defenses at Harlem Heights.

The rebels had built the forts largely to protect the Hudson River. Of the major rivers in America, the Hudson was the most important during the War for Independence. The Hudson or "North River," as it was also called by the colonists, was navigable by ocean-going ships for 150 miles from its mouth at New York City to Albany. Along its banks lived tens of thousands

---

Quebec late in 1775, he was forced to prematurely attack the city on New Year's Eve, 1775 because the enlistments of many of his troops would expire the following day. He was killed and the assault was a failure. In his letter to Washington of September 24, 1776, Hancock said that "the untimely Death of General Montgomery alone, independent of other Arguments, is a striking Proof of the Danger and Impropriety of sending Troops into the Field, under any Restriction as to the Time of their Service."

[1] Following the Battle of Kip's Bay, the British established a defensive position across Manhattan at about the site of present 91st Street. The Americans facing them at Harlem Heights occupied positions corresponding to the ground from modern 147th to 161st Streets. On September 16th, the day following the British landing at Kip's Bay, there was some fighting between the two armies which ended in a draw, but at least the Americans acted with courage. This incident is known as the Battle of Harlem Heights.

[2] Lesser, ed., *The Sinews of Independence*, 32-33. This figure was the total American strength in the New York City area and includes approximately 3,500 officers and men in New Jersey under Nathanael Greene.

[3] The volcanically-formed cliffs which soar upward from the banks of the Hudson River were known simply as the "Steep Rocks" at the time of the American Revolution. The cliffs north of Tenefly, New Jersey were called Closter Mountain. These cliffs began to be called "The Palisades" about 50 years after the end of the Revolution. However, for ease of identification, I will use the modern term Palisades to describe these cliffs.

of people cultivating rich farmlands. The Hudson provided easy access into the heart of New York and New England.[1]

The defense of the Hudson became problematic when Washington realized that British warships could sail up river and land troops behind the American lines. Equally threatening was the fear that a British naval force on the Hudson would encourage the numerous New York State Loyalists, who were only waiting for leadership and arms from the British, to rise up against the rebels. British ships on the Hudson also could block vital rebel supply routes, especially troop reinforcements and food coming to New York City from patriot strongholds in New England.

There was another reason to defend the lower Hudson River. The Continental Congress had authorized the construction of eleven frigates, and the largest of these warships, *Congress* and *General Montgomery*, were under construction at Poughkeepsie, New York. The infant men-of-war had to be protected against efforts by the British to destroy them before they could get to sea.

The only American naval force available to defend New York City consisted of some lightly armed converted merchant ships and boats mounting a few cannons. This scratch force was no match for the British, who had the most powerful navy in the world. Unable to match the British at sea, the rebels had to depend on forts and gun batteries to defend New York harbor and the Hudson River.

Only a few places along the Hudson River's 150 mile length offered an opportunity for defense. One excellent defensive position was 45 miles north of New York City where the river took a bend, forcing sailing ships to slow down and making them easy targets for shore-based artillery. The American fortress at that location eventually was named West Point. The

---

[1]At the time of the Revolution, there were two great water routes that led from the Hudson River to the interior of North America: New York City to Lake Ontario, which took travellers north on the Hudson River to a point just below Albany, where the Mohawk River meets the Hudson; then west along the Mohawk River and across a carrying place protected by Fort Stanwix (modern Rome, New York), to the headwaters of the Oswego River; then north on the Oswego River to the Great Lakes and the interior of the North American continent. The second critical route connected New York City with Montreal: north on the Hudson from New York City beyond Albany to a 60 mile carrying point where there was a road. The carry was protected by the British outposts of Fort Anne and Fort Edward, New York. The 60 mile carry ended at the southern shore of Lake George, protected by the British post of Fort William Henry; then the route continued north on Lake George and into Lake Champlain, past the old French Fort of Crown Point and onto the Richelieu River; next past French-built Fort Chambly and onto the St. Lawrence River near Montreal.

other good defensive position lay at a point where the river squeezed between the rocky northern end of Manhattan Island and the cliffs of the New Jersey Palisades. With the defense of the lower Hudson River in mind, Washington reconnoitered the rugged, forested terrain on the uninhabited northern tip of Manhattan Island on June 12, 1776, accompanied by Colonel Rufus Putnam, the chief engineer of the American army. They found a hill which dominated the island's densely wooded northern tip and which butted against the Hudson, affording an excellent position to defend the waterway 220 feet below. The hilltop was christened Mount Washington.

Rebel troops were soon busy fortifying the postion. "In the course of some weeks, wrote Captain Alexander Graydon, "our labours had produced immense mounds of earth, assuming a pentagonal form, and finally issuing in a fort of five bastions." Graydon thought little of Rufus Putnam, whom he saw as "a self-educated man with want of experience."[1] Nevertheless, Putnam was one of the few men available at the outbreak of the Revolution who knew anything about military engineering.[2]

The patriots labored away on their defenses in and around New York City during the summer of 1776 while the British army and navy continued to strengthen their forces on Staten Island. The first test of the American's Hudson River defenses came on Friday afternoon, July 12, 1776, the anniversary of James Wolfe's victory over the French at Quebec in 1761 and a day which the British army liked to celebrate. In addition, General William Howe's older brother, Admiral Lord Richard Howe was expected to enter New

---

[1]Rufus Putnam, a Massachsetts native, served as a colonial officer with the British during the French and Indian War and as Deputy Surveyor of West Florida (1773). In 1775, Putnam was commissioned a lieutenant colonel in the American army, and became an engineer quite casually. "Some of my acquaintance," he recalled, "mentioned me as having been imployed in that line in the Late war against Canada." He told Washington that "I had never read a word on the Subject of Fortification, that it was true that I had ben imployed on Some under British Engineers, but pretended to no knowledge of Laying works." Nevertheless, the Commander-in-Chief gave him the job (with the rank of colonel), and Putnam said that he finally got to read a book about engineering during the winter of 1776. Rowena Buell, *The Memories of Rufus Putnam and Certain Official Papers and Correspondence* (New York: Houghton, Mifflin and Company, 1903), 55-57.

[2]In November 1776, Putnam resigned his post as Chief Engineer to command an infantry regiment. He served as an infantry officer for the balance of the Revolution. The Americans got some competent military engineers when several French engineers arrived in 1777 as "volunteers." The British had established an engineering school at Woolwich, England in 1757 and they had skillful engineers serving with their army. The French had a similar school at St. Etienne.

York harbor that day with a fleet bringing additional troops from England. The rebels expected the British to salute this important day, and the British did, but in an unexpected manner.

At 3:30 in the afternoon, the stillness of the summer day was broken when two British frigates suddenly came alive, hoisted their sails, ran out their cannons and started racing across New York harbor for the mouth of the Hudson River. The two warships were the 44-gun *Phoenix* and the 24-gun *Rose*. They were accompanied by a schooner and two supply tenders. On board the five craft were about four hundred men, including a complement of Royal Marines. Rebel sentinels saw the frigates and sounded alarm cannons; church bells rang and the beat of drums called men to arms throughout the city. Artillerymen ran to their posts; this was the moment they had been waiting for.[1]

A number of witnesses recorded the action. Stephen Kemble, a New Jersey Loyalist, saw the affair as it developed from aboard a British warship at anchor near Staten Island. "About half after 3 in the Afternoon," he wrote, "His Majesty's Ship Phenix, Commanded by Capt. Parker, and the Rose, by Capt. Wallace, with the Tryal Schooner and two Tenders, got under Sail to pass the Town of New York; in about forty minutes they got abreast of Paulus's Hook [now Jersey City, New Jersey], before which time they did not fire a Shot, tho' they received the whole of the Rebels fire from Red Hook [part of modern Brooklyn], Governors Island, the Battery [today's Battery Park in lower Manhatten] and from some Guns in the Town." Kemble counted 196 shots fired at the squadron.[2] When the frigates got within range of the American batteries at Paulus Hook, they returned fire and drove the rebels from their guns. The warships also fired thundering broadsides into New York City, causing general consternation. "When they came this side of Trinity Church, they began to fire smartly," one civilian remembered. "The balls and bullets went through several houses between here and Greenwich [Greenwich Village]....The smoke of the firing drew over our street like a cloud, and the air was filled with the smell of powder. This affair caused a great fright in the

---

[1] The British fleet of transports and warships that eventually gathered in the waters around Staten Island was the largest concentration of warships up to that time in history. It was only exceeded in numbers by the Allied fleet which was assembled for the invasion of Normandy in 1944.

[2] *Journals of Lieut.-Col. Stephen Kemble* (New York: New York Historical Society, 1883), I: 80.

city. Women and children and some with their bundles came from the lower parts, and walked to the Bowery, which was lined with people."[1]

The Americans never did stop the men-of-war. Patriot artillery performed miserably. Some of their old cannons blew up under the pressure of live ammunition, killing or wounding their crews. A number of the casualities belonged to the New York State Provincial Company of Artillery commanded by Captain Alexander Hamilton, a student from Kings College (now Columbia University). Farther up river, the frigates ran past the guns of Fort Washington. The ships returned "our fire in great style," Graydon reported. "We were too high for their guns to be brought to bear upon us with any certainty; though one ball was thrown into the fort. Our elevated situation was nearly as unfavorable to the success of our fire upon them."[2] Carried by a favorable wind, the British squadron sailed majestically north, some thirty miles above the American defense lines before coming to anchor in the Tappan Zee region. It was a dazzling exploit to celebrate the anniversary of Wolfe's great victory at Quebec!

The sudden appearance of two powerful British warships on the Hudson River fulfilled Washington's worst fears of an enemy squadron operating on the river above New York City. The ships lingered deep in rebel territory for over a month, always a threat to patriots ashore and on the river, as well as to American ferry and other riverine interests and communications. Washington went to extraordinary lengths to trap or drive them away. For a month, he worked heatedly to block enemy navigation with various river obstructions, and even attempted an attack with fire rafts.[3] Nothing worked, and the enemy flotilla sailed home in mid-August unscathed but for a few lucky cannon hits.

---

[1]*Diary of the Reverend Mr. Shewkirk*, in Henry Steel Commanger and Richard B. Morris, eds., *The Spirit of Seventy-Six* (New York: Harper & Row, 1975), 422.

[2]John Stockton Littell, ed., Alexander Graydon, *Memoirs of His Own Time* (Philadelphia: Lindsay & Blakiston, 1846), 152.

[3]For the various schemes, see Fitzpatrick, ed., *Writings of Washington*, 5: 344; Edward Tatum, ed., *The American Journal of Ambrose Serle* (San Marino, CA: The Huntington Library, 1940), 54. Henry Duncan, Captain of H.M.S. *Eagle*, anchored off Staten Island, reported in his journal that "during the time we have been here, we have observed the rebels very busy in erecting batteries, fitting out row galleys, and making large and high buildings of wood to sink in the river to destroy the navigation above the town." What Duncan saw were river obstructions called *chevaux-de-frise*.

The passage of the two British frigates up the Hudson made it apparent that Fort Washington alone could not stop warships. Washington hoped that if he could mount gun batteries across the Hudson from Fort Washington, British ships would be caught in a murderous crossfire. There was an ideal site in New Jersey for such a battery. The ground was a little south of Fort Washington above a breach in the New Jersey Palisades. A narrow road ran through the opening from the crest of the Palisades to the Hudson River where Burdett's Ferry carried passengers and freight between New Jersey and Manhattan Island. By mid-July, Washington had his army hard at work on the project, and patriot guns on the Palisades subsequently blazed away (however ineffectually) at *Phoenix* and *Rose* when they returned south in August.

Despite their poor initial performance against the enemy ships, Washington appreciated the importance of the Palisades battery to the defense of New Jersey, and he ordered an expansion of the position above Burdett's Ferry. He gave the assignment to General Hugh Mercer, the rebel commander in New Jersey, who had a strong build-up underway by late September.[1] In mid-October, the growing fortification at Burdett's Ferry was renamed Fort Lee, in honor of General Charles Lee, now second in command of the Continental army.

While its name was impressive, Fort Lee was not a great citadel. It was really a fortified camp to support the gun batteries mounted on the crest of the Palisades. Thomas Paine, the author of *Common Sense* and civilian aide to General Nathanael Greene during November 1776, recalled Fort Lee as a "field fort," which was eighteenth-century nomenclature for a temporary earthen fortification. The post was a four-sided work about 2,500 feet square located on a flat tableland about a quarter mile behind the batteries on the

---

[1] The diary of soldier John Adlum has an entry for August 28th, 1776 which supports the belief that there were no major defenses at the Burdett's Ferry site during the early summer of 1776. Adlum said that he was at Paulus Hook and "in a few days after, we re-marched to the ground where Fort Lee was afterwards erected." Howard Peckham, ed., *Memoirs of The Life of John Adlum in The Revolutionary War* (Chicago: The Caxton Club, 1968), 19. Despite the many places in New Jersey named in honor of Hugh Mercer (1725-1777), he was a Scotsman by birth who emigrated to Virginia. In Scotland, Mercer was a physician and a supporter of Prince Charles Edward Stuart, remembered in history as "Bonnie Prince Charlie." Mercer supported the Jacobite uprising and participated in the Battle of Culloden in 1745 in which the English defeated the Scots and ended the rebellion. Many of the Highlanders, including Mercer, came to America following their defeat and sided with the rebels during the Revolution. Mercer was mortally wounded at the Battle of Princeton on January 3, 1777.

Palisades. Over 300 huts arranged in a regular street pattern surrounded the fort, housing some 3,000 American soldiers. If the fort were in existence today, it would sit within the center of the modern town of Fort Lee, New Jersey. Just to the east were the guns on the crest of the Palisades, well placed in a natural defensive position 300 feet above the Hudson and protected by rudimentary earthworks. The gorge, which descended from the crest of the Palisades to the river, separated the fort from the batteries. There were no fortifications on the river shore. The earthen fort, the streets of huts, and the gun batteries on the Hudson were collectively called Fort Lee.

The guns at Fort Lee were already in operation when Washington and his army arrived at Harlem Heights on September 15, the same day they lost the Battle of Kip's Bay. On October 9, the troops watched from across the river as Fort Lee engaged a second foray by British shipping up the Hudson. Again the warships sailed passed the rebel river defenses "without any kind of damage or interruption." Colonel Thomas Ewing, an American officer who watched the incident, reported that the rebel gunfire was so ineffective that he could see a gentleman walking the deck of one of the frigates, seemingly in command, as if nothing was the matter. Ewing could see no damage being done to the British vessels.[1]

The dispatch of three warships to control the Hudson above the rebel army at Harlem Heights was ominous. Three days later, on October 12, General Howe further revealed his hand when he landed troops on Throgs Neck, a narrow peninsula jutting out from the Bronx into Long Island Sound. From Throgs Neck, Howe moved inland to outflank the rebels and cut off their retreat from Harlem Heights into Westchester County. In addition, more Royal Navy ships sailed above the Fort Washington-Fort Lee line to block any American move across the Hudson into New Jersey.

Faced with the threat of being surrounded, on October 16 Washington called his senior officers together for a council of war. There was much excitment at the council because General Charles Lee was present. Lee had

---

[1]The three British warships that ran past the American batteries were *Phoenix*, *Roebuck* and *Tartar*. The squadron was commanded by Captain Parker of *Phoenix*. The Americans watching from Harlem Heights, Fort Lee and Fort Washington may not have seen it, but the three ships had casualties as they passed the rebel batteries. Captain Parker reported a total of nine killed and eighteen wounded aboard the three ships. Force, ed., *American Archives*, Fifth Series, III: 818.

returned triumphantly from Charleston, South Carolina, where he had commanded Southern troops in a brilliant defense of Charleston in June 1776.[1] The generals debated whether to await attack in their position at Harlem Heights or to retreat to open country while there was still time. Lee favored retreat, scoffing at the idea of a position being good merely because its approaches were difficult.   Further, he pointed out that there was only one escape route open to them from Harlem Heights, and that was via the Kings Bridge which connected Manhattan Island with the Bronx. "For my part," said Lee, "I would have nothing to do with the islands [Long Island and Manhattan] to which you have been clinging so pertinaciously."[2] Influenced by Lee's arguments, Washington decided to move while he had the chance.

On October 21, Washington abandoned Harlem Heights and crossed to the Bronx. His goal was the village of White Plains in Westchester County. However, at the insistence of the Continental Congress, and with the unanimous approval of his senior officers, he left a sizable garrison at Fort Washington with orders that the post " be retained as long as possible."[3]

General Howe and his army pursued Washington to White Plains with a splendid army of 20,000.   The stand-off Battle of White Plains was fought on October 28, and the British then began positioning artillery for a renewed action.   They planned another attack for October 31, but a heavy rainstorm canceled their assault.   Washington used this rain shower to conceal the evacuation of his army from White Plains, and the rebels retreated north into rugged country on the Croton River in North Castle, New York, where they constructed a strong defense. Watching from a respectful distance, Howe's reconnaissance parties mistook piled-up cornstalks, with dirt still attached to their roots, for sturdy redoubts. The British general decided not to attack.

---

[1]In his memoirs, Sergeant Roger Lamb of the British army wrote that "During this attack [on Charleston] general Lee exposed himself to great danger; as the balls whistled about he observed one of his aid-de-camps shrink every now and then, and by the motion of his body seemed to evade the shot. 'Death sir,' cried Lee, 'what do you mean, do you doge? Do you know that the king of Prussia lost above an hundred aid-de-camps in one campaign.' "'So I understand, sir,' replied the officer, 'But I did not think you could spare so many.'" Roger Lamb, *Journal of Occurrences During the Late American War* (Dublin, Ireland: Wilkinson & Courtney, 1809), 99.

[2]Lee's comment was reported in Washington Irving, *The Life of George Washington* (New York: G.P. Putnam and Co.,, 1855), II: 381.

[3]Proceedings of a Council of General Officers, October 16, 1776, Force, ed., *American Archives*, Fifth Series, II: 1117-1118. Alden, *General Charles Lee*, 144.

The unbroken string of defeats and retreats had its effects on the American army. Many of the soldiers were demoralized and, with winter approaching, desertions ran higher than ever. Patriots had counted 18,730 fit for duty on September 28, 1776; but by the end of October, the number had dropped to 16,969.[1] The enlistments of the Massachusetts militia would expire on November 17 and they were determined to go home. Almost all the Continental regiments were eligible to disband on November 30 or December 31; few fresh troops were arriving to take their place. Enlistments were slow, which was no surprise since the Americans had lost every major engagement in the New York campaign and were on the run. Washington was aware that his army was diminshing with each passing day and wrote Congress to say "how essential it is to keep up some shew of force and shadow of an Army."[2]

Logistics added to Washington's problems. Food and equipment were in short supply, and the rebels had lost many of their blankets and tents during the months of fighting. By late October, the troops were sleeping unprotected on the frozen ground. Some men were losing heart and silently questioning whether George Washington was the right man to command the patriot army.

Washington's chief problem, however, remained General Howe. Over November 5 and 6, the British commander shifted his army from White Plains to Dobb's Ferry on the Hudson, where the Navy had supplies waiting.[3] These ships had successfully run past the rebel gun batteries at Forts Washington and Lee the previous day.

Unsure what Howe was up to, Washington again called a council of war. Some officers believed the British were finished campaigning for the year and heading for winter quarters in New York City. Others felt that Howe would try to penetrate deeper into New England or move north on the Hudson River towards Albany. Washington's assessment of the situation was that Howe definitely planned to continue to campaign before going into winter quarters. The Virginian believed that his opponent would use a part of his army to attack Fort Washington and another part to invade the rich farmlands

---

[1]Lesser, *The Sinews of Independence*, 32-36.

[2]Washington to the President of Congress, November 6, 1776, Fitzpatrick, ed., *Writings of Washington*, 6: 250.

[3]Kemble,*Journals*, I: 97-98. Kemble reported that the the the march of the troops to Dobbs Ferry was "marked by the Licentiousness of the Troops, who committed every species of Rapine and plunder."

of New Jersey. After discussing the situation, the officers unanimously agreed to "throw a body of troops into the Jerseys immediately" and to detach 3,000 troops for the defense of the Hudson Highlands.[1]

On November 7, the day following his decision to send part of the army to New Jersey, George Washington wrote to inform Governor William Livingston of the situation. He gave the New Jersey leader the latest war news and warned that Howe was not finished for the year. The Commander-in-Chief thought it probable that the British general would press into New Jersey with at least part of his force, if only to affirm his reputation. He assured Livingston that if this occurred, he would at once "throw over a body of our Troops, with the utmost expedition, to assist in checking their progress."[2]

Such a move, however, would not be easy. Washington faced the problem of deciding how to split his little army to defend New Jersey and still protect the Hudson River and New England. His solution went against all established military doctrine: he decided to divide his small army in the face of a superior enemy. The plan called for splitting the army into three unequal pieces. Believing that New Jersey would become the focus of the war, Washington decided that he would personally lead all the troops whose homes were south of the Hudson River to New Jersey to help defend that state.[3] They totalled about 5,000 men. This force was too small to defend New Jersey. However, Washington calculated that he could add to this number the 2,146 men under Greene's command at Fort Lee, as well as the 1,500 Pennsylvania troops garrisoning Fort Washington.[4]

---

[1]Force, ed., *American Archives*, Fifth Series, III: 543-544.

[2]Fitzpatrick, ed., *Writings of Washington*, 6: 255-256. In this same letter Washington recommended that the New Jersey governor alert the state's militia, make any necessary repairs to the barracks in Elizabethtown, Perth Amboy and New Brunswick, and to remove all "Stock, Grain, Effects and Carriages" from the the seacoast to the safety of the interior of the state.

[3]On November 7, Washington wrote Greene from North Castle: "If you have not already sent my Boxes with Camp Tables and Chairs, be so good as to let them remain with you, as I do not know but I shall move with the Troops designed for the Jersey's, persuaded as I am of their having turned their Views that Way." Fitzpatrick, ed., *Writings of Washington*, 6: 254-255.

[4]On October 26, Greene reported to Washington that he had 2,146 officers and men present and fit for duty. Force, ed., *American Archives*, Fifth Series, II: 1250. A few weeks later, on November 14, Greene reported 2,667 troops under his command . Greene's

As agreed at the November 6 council of war, 3,000 troops would be headquartered at Peekskill, New York, and assigned to defend the Hudson Highlands. Washington gave this command to the unimaginative but reliable General William Heath. The third and largest portion of the army, consisting of 7,500 soldiers, would remain at North Castle under the command of General Charles Lee. Lee's mission was to deter any British thrust into New England and to wait as a reserve until General Howe's intentions became clearer.

At the same time, some decision was necessary regarding the future of the Fort Washington garrison on northern Manhattan. Preoccupied with defending the Hudson Highlands and New Jersey, Washington at first gave relatively little thought to the fort. Yet there was not much trepidation within the walls of the post. The officers in command felt confident that their sturdy fortress could withstand a siege for a considerable time. Greene assured the Commander-in-Chief that if Fort Washington was threatened, the men could be ferried across the Hudson River to the safety of rebel-held New Jersey. For the time being, then, the fort and its considerable garrison seemed safe enough.

Washington began his troop movements on November 8. The reports of spies and the sudden movement of enemy boats around Dobbs Ferry convinced him that an invasion of New Jersey was imminent.[1] He ordered part of his army across the Hudson River to New Jersey, and the Virginia, Delaware and Pennsylvania troops commanded by General William Alexander, better known as Lord Stirling, were quickly on their way. Once across the Hudson, Sterling's Brigade provided protection for 2,700 additional soldiers who made the crossing the followng day. Stirling reached Hackensack, New Jersey, with his brigade on November 12. Washington followed, leaving North Castle early on the morning of November 10, making various stops along the way to inspect fortifications and to consult with senior

---

force was spread out on or near the Hudson River from Sneeden's Landing opposite Dobbs Ferry to Clinton Point, which lay opposite Spuyten Duyvil. Greene mentioned other American strong points at Bergen, Hoboken, Bull's Ferry (present day West New York, New Jersey), and Hackensack. However, this figure is misleading because it included 1,510 who were sent by Greene from New Jersey to reinforce Fort Washington. Thus it is difficult to determine the exact number of American troops in New Jersey in mid-November, 1776. Adrian C. Leiby, *The Revolutionary War in the Hackensack Valley* (New Brunswick, NJ: Rutgers University Press, 1962), 58.

[1]Washington to Greene, November 8, 1776, Fitzpatrick, ed., *Writings of Washington*, 6: 257-258.

commanders.[1] By this time, the Commander-in-Chief was more concerned with the situation at Fort Washington and with the security of vital supplies at Fort Lee. He reached Fort Lee on November 13, consulted at length with General Greene, and rode on to Hackensack, a farming village six miles west of Fort Lee, where he established his headquarters at the Zabriskie Mansion.[2]

Having arrived in New Jersey, Washington now had to await events. In effect, the rebel commander had placed his faith in a plan that left his army divided in the face of a concentrated enemy who held the initiative. When the anticipated assault came, he had to trust that his subordinates, especially Lee, could quickly discern enemy intentions and react accordingly. Such a strategy was inherently risky even when undertaken by well-equipped and experienced armies, and Washington's was neither. But it was a gamble the general felt he had to take.

In the patriot commander's view, success depended chiefly on a quick response by Lee if the British launched a major invasion of New Jersey. He was counting on just such a reaction. If Howe moved, the general wrote one American officer, he was positive "that the troops under General Lee, will also cross Hudson's River, if it should be necessary in consequence of the Enemy's throwing their force over." Washington further emphasized his thinking on this point in his instructions to Lee dated November 10: "If the enemy should remove the whole, or the greatest part of their force, to the West side of Hudson's River, I have no doubt of your following with all possible dispatch."[3] At least that was the plan.

---

[1]Fitzpatrick, ed., *Writings of Washington*, 6: 272, and Heath's *Memoirs*, 95.

[2]Fitzpatrick, ed., *Writings of Washington*, 6: 279.

[3]Fitzpatrick, ed., *Writings of Washington*, 6: 266. There are other references to Washington's dependence on Lee if General Howe invaded New Jersey. Washington ended a letter to Colonel (later General) Henry Knox, dated November 10, 1776, "It is unnecessary to add, that if the Army of the Enemy should wholly or pretty generally throw themselves across the North River, that General Lee is to follow." *Ibid.*, 6: 267.

CHAPTER TWO

Fort Washington

The Importance of the North River, and the sanguine wishes
of all to prevent the enemy from possessing it, have been
the causes of this unhappy catastrophe.
—Washington to Governor Jonathan Trumbull,
November 17, 1776

Washington had lost all direct contact with Fort Washington from the moment he left Harlem Heights on October 21. Until he arrived at Fort Lee on November 13, when he was able to discuss Fort Washington with General Greene, he had received only a few letters about affairs on the Manhattan side of the Hudson, and they were not reassuring. While he was still at Harlem Heights, Washington had witnessed the failure of the batteries at Forts Washington and Lee to prevent the Royal Navy from sailing up the river. The incident, which took place on October 9, had deeply disturbed the general, and he was hardly pleased to learn that similar events had recurred. How much faith could he place in the ability of his forts to defend the vital Hudson River?

Washington had not seen the next tests of the river forts. The first came on October 27, when the general and the Grand Army were at White

Plains. Two British frigates brazenly stopped below Forts Washington and Lee as part of a probe of the American defenses. The two frigates engaged the rebel batteries in an intense cannon duel and took a terrible beating for several hours; but neither was sunk, and they returned safely down river. On November 5, as Howe was moving towards Dobbs Ferry, three additional British ships successfully ran the Fort Washington-Fort Lee defensive line. The journal of H.M.S. *Pearl,* one of the ships involved, recorded a brisk fire from the Americans, which the British returned. "We recd a number of shot in our Hull & several between Wind & Water," the log noted, and "had the Major part of our running Rigging & and a great part of our lower Cut to pieces. found Wm Brown, Seaman Kill'd & several wounded. The Sails much torn our Mizen & Mizen top-mast shatter'd & and Boats much damaged." The British were under fire for about an hour and a half and, as *Pearl* candidly admitted, suffered battle damage and casualties; but the American batteries failed to sink any of the enemy ships or force them back down river. Once more, the rebel guns had come off second best.[1]

General Greene brushed off this latest failure of his river forts to stop enemy shipping on the Hudson River.[2] But when Washington received a report on the incident, he questioned the value of maintaining Fort Washington when it was unable to stop the enemy from sailing up and down the Hudson River at will. "The late passage of the 3 Vessels up the North River," he wrote to Greene on November 8, "is so plain a Proof of the Inefficacy of all the Obstructions we have thrown into it" "If we cannot prevent Vessels passing up, and the Enemy are possessed of the surrounding Country, what valuable purpose can it answer to attempt to hold a Post from which the expected Benefit cannot be had."[3] In fact, Washington had a point, and had he pushed it further he might have spared the army, and himself, some real pain.

Greene, however, had a seemingly plausible explanation. He fired back a detailed reply, dated November 9, in which he assured Washington

---

[1] The engagements, including *Pearl's* journal, are noted in William James Morgan, ed., *Naval Documents of the American Revolution*(Washington, DC: Naval History Division, Navy Dept., 1972), VI: 1428-29. Another account of the incident on November 5 is in *The Diary of Frederick Mackenzie*, I: 98.

[2] In fact, Greene mistakenly reported to Washington that fire from the forts seriously damaged the British ships; see Showman, ed., *Papers of Nathanael Greene*, I: 337-38.

[3] Fitzpatrick, ed., *Writings of Washington*, 6: 257-258.

that the fort was safe from being overrun and should not be abandoned. Greene insisted that the garrison at Fort Washington was in no danger because they could be quickly evacuated across the Hudson River to Fort Lee. Further, the fort was holding down a large number of enemy troops who had surrounded it. Even though the British were getting ready to besiege the fort, he promised Washington that it would take the enemy until the end of December to capture the post.[1] In short, there was no reason for undue concern. Washington's instinct still was to evacuate Fort Washington; but he had no first hand knowledge of the situation and he instead chose to rely on Greene's assurances.

General Greene, inexperienced with military engineering and lacking trained engineers to advise him, was mistaken about Fort Washington. It looked impressive because of its excellent natural defensive location, a hilltop which dominated the surrounding countryside. The American defensive works were a mile long. Well-placed outer works defended the fortifications from all land approaches and rugged cliffs rendered it unassailable from the Hudson River side. But Fort Washington was constructed of earth and wood and lacked most of the features necessary to resist siege or attack; there were no ditches, casements, palisades, or barracks, and the outer works were weak. The post lacked food, fuel and water to sustain a siege. Water had to be carried to the fort from the river, 280 feet below, and the British could easily sever this source if they attacked. Much of the garrison of Fort Washington was spread out in positions outside the earthen walls and the fort was too small to hold the entire command if the outer works were overrun.[2]

Fort Washington was essentially a Pennsylvania garrison. The commander was Colonel Robert Magaw, a thirty-five year old lawyer and patriot from Carlisle, Pennsylvania, who commanded the Fifth Pennsylvania regiment. Magaw's second-in-command was Lieutenant Colonel Lambert Cadwalader from Philadelphia. The regimental staff included yet another Pennsylvanian, William Demont, the adjutant. Unfortunately, he was also a traitor.

Demont was an Englishman by birth, and he deserted to the enemy on

---

[1] Showman, ed., *Greene Papers*, I: 344.

[2] Historians Douglas Marshall and Howard Peckham said that some American officers realized the shortcomings of Fort Washington, but their qualms were never effectively communicated to Greene. Douglas Marshall and Howard Peckham, *Campaigns of the American Revolution* (Ann Arbor: University of Michigan Press, 1976), 26.

the night of November 2, carrying with him a plan of Fort Washington, including the positions of its critical outer works. Demont passed safely between the lines and reached the British army where he turned over his valuable plans to Earl Percy who eagerly passed them on to Howe. Howe probably received Demont's plan from Percy on November 3 or 4. For Howe, it was a lucky stroke. Although the British general was planning an attack on Fort Washington, possession of Demont's plans gave him an incentive to accelerate his timetable for the assault. In fact, getting the plan of Fort Washington may have accounted for Howe suddenly breaking contact with the rebel army near White Plains on the night of November 5.[1]

At noon, on November 6, Howe arrived at Dobbs Ferry. To the south, the Hessian General Wilhelm von Knyphausen had already driven in the American outposts near Fort Washington.[2] This meant that the only escape route open to the garrison was to climb down the high cliffs to the west and to cross the Hudson River to Fort Lee. Howe proceeded to move against his prey. From Dobbs Ferry, the general marched southward while Cornwallis moved his corps to the east bank of the Harlem River.[3] Lord Percy brought up troops from New York City to a position below Fort Washington on the Harlem Plains. Fort Washington was now cut off and the garrison's only escape was across the Hudson River to Fort Lee.

In response to Howe's maneuvers, Greene sent Magaw additional troops from Fort Lee. It was a substantial reinforcement, which brought the

[1] Historian David Ramsey pointed out that Howe realized that Washington's army could not come to the aid of Fort Washington. "The Americans having retired (to North Castle)," he wrote, "Sir William Howe determined to improve the opportunity of their absence, for the reduction of Fort Washington." David Ramsey, *History of the American Revolution* (Philadelphia, 1793). Mackenzie reported in his diary on November 2 that a man named Diamond, "who says he was Ensign and Adjutant" deserted from Fort Washington. It is extraordinary, but Mackenzie appears to have interviewed Demont on November 2, and reported that Demont said that there was much disagreement and dissension at Fort Washington, "everybody finding fault with the mode of proceeding, and the inferior officers, even Ensigns, insisting that, in such a cause, every man has a right to assist in Council, and to give his opinion." *Mackenzie Diary*, I: 95.

[2] General von Knyphausen had recently arrived in America with a large number of Hessians to reinforce Howe's army. He was 60 years old at the time and a professional soldier of great personal courage although he is best remembered in the American Revolution as the German officer who buttered his bread with his thumb.

[3] In the eighteenth century, the term "brigade" or "corps" meant a minimum of three regiments which usually operated together under the command of a brigadier general.

Fort Washington garrison to some 2,900 men. But the odds were still grim: facing them were twelve British and fifteen Hessian regiments, totaling about 13,000 men. Colonel Magaw dispersed his troops into a wide arc of outer works in an area about four miles long and three-quarters of a mile wide between the Hudson and the Harlem Rivers and waited.[1]

Washington had arrived at Fort Lee with his staff on November 13, staying at Greene's headquarters in a farmhouse a few miles from the fort itself.[2] Again reassured by Greene that Fort Washington could withstand an assault, the Commander-in-Chief went to his headquarters in Hackensack and turned his attention to defending the interior of New Jersey against a possible British attack. Apparently, he planned to push on to Perth Amboy the next day.

But unknown to Washington, the situation at Fort Washington was changing rapidly for the worse. In fact, a crisis was in the making. On November 15, Colonel James Patterson, Howe's adjutant-general, approached Fort Washington accompanied by a drummer beating the parley.[3] Patterson was carrying a white flag and called upon Magaw to surrender the fort or suffer death by the sword. Magaw gave Patterson a written refusal and the parley ended.

Washington received word of the British ultimatum and quickly determined to go to Fort Washington and talk personally with Magaw. That night, he mounted his horse and rode hard from his headquarters in Hackensack to Fort Lee. Upon arriving at the fort, junior officers told him that Generals Greene and Putnam were across the river conferring with Colonel Magaw. Washington followed his generals and was in the middle of the Hudson River in a boat when he was met by Greene and Putnam returning

---

[1]Christopher L. Ward, *The Delaware Continentals* (Wilmington: Historical Society of Delaware, 1941), 92. Showman, ed., *Greene Papers*, 1: 358. Four battalions from the Flying Camp are identified as having been dispatched from Fort Lee by Greene to reinforce Fort Washington. They were all Pennsylvania units: Swope's, Watts', Montgomery's and Baxter's Bucks County Militia. Bradley's Connecticut Regiment, half of John Durkee's 20th Continentals (Connecticut) and 250 Maryland and Virginia riflemen commanded by Colonel Moses Rawlings are also identified as being sent to reinforce Fort Washington. Douglas Southall Freeman, *George Washington* (New York: Charles Scribner's Sons), IV: 248, note 111; Fitzpatrick,ed., *Writings of Washington*, VI: 285, 293.

[2]Leiby, *Revolutionary War in the Hackensack Valley*, 64.

[3]Beating the parley was a drum call designed to inform one's enemy that you wished to talk. The term is derived from the French word "parle": to converse.

from Fort Washington in their rowboat. The generals sat bobbing and talking with each other as the oarsmen held the boats together. Greene and Putnam said they had just come from a conference with Magaw who insisted that he could repel an attack. They assured Washington that everything possible had been done. Washington returned to Fort Lee, determined to see Magaw himself the following morning and make a final decision on whether the fort should be defended or abandoned. [1]

At sunrise, Washington was again in a boat with Generals Putnam, Greene, and Mercer. Just as they were about to pull away from the New Jersey shore, the generals heard the sounds of cannon fire from across the river. Washington ordered the boat to pull hard for the Manhattan shore; the British assault on Fort Washington had begun. As soon as their boat bumped the shoreline, the generals were out and climbing toward the crest. They found Magaw, and after conferring with him decided that the attack was the opening round of a long siege. Everything seemed well-managed by Magaw, and Washington was urged to return to the safety of Fort Lee. Washington saw that nothing more that could be done and he returned with his entourage to New Jersey. Once back, the generals quickly got to the crest of the Palisades to get a clear view of the action across the river. They were about to become spectators to one of the greatest defeats in American military history.

The morning of November 16 passed with the sound of intense gunfire from across the river. Much of the battle was hidden from view by the rugged hills and forests surrounding Fort Washington. But everyone at Fort Lee could hear the constant reports of artillery and small arms, and could see a great cloud of smoke above the tree line.

Through his telescope, Washington had an unobstructed view of the open terrain south of Fort Washington, and he could see clearly the noble defense of the fort's outer works by Colonel Lambert Cadwalader and his 800 Pennsylvanians. They fought well against imposing odds. Unknown to either Cadwalader or Washington, the patriots were under assault by a force over double their strength, commanded by Lord Percy. Washington could see Percy's troops advancing and Cadwalader's men being cut down. The British advance was inexorable. According to historian Washington Irving, the sight was almost too much for the patriot general: "It is said so completely to have

---

[1] General Israel Putnam (1718-1790) from Connecticut was technically in charge of the American defenses on northern Manhattan Island. See Fitzpatrick, ed., *Writings of Washington*, 6: 206. But Washington thought little of Putnam and worked with Greene on any serious matters, including the defense of Fort Washington.

overcome him, that he wept, with the tenderness of a child."[1] Perhaps. But whatever his emotional state, it was clear to the general that he was not watching a siege; Howe was assaulting Fort Washington from every side with 8,000 British and German troops. The British were moving in for the kill.

By mid-day, after hard fighting north of the fort, Crown forces had broken through the critical outer works, forcing the remaining 2,400 American defenders to retreat to the small earthen fort on the top of the hill. Fort Washington became a trap. It had been built to hold 1,000 men and it was now holding over twice that number. "A single shell," General Heath observed, "dropping among them, must have made dreadful havoc."[2]

As the battlefield fell silent, and Washington thought that the fighting had stopped so that the British could reiterate their surrender demand. At this point, the general sought to take advantage of the lull in the action to contact Magaw. An officer at Fort Lee, Captain John Gooch, volunteered to carry a message to Magaw. It was a promise of help. Washington told Magaw that if he could hold out until nighttime, some way would be found to evacuate his men.[3] In this version of a Revolutionary War marathon, the intrepid and obviously fit Gooch ran down to the Hudson River, jumped into a small boat, rowed himself across, raced up the steep cliff and through the enemy lines to Fort Washington. He found the fort so crowded that it was difficult to pass through. But Gooch found Magaw and delivered Washington's message.

The daring Gooch got a reply, and again braved enemy bullets and bayonets as he ran back through the enemy positions to his boat and rowed back to Fort Lee. He delivered Magaw's message to Washington: It was too late. Fighting on was impossible, and the surrender negotiations were too far advanced for Magaw to break them off. The gallant but distressed colonel

---

[1] Irving, *Life of Washington*, II: 424.

[2] William Heath, *Memoirs of Major-General Heath* (Boston: I. Thomas and E.T. Andrews, 1798), 97.

[3] Heath said that Gooch was a "brave and daring man" and identified him as being from Boston. *Ibid.*, 97. But Freeman says he was a Rhode Islander, a captain in the Ninth Continental Infantry, and cites Heitman. Freeman, *George Washington*, IV: 251, footnote 4; and Frances Heitman, *Historical Register of Officers of the Continental Army* (Washington, DC: Rare Book Shop Publishing Company, 1914), 251. The problem is that the Ninth Continental Infantry was with Charles Lee in Westchester, New York at the time of the British assault on Fort Washington. Lessor, *Sinews of Independence*, 41. It is probable that Gooch, who was Greene's friend, was on detached duty from his regiment and was present at Fort Lee on November 16, 1776.

had no real choice but to proceed with the capitulation, and even as Gooch had reached him, he was about to surrender the fort and its entire garrison. As Gooch returned to the New Jersey side of the Hudson, enemy regiments already were forming to receive the formal surrender. The defeat was total.[1]

The enduring silence at Fort Washington soon made clear the reality of surrender. Shocked rebel troops at Fort Lee, who saw quickly the gravity of the moment, ceased their frantic preparations to bring the men from Fort Washington across the river. Washington and his senior officers, including Greene, Putnam and Mercer, stood silently on the crest of the Palisades as they watched the American standard being lowered from the flagpole at Fort Washington.[2] They were a grim and bewildered audience. A patriot soldier

---

[1]Alexander Graydon was captured at Fort Washington. He noticed that the enemy seemed to have a perfect knowledge of the terrain and the American positions during their assault. Graydon wrote, "In the affair of Fort Washington, he [General Howe] must have had a perfect knowledge of the ground we occupied. This he might have acquired from hundreds in New York; but he might have been more thoroughly informed of every thing desirable to be known, from one Dement, an officer of Magaw's battalion, who was intelligent in points of duty, and deserted to the enemy, about a week before the assault." John Littell, ed., *Alexander Graydon, Memoirs of His Own Time* (Philadelphia: Lindsay & Blakiston, 1846), 215. In 1792, sixteen years after he deserted from Fort Washington, William Demont asked for compensation from the British government. His request stated his service to the British: "On the 2d of Nov 1776 I Sacrificed all I was Worth in the World to the Service of my King & Country and Joined the then Lord Percy brought in with [me] the Plans of Fort Washington by which Plans that Fortress was taken by his Majestys Troops the 16 instant, Together with 2700 Prisoners and Stores & Ammunition to the amount of 1800 Pound, at the same time I may with Justice Affirm from my Knowledge of the Works I saved the Lives of Many of his Majestys Subjects." Edward Floyd de Lancey, ed., Thomas Jones, *History of the New York During The Revolutionary War* (New York: New York Historical Society, 1879), 630. The story of John Gooch's exploit is from Force, ed., *American Archives*, Fifth Ser., III: 741, and Heath, *Memoirs of the American War*, 97.

[2]While marine artist Dominic Serres shows a red and white striped flag flying over Fort Washington, the Continental Army probably did not have a national flag at this point in the Revolution. More likely, since the fort was mostly garrisoned by Pennsylvania troops, a Pennsylvania regimental flag probably flew over it. The British recorded capturing two Pennsylvania rifle regiment standards ("2 Standards with a Rifleman on") and Colonel Magaw's purple standard. Edward Richardson, *Standards and Colors of the American Revolution* (Philadelphia: University of Pennsylvania Press, 1982), 113. There is also the possibility that the fort fought under a red standard with the motto "LIBERTY." Eleven such flags were captured at the Battle of Long Island. A red damask flag with the motto "LIBERTY OR DEATH" is reported to have been captured from the Americans at the Battle of White Plains, less than a month before the surrender of Fort Washington. *Ibid*, 105-106.

standing near the solemn generals recalled the seriousness of the occasion. Washington, he related, "seemed in any agony when he saw the fort surrendered."[1] Only a moment later, the King's colors rose to replace the rebel ensign. The victors savored the moment. The sound of wild cheering drifted across the river along with the music of the combined British and German military bands. The bitter Americans took no pleasure in the celebration.

The disaster was complete. The captured garrison of Fort Washington was marched off to makeshift prisons in New York City. Conditions for many of the prisoners were deplorable. A few of the lucky ones would be exchanged, but over time, most of the unfortunates would die from disease and mistreatment.[2] For all other rebels, the defeat only drove home the seeming invincibility of Howe's army.

While most patriots were still reeling, Charles Lee lost no time in distancing himself from the catastrophic events at Fort Washington. In fact, he used the disaster to enhance his own reputation with other patriot leaders. Lee wrote Doctor Benjamin Rush, his friend and influential member of the Continental Congress, shortly after the surrender: "The affair at Fort Washington cannot surprise you at Philadelphia more than it amazed and stunned me. I must entreat that you will keep what I say to yourself; but I foresaw, predicted, all that has happened; and urged the necessity of abandoning it." Even if the post had managed to hold out, he told Rush, it was useless to the patriots. On the other hand, Lee was not willing to broadcast his opinion of the disaster. Still, he wanted Rush to understand that Washington

---

[1] Joseph White, *A Narrative of Events... Charlestown, Mass., 1833*, reprinted in *American Heritage* 4 (June 1956): 74-79.

[2] Howe reported capturing 2,818 Americans at Fort Washington. British army casualties were stated at 460 men killed or wounded, the majority of whom were Germans. Blanco, ed., *The American Revolution: An Encyclopedia*, I: 578. There were some hard feelings over the surrender among the Americans, with at least one prominent New Englander remarking on the garrison's Pennsylvania origins. Joseph Trumbull, Commissary General of the Continental Army and influential son of Governor Jonathan Trumbull of Connecticut, remarked on this fact in a letter to a friend dated November 18, 1776. Trumbull's letter was intercepted by the British and published in a New York City newspaper. "It is said Mount Washington has surrendered," he wrote. "We don't yet hear particulars. I am glad a Southern officer [Magaw from Pennsylvania] commanded. The story is not told to his advantage here; be it as it may, we should not have heard the last of it from Reed [Joseph Reed from Pennsylvania] and some others of his stamp, if a New-England man had commanded." Joseph Trumbull to William Williams, November 18, 1776, and published in the *New York Gazette*, December 9, 1776; Force, ed., *American Archives*, Fifth Ser., III: 1498. New Englanders sometimes referred to people from New Jersey or Pennsylvania as "Southerners."

had clung to the post against his advice. "Let these few lines be thrown into the fire," he cautioned, "and in your conversation only acquit me of any share of the misfortune—for my last words to the General were—draw off the garrison, or they will be lost."[1]

Some 2,700 American troops were killed, wounded or captured at Fort Washington. It was an appalling defeat for the patriot cause, by far the worst they had suffered so far in the war.[2] Nathanael Greene's inexperience had led to his mistaken belief that Fort Washington was invincible. But the real blame for the catastrophe falls on Washington's shoulders; the crisis stemmed directly from his hesitation in ordering the fort to be abandoned while there was still time. For weeks before the British assault, Washington instinctively knew that trying to hold Fort Washington was folly. Its capture was one of the biggest mistakes Washington made during the entire course of the Revolution (if not *the* biggest mistake). The debacle was a sharp military setback for the rebellion and seriously damaged Washington's personal prestige.

Indeed, events had wounded the Commander-in-Chief to an extent he may not have immediately understood. Some critics saw the loss of Fort Washington and the gravity of the patriot difficulties that followed it as evidence that Washington was losing his grip; he had become too mentally and physically exhausted to make effective decisions. In the Continental Congress, some members bluntly said that Washington had made a mess of things. Maryland delegate Samuel Chase, after learning the details of the staggering losses at Fort Washington, sent a report back home which bitterly recorded that "2,200 of our Troops are prisoners. The fort was victualed for three Months & amply supplied with Cannon and all military stores. If this account be true, we have again blundered."[3] The account was true enough, and so was the blunder.

---

[1]Charles Lee to Benjamin Rush, November 20, 1776, *Lee Papers*, II: 288. Lee claimed that he had argued that Fort Washington should be evacuated, but that his proposal had been ignored. James Flexner, *George Washington in the American Revolution* (Boston: Little, Brown, 1967), 145.

[2]Only the surrender of almost 5,500 American troops at Charleston, South Carolina, in May 1780 surpassed the losses sustained at Fort Washington.

[3]Samuel Chase to the Maryland Council of Safety, November 21, 1776, Paul H. Smith, ed., *Letters of Delegates to Congress, 1774-1789* (Washington, DC: Library of Congress, 1976-): 5: 525.

CHAPTER THREE

Fort Lee

Gen. Howe must exert every nerve to effect something more than he has yet done with a land and marine force that all Europe had been taught to believe would in one Campaign crush America.
—Richard Henry Lee, November 1776

Despite the intense military activity at Fort Lee in the autumn of 1776, there was little else in the surrounding New Jersey countryside to indicate a state of war. Traveling west, beyond Fort Lee, the narrow farm roads quickly left the war behind as they passed considerable salt meadows and tidal marshes, then opened onto the rich and broad farmlands of the Hackensack Valley. This flat, abundantly watered valley was populated by prosperous farmers descended from the original settlers of New Netherland. From all accounts, the Hackensack Valley was delightful and prized farm country with handsome houses, active mills, and barns and yards brimming with livestock and grain.

The center of activity in the valley was the village of Hackensack, which lay along the Hackensack River five miles west of Fort Lee. This peaceful hamlet surrounded a village green. On the north side of the green was a church with a short white steeple, and next to it was a small stone building which served as the Bergen County courthouse. Near the courthouse was a tavern kept by Archibald Campbell. Also clustered around the green were a few small buildings that housed tradesmen including a blacksmith and a tanner.

The largest and most elegant building in Hackensack was the home of Peter Zabriskie, a local judge and wealthy landowner.[1] The Zabriskie Mansion, as it was called locally, was built of stone three feet thick and stood on the north side of the village green near the church. The road extending north from the village along the Hackensack River was dotted with pleasant farmhouses. Two miles along this road was a bridge across the Hackensack River. Built in 1745, it was called "New Bridge." It was also possible to cross the Hackensack on one of the several mill dams that had been constructed across the river. Enterprising farmers living along the river ferried passengers across the river for a fee. Three miles to the south of the village was a ferry called "Little Ferry" (today the town of Little Ferry).

A few miles to the west of the Hackensack River lay a meandering river named the Passaic, that could be traced to its source in the Great Swamp around Basking Ridge, New Jersey. A dilapidated bridge crossed the Passaic on the road from Hackensack, leading to another village named Acquackanonk (modern Passaic). There were other small farming communities spread over the countryside of northern New Jersey with quaint Indian and Dutch names like Totowa, Teaneck, Pascack and Paramus. From all accounts, the Hackensack Valley had some of the best farmland in all of the original Thirteen Colonies.

The majority of the people living in the Hackensack Valley were neither townsmen nor great landowners. They were independent farmers, usually owning seventy-five or a hundred acres of land from which they derived a comfortable existence. A fair number of the farms used slave labor.

People of Dutch ancestry were numerous in the Hackensack Valley. They doggedly spoke Dutch in their homes and churches and kept their Old World customs even though Holland had finally surrendered New Netherland to the English a century prior to the American Revolution. As the earliest settlers to arrive in New Jersey, the Dutch were among the largest land-owners in Bergen County, and they also owned the rich land along the banks of the Raritan and Millstone Rivers in the central part of New Jersey.

---

[1]This account is drawn from Adrian C. Leiby, *The Revolutionary War in The Hackensack Valley* (New Brunswick: Rutgers University Press, 1962), 7.

At the outbreak of the Revolution, New Jersey was a quiet, comfortable agricultural colony with no great commercial centers or seaports. The land was bountiful and New Jersey was known in the eighteenth century as the Garden of America. Produce from New Jersey's farms moved along country roads to the colony's river ports for shipment to nearby cities. In the eastern part of New Jersey, the roads led to the river ports of Perth Amboy, New Brunswick, Raritan Landing, Newark, and Elizabethtown. These port towns sent the bulk of their boats to New York City. In the western part of New Jersey, produce was sent to Philadelphia from the Delaware River port towns of Burlington, Salem, Bordentown, and Trenton.[1]

New Jersey's population had been steadily increasing in the years prior to the Revolution. In 1745, it was estimated at 61,000. By 1754 it had risen to 80,000 and reached approximately 115,000 by 1772.[2] On the eve of the American Revolution, Elizabethtown (present- day Elizabeth) had grown to between 200 and 300 houses, making it the largest and most important town in New Jersey. Trenton, Perth Amboy and New Brunswick had about a hundred houses each. Newark and Princeton were smaller but growing.

People of Dutch ancestry made up over one-sixth of the population of New Jersey. The vast majority belonged to the Dutch Reformed Church. The Scotch, Scotch-Irish, and Germans followed the Dutch to New Jersey and settled in the interior of the province, especially in Somerset and Hunterdon Counties.[3] The Scotch and Scotch-Irish were Presbyterians and the Germans were Lutherans. There were also Quakers who settled in the western part of New Jersey, along the Delaware River in Burlington County. People of Puritan stock had emigrated from New England to New Jersey, establishing themselves in Essex and Morris Counties with their commercial centers at Newark, Elizabethtown, and Morristown. There were also some 10,000 blacks in New Jersey in 1775, most of whom were slaves.

Like many of her sister colonies, New Jersey had moved slowly from

---

[1]Wheaton Lane, *From Indian Trail to Iron Horse* (Princeton: Princeton University Press, 1939), 50.

[2]Carl Woodward, *Ploughs and Politicks* (New Brunswick: Rutgers University Press, 1941), 146.

[3]The term Scotch-Irish referred mostly to refugees from Scotland who were forcibly removed to Ireland by the British government following the Scottish uprising of 1745. These people preferred to call themselves "Ulstermen," the county in Northern Ireland where they lived before coming to America.

protest to rebellion. Much of the support for the rebellion came from the poorest and least educated people in the colony; the Scotch-Irish farmers in the hilly regions of Morris County and those living on the borders of the great swamps and marshlands. Looking at each county in the colony, there was some support for the rebellion in Somerset and Hunterdon Counties. Bergen and Monmouth Counties were two of the biggest Loyalist centers in New Jersey. Less populated Sussex County also held many Loyalists. Middlesex County was generally for the rebellion as were Essex, Salem, and Cumberland Counties. Cape May County had too few people to matter. On balance, New Jersey was a largely patriot state, but with enough support for the King to make for bitter civil strife during the war.

New Jersey was slow to respond to the outbreak of the Revolution. However, within six months after the start of the war, the colony had raised three regiments which marched off to fight in Canada. By 1776, however, with these regiments gone, New Jersey had only a weak, poorly organized militia at home for regional defense. In June 1776, to help defend the state, the Continental Congress voted to raise militia companies from Maryland, Delaware, and Pennsylvania to form a mobile reserve named the Flying Camp. General Hugh Mercer was appointed commander of the Flying Camp and militia were recruited to serve until December 1 or December 30, 1776. The Flying Camp was, in theory, to rush to any point along New Jersey's shoreline where the enemy might attempt an invasion.

George Washington was desperate for manpower during the New York campaign and he depleted the Flying Camp to fill the ranks of the Grand Army. By November 14, the remaining poorly trained and equipped militia regiments of the Flying Camp had moved to Fort Lee or were guarding the Hudson River.[1] In the days following the loss of Fort Washington, General Washington came to the grim realization that these poorly disciplined and dispirited troops represented a significant portion of the men still available to him. It was not a comforting prospect.

It rained in northern New Jersey on the night of November 19, 1776. Major General Nathanael Greene was sleeping soundly at Fort Lee, knowing that five hundred American soldiers were patrolling the New Jersey side of the Hudson. The patrols ran from opposite Spuyten Duyvil to Sneden's Landing watching for a surprise attack.

Five miles away, in Hackensack, Washington was also sleeping. Before retiring, he had finally completed a private letter which he had started

---

[1]Force, ed., *American Archives*, Fifth Ser., 3: 663.

two weeks earlier to his confidant and brother, John Augustine. In this revealing letter (dated Hackensack, November 19), Washington wrote about what had happened since his arrival at White Plains in October. He was especially bitter at the loss of Fort Washington, writing that when he learned that a British squadron had sailed safely past the rebel gun batteries on the Hudson River on November 5, he had wanted to abandon the position. It was held contrary to his "wishes and opinion," he wrote, and he constantly faced "perplexities and mortifications." These included, he painfully reported, the poor quality of the officers in his army. "The different States," the general complained, commissioned men "without regard to the merits or qualifications of any officer, quarreling about the appointments, and nominating such as are not fit to be shoe blacks." Washington closed his letter with a passage that would later become famous. "I am wearied almost to death with the retrograde motions of things," he told John, and "solemnly" protested that a reward of twenty thousand pounds a year "would not induce me to undergo what I do." He wished his brother "all health and happiness," adding that "nothing in this world would contribute so much to mine as to be once more fixed among you in the peaceable enjoyment of my own vine and fig tree."[1] It was one of the general's most heartfelt letters of the war.

Since the dreadful surrender of Fort Washington, the morale of the Grand Army had reached a new low. There was whispered criticism of Washington's generalship from the officer corps and among politicians, all of which was a heavy burden for the sensitive Virginian to bear. Those closest to him knew that he felt himself wronged by such criticism. "We were in a fair way of finishing the campaign with credit to ourselves," wrote Tench Tilghman, one of the general's young aides, "and I think to the disgrace of Mr. Howe, and had the General [Washington] followed his own opinion, the [Fort Washington] garrison would have been withdrawn immediately upon the enemy's falling down from Dobb's Ferry. But General Greene was positive," Tilghman explained, "that our forces might at any time be drawn off under the guns of Fort Lee. Fatal experience has evinced the contrary."[2]

---

[1]Fitzpatrick, ed., *Writings of Washington*, 6: 242-247.

[2]Tench Tilghman wrote Robert R. Livingston from Hackensack on November 17, the day after the loss of Fort Washington. Force, ed., *American Archives*, Fifth Ser., III: 740. Tilghman (1744-1786) was a successful Philadelphia businessman, the son of a prosperous Maryland tobacco grower. He was a graduate of what today is the University of Pennsylvania, was an active patriot, and joined the American army at the start of the rebellion. Tilghman was an officer in the Flying Camp in the summer of 1776 and joined

The Commander-in-Chief did not hesitate to take decisive action following the loss of Fort Washington. Wisely, he did not seriously consider a stand at Fort Lee. Rather, he ordered all the equipment and stores at Fort Lee removed as quickly as possible in preparation for abandoning that post and retreating deeper into New Jersey. But a lack of transportation frustrated his efforts to move the vast amounts of equipment and foodstuffs to the safety of the interior of the state. The delay was frustrating and potentially dangerous. Still, the general worked energetically.

But the patriots had run out of time. On the morning of November 20, after a rainy night, Washington was up early and again working with his staff to get the Fort Lee stores away. At 10:00 a.m., he was absorbed in his work when a rider came galloping up to the Zabriskie Mansion from Orange-Town, New York, with urgent news: Howe's army had crossed the Hudson. The invasion of New Jersey had begun.[1]

The moment Washington finished reading the communication he immediately swung into action. He jumped to his feet and gave instructions for troops from his skeleton force at Hackensack to secure the strategic points between the crossroads of Liberty Pole (modern Englewood) and Fort Lee, especially the New Bridge. The Commander-in-Chief then mounted his horse

---

Washington's staff as an aide on August 8, 1776. He was an aide to Washington until the end of the Revolution, and Washington allowed him the honor of having him bring the news of Cornwallis's defeat at Yorktown (1781) to the Continental Congress. He was one of thirty-two men who served on Washington's military staff during the Revolution, and he served the longest, seven years. Many of Tilghman's staff colleagues were talented officers, but the rebels never developed a fully organized or effective staff during the war.

[1]The time of the arrival of the courier is mentioned in a letter from Robert H. Harrison to General Schuyler, dated Hackensack, November 20, 1776, Force, ed. *American Archives*, Fifth Ser., III: 781. Harrison's comments offer the most detailed account of how General Washington learned about the British invasion of New Jersey. Orange-Town, New York (modern Orangetown), is near the New Jersey border and close to the Hudson River. At the time, Orange-Town was probably an American outpost. Colonel Harrison's comments demonstrate that news of the invasion did not come from General Greene at Fort Lee, as some historians have believed; e.g., Freeman, *George Washington*, IV: 256. Having learned of the attack, Washington did not ride all the way to Fort Lee. He only went as far as the strategic crossroads of Liberty Pole to await the arrival of Greene with the Fort Lee garrison. Greene must have learned independently that the British army had landed. We can also speculate that upon receiving the news of the invasion, Washington sent an urgent dispatch to Greene with orders to abandon Fort Lee. This would account for Greene's noting, a few days later, that "His Excellency ordered a retreat immediately." Nathanael Greene to Governor Nicholas Cooke, December 4, 1776, Showman, ed., *Greene Papers*, 1: 360.

and, accompanied by Major General Israel Putnam and two of his aides (William Grayson and Robert Hanson Harrison), he rode east to the Hackensack River. He crossed using either one of the boats held there for the use of the army or by riding over one of the mill dams, and then galloped with his party down the road towards Fort Lee.

At the same time that Washington received the fearful news, an American officer arrived at Fort Lee with the same intelligence. A large British force, he said, had landed at dawn seven or eight miles above the fort.[1] General Greene could only conclude that they were coming hard, and he immediately began preparing to evacuate Fort Lee.

The Commander-in-Chief, who had questioned Greene's judgment in the aftermath of Fort Washington, now was in full accord. As Washington raced his horse eastward towards the Hudson River and Fort Lee, he knew that the post was nothing more than an incomplete earthen work garrisoned by a small, untrained force. Defense was folly. The Fort Lee garrison must be evacuated across the Hackensack River, but Washington knew that such a large number of men could only cross the river on the New Bridge. If the British seized the bridge before he could get the retreating troops across, or if the enemy gained control of the strategic crossroads at Liberty Pole, the Fort Lee garrison would be trapped. It would be a debacle that could easily finish the rebel army.

General Howe's hopes for the operation were probably not as high. But he wanted to do real damage at Fort Lee, and then to press the invasion of the New Jersey interior. Howe's units had moved the night before, under cover

---

[1] There was never any lack of opinion on how the warning of the attack reached Fort Lee. Thomas Paine, an aide to General Greene, recorded the time of the American officer's arrival at the fort, and Paine was there at the time. Eric Foner, ed., *Thomas Paine, Collected Writings* (New York: Literary Classics of the United States, Inc., 1995), *The American Crisis*, I: 93. The diary of Ensign Thomas Glyn contradicts Paine regarding the warning, saying that it came from a "Countryman" (a farmer). But Glyn is a less reliable source than Paine, who was actually at Fort Lee. Charles Stedman, who also witnessed events from the British side, told yet another version. He said that a British deserter warned Fort Lee. "Lord Cornwallis began his march with great secrecy and dispatch," Stedman wrote. "In all probability he would have surprised the fort and made the enemy prisoners of war, had not a deserter informed them of his approach." Charles Stedman, *History of the American War* (London, 1794), I: 219. There is also a legend that a slave girl later given the name Polly Wyckoff gave the first alarm. She supposedly was working in the kitchen of the Matthew Bogert farm when she looked out the window and saw British soldiers. Running into the living quarters where the family was seated, she exclaimed "Bogert's fields are full of Red Coats!" The story is in T. Earle Thompson, *An Elementary History of New Jersey* (New York, Hinds, Hayden & Eldredge, 1924), 56.

of the rainstorm. By dawn of November 20, a division of the British task force had landed and secured a landing at Closter, New Jersey. As Washington rode towards Fort Lee, the entire British invasion force of 5,000 had landed safely in New Jersey.

Historians do not know exactly when Howe decided to invade New Jersey. However, the operation seemed the logical next step after the fall of Fort Washington. This much was clear even to junior officers. As early as November 15, Captain Frederick Mackenzie wrote in his diary that "from the general appearance of matters, it is probable, that the moment Fort Washington is taken, General Howe will land a body of troops in Jersey from the right of his Army, and after taking Fort Constitution [Fort Lee] penetrate into that Province towards Philadelphia."[1]

The first evidence of Howe's intentions came in his order calling for fifty flatboats to move up the Hudson River from New York City. These boats would ferry the invasion force to New Jersey. Some of the boats floated undetected past the sentries at Fort Lee and were moored out of site of rebel observers at Spuyten Duyvil.[2] In a general order dated November 19, 1776, General Howe actually put the invasion of New Jersey into motion under the command of General Charles Earl Cornwallis, an aggressive career officer.[3]

---

[1]Mackenzie, *Diary*, 1: 105.

[2]On November 23, 1776, Vice Admiral Lord Richard Howe reported to the Admiralty that "Thirty flat boats were ordered up to Kingsbridge by the North River the Night of the 14th." Boats crews came from Navy transports. Twenty additional boats made the trip, "undiscovered" by rebel batteries, on the night of November 18. Donald M. Londahl-Smidt, "British and Hessian Accounts of the Invasion of Bergen County," *Bergen County History*, 1976 Annual, 45-47. The original letter is in Great Britain, Public Record Office, Admiralty, Class 1, vol. 487. The barges used by the British for their invasion of New Jersey were depicted in a watercolor by Captain Thomas Davies of the Royal Artillery. They had one mast and were manned by British sailors. Built in England, specially-modified transports brought them to America. There were also smaller boats in the British New Jersey invasion flotilla; called "batteau," they were long, light, flat-bottomed boats with a sharply pointed bow and stern.

[3]The general order, dated Nov. 19, which started the British invasion of New Jersey read as follows: "The following Corps are to Strike their Tents Load their Waggons & be in reddiness to March with their Blanketts & Provision this Night at Nine O'Clock. Two Compy Chassuiers 1st & 2d Lt. Infantry 1st & 2d Grenadiers 33d Regt 42 Regt. 3 Battns Hessian Grenadiers---2 Battn of Guards 100 Men of Roger's Corps without Arms two Engineers with twelve Carpenters & three Guides. They will receive their Orders from Lt. Gl. Ld. Cornwallis." Orderly book of the 1st battalion, detachment of the Brigade of

Lord Cornwallis, Sixth Earl of Eyre, and a member of the House of Lords, was a good choice to command the critical New Jersey mission. He was an ambitious and experienced officer, a man who had wanted to be a soldier from childhood. Just prior to his eighteenth birthday, his rich and indulgent father bought him an ensign's commission in the prestigious First Regiment of Foot Guards. But instead of joining his regiment, Cornwallis toured Europe with a Prussian officer and attended a military academy in Italy. When the Seven Years War broke out in 1757, Cornwallis abandoned his studies and rushed to join the fighting. He proved to be a bold and enterprising young officer who was beloved by his men. His youthful experience was the opening chapter in an illustrious military career.

At the time of the New Jersey invasion, Cornwallis was a seasoned veteran. He had seen plenty of combat during the Seven Years War, and his courage and intelligence were undoubted. Thirty-eight years old in his American command, he was described as short and thick set, his hair somewhat gray, his face pleasant, and his manner easy. He also had a cast in one eye, the result of a sports injury inflicted on him by a fellow classmate while in school at Eton. Cornwallis was married and deeply devoted to his wife, who had begged him not to leave her for the war in America. (Perhaps he should have listened to her. But in 1776, who would have predicted his fate at Yorktown in 1781?)

Under Cornwallis' command, the five thousand-man amphibious assault of New Jersey commenced at 11:00 p.m. on the night of November 19. The secretly-gathered boats emerged from Spuyten Duyvil onto the Hudson River, concealed under a driving rainstorm and a heavy fog, which was common along the Palisades.[1] The boats quietly ferried the first division, consisting of half of Cornwallis' force, to a point in New Jersey about five miles north of Spuyten Duyvil.

A variety of contemporary sources revealed the composition of the British invasion force. Lord Cornwallis commanded elite troops, mostly veteran infantry units. The force was composed of the First and Second Battalions of Light Infantry, the Forty-second (or Royal Highland) Regiment of Foot (better known as the "Black Watch"), and two companies of Hessian

---

Guards, August 2, 1776 to January 28, 1777, Manuscripts Division, New York Historical Society, New York.

[1]The exact number of soldiers taking part in the invasion varies from source to source, but 5,000 men is the generally accepted figure.

Jaegers.[1] In addition, Cornwallis was assigned his own Thirty-third Regiment of Foot, "The Detachment of the Brigade of Guards," three battalions of Hessian grenadiers commanded by Colonel Carl Emilius von Donop, and a hundred men from Lieutenant Colonel Robert Rogers' provincial Queen's American Rangers.[2]

Also important to the mission were three Bergen County loyalists. They were probably John Aldington, who owned a farm and brewery in English Neighborhood (now Leonia), John Ackerson, a Closter farmer, and William Bayard, who operated the Hoboken ferry. Traveling with Cornwallis, they led his men to a remote and unguarded landing site. There, the King's troops found a pitching place with a narrow path leading from the river's edge to the crest of the Palisades and onto the farm country of Tenafly, New Jersey.[3]

---

[1]The English translation of jaeger is hunter. In 1775, the British needed rifle units of their own to counter the dangerous patriot riflemen, most of whom came from the frontier counties of Pennsylvania, Maryland, and Virginia and carried the long, light and often skillfully made Pennsylvania long rifle. The jaegers were recruited from forest wardens and game keepers, wore green uniforms, and carried a short, accurate rifle with a large bore and an octagonal barrel of about 28 inches. George Neumann, *The History of Weapons of the American Revolution* (New York: Harper & Row, 1967), 134. The jaegers were fine marksmen as well as skilled and motivated soldiers. The two companies arrived in America in 1776, and if later outfits were not always up to the quality of the initial companies, they generally proved to be excellent troops. They were often used as scouts and frequently they provided marching columns with flank, rear, or advance security. The presence of the two jaeger companies with Cornwallis was further evidence of the high quality of soldiers who assaulted New Jersey on November 20.

[2]Donald M. Londahl-Smidt, "British and Hessian Accounts of the Invasion of Bergen County, 1776," 37 -38. Londahl-Smidt's extensive research has yielded a detailed list of the troops that comprised the Cornwallis expedition. Rogers, who commanded an elite corps of provincial scouts called Rogers Rangers during the French and Indian War, remained loyal to the King during the Revolution and raised the Queen's American Rangers. In the British army, the First, Second (also called the Coldstream Guards), and Third Regiments of Foot comprised the Brigade of Foot Guards. In February 1776, fifteen men were selected from each of the companies of the three regiments for service in America. The 1,101 officers and men were commanded by acting Brigadier General Edward Mathew and were known as The Detachment of the Brigade of Guards.

[3]"Pitching places" were used to throw logs down to the shore, where boats took them to New York. Historian Richard P. McCormick was the first to speculate on Aldington's role as a guide, but there is no definitive proof connecting any specfic Tory to the invasion force. Any number of local residents knew the terrain and could have helped the British. See "John Aldington," *Bergen County History*, 1970 Annual; John Spring, "The 1776 British Landing at Closter," *Bergen County History*, 1975 Annual.

Cornwallis's landing place has confused historians for over two hundred years. At the time, no one recorded the name of the exact site, and during the first decades of this century, historians decided the British came ashore at Upper Closter Landing (also known as Old Closter Dock Landing), which is seven and a half miles north of Fort Lee. However, compelling evidence now shows that the British army actually landed at Lower Closter Landing (later called Huyler's Landing) which is a one and a half miles closer to Fort Lee.[1]

The British next faced the arduous task of getting themselves and their artillery up the narrow and steep path from the river to the crest of the Palisades. Lieutenant Henry Stirke of the Light Infantry was one of the first men ashore. He looked up to see a "Precipice, above a half mile in length" and

---

[1]In 1898, William S. Stryker published his classic account of the Battles of Trenton and Princeton. Stryker briefly described the New Jersey retreat of 1776, and without supporting documentation placed the landing site at Old Closter Dock. William Stryker, *The Battles of Trenton and Princeton* (Boston and New York: Houghton, Mifflin and Company, 1898), 2. Later historians assumed the accuracy of Stryker's account, thus perpetuating the story.

The distance of these two landing sites from Fort Lee was important, but so was the road system that extended from the landings into the interior of New Jersey. In 1776, it was three miles longer to Fort Lee from Upper Closter Landing than from Lower Closter Landing. Based on the time of the British landing and their arrival at Fort Lee, it seems likely that Cornwallis came ashore at Lower Closter Landing. Historian John Spring explained that a fault in the Palisades at Lower Closter Landing created a steep but passable natural path from the shoreline of the Hudson to the crest. General Anthony Wayne surveyed the path in 1780 and reported that it was approximately four feet wide. This path is clearly shown in Captain Thomas Davies's watercolor painting. A local landowner and businessman named George Huyler widened and graded the path in 1840, which erased the original track. Other development along the Hudson Palisades in the last century altered the terrain and confused historians even further.

Historian Kevin Wright suggests that guides with Cornwallis may have overshot Lower Closter Landing on the night of Nov. 19 and arrived at Upper Closter Landing instead. Realizing their mistake, they brought the boats to Lower Closter Landing. This could account for the story that Cornwallis stopped at the Blackledge-Kearny House at Upper Closter Landing on the morning of Nov. 20. The house, built in 1750, is still standing at the water's edge.

Another theory is that the guides first brought Cornwallis to Lower Closter Landing, which he initially rejected as unsuitable. Looking at other landing sites, including Upper Closter Landing where he went ashore briefly, Cornwallis then returned to Lower Closter Landing where his troops landed and scaled the Palisades. The diary of Ensign Thomas Glyn, who took part in the operation, gives a tempting bit of information about the confusion over the landing site. The site was, he wrote, "beyond the usual landing place and considered inaccessible for any body of men." Thomas Glyn, "Ensign Glyn's Journal on the American Service with the Detachment of 1,000 Men of the Guards Commanded by Brigadier General Mathew in 1776," Nov. 20, 1776, unpublished manuscript, Princeton University Library, Special Collections, Princeton, NJ.

"impassable for Horses." Stirke said that his company, with another, was ordered to, "push up the hill, with as much expedition as possible to take post; and maintain it, till sustain'd."[1] The path that the light infantry companies struggled to climb was scarcely four feet wide, but that was enough. When they reached the top, the Light Infantry and German Jaegers secured a semi-circular defensive perimeter while other units made the climb. A Hessian officer, after ascending the rocky height, felt that the British were lucky to have landed unopposed. "Our disembarkation appeared terrible and impracticable as we landed at the foot of a rocky height and had to go up a very steep and narrow path. Fifty men," he said, " would have sufficed to hold back the entire corps if they had only hurled stones down on us."[2]

There were not enough boats to carry the five thousand British across the Hudson at one time. Thus Cornwallis had to split his invasion force into two divisions. The second division waited for the boats to return from New Jersey at the Philipse Farm, a vast tract in Westchester County directly across the Hudson from the New Jersey landing site. The farm was only a part of Philipsburg Manor, the seat of the influential Philipse family. The manor encompassed all the land along the eastern shore of the Hudson River from Spuyten Duyvil to the Croton River. The farm itself stretched along the Hudson River from Spuyten Duyvil to Yonkers, and the British used the Philipse dock, which reached three hundred feet across the river. (A large section of the Philipse Farm is located in the center of modern Yonkers.)

Waiting to embark in the second wave was Hessian Colonel Karl von Donop. An officer with many years of service, he found the crossing a time-consuming operation. Von Donop had started with his brigade from camp at Westchester County at 9:00 p.m. on November 19, proceeding to "Colonel Courtland's house" where he met the English Guards detachment. This combined force left the Courtland House at 3:00 a.m. and marched to the Philipse Farm, which they reached about two hours later. "It was only at 8 o'clock that we could be embarked." wrote Von Donop, "as the boats, which took over 2 battalions of light infantry, two Batt'ns of English Grenadiers and

[1]Henry Strike, "A British Officer's Revolutionary War Journal," ed. S. Sydney Bradford, *Maryland Historical Magazine* 56, No. 2 (June 1961): 165.

[2]Translation of original manuscript, Military Reports and Narrations of the Hessian Corps in America, Item Z, Lidgerwood Collection, Morristown National Historical Park. The letter was from Lieutenant Johann Emanuel Wagner to Lieutenant General Wilhelm von Dittfurth, and dated, "In Camp at [English] Neighbourhood below Fort Lee, in the Province of Jersey, November 22nd, 1776."

the 33rd and 42nd Regiments to the New Jersey Coast opposite to Philips house, did not get back before that time." Most of the expedition's artillery was with the second division as well, which meant that the British had to avoid heavy fighting until the entire force was across the Hudson.[1]

Ensign Thomas Glyn provided another eye-witness account of the invasion. Glyn, who served in the Detachment of the Brigade of Guards, also crossed to New Jersey with Cornwallis's second division. He said the first division landed in New Jersey at daybreak, and, "as soon as the boats could return, the 2nd Division embarked at Philipses Farm and the whole Corps made to the crest of the Palisades good their landing without any opposition."[2]

The lack of opposition was fortunate, because the troops had a hard time getting up the Palisades. Both Glyn and von Donop recalled the climb with evident distaste. The Hessian complained that the landing place "appeared horrible and impracticable," and that the troops had to climb up a very steep path which was hardly four feet wide. "The rebels," he said, "must have considered it an impossible landing place, for they had no sentries posted at the place; for 50 men would have been sufficient to check our whole corps." Glyn made very similar observations. The Palisades, he wrote, had "a very perpendicular bank of rock 80 feet high to ascend," which made reaching the top very difficult; it was a poor "landing place and considered as unacceptable for any body of troops."[3]

---

[1]Donop to Lt. Gen. Baron von Heister, November 19, 1776, translation of original manuscript, Lidgerwood Collection of Hessian Manuscripts, Letter A, Morristown National Historical Park, 12-14. The best evidence shows that the Cornwallis's entire force gathered on the night of November 19 at Spuyten Duyvil where the first division embarked. The troops of the second division marched up the east side of the Hudson River six miles to the Ludlow area of Philipse's Farm. See Howe to Lord Germain, November 30, 1776: "The 1st Division for Embarkation landed next Day at 8 o'Clock in the Morning about seven Miles above the Fort, while the 2d. Division marched up the East Side of the River, by which Movement the whole Corps, were landed with their Cannon by 10 o'Clock under the Command of Lieutenant General Earl Cornwallis." Quoted in Donald M. Londahl-Smidt, "British and Hessian Accounts of the Invasion of Bergen County, 1776," *Bergen County History*, 1976 Annual, 47- 48. Lieutenant Strike's journal noted that "The Guards, with ye British, and Hessian Grenadiers; *and the Cannon succeeded us.*" S. Sydney Bradford, "A British Officer's Revolutionary War Journal, 1776-1778," *Maryland Historical Magazine* 56, No. 2 (June 1961): 164.

[2]Thomas Glyn, "Ensign Glyn's Journal on the American Service with the Detachment of 1,000 Men of the Guards Commanded by Brigadier General Mathew in 1776." Unpublished manuscript, Princeton University Library, Special Collections, 28.

[3]Donop to von Heister, Nov. 19, 1776, Lidgerwood Collection; Glyn, "Journal," 28.

The soldiers also had to drag the artillery up the Palisades. There were eight pieces of artillery with the expedition: two light six-pounders, two howitzers, and four English three-pounders, all of which were manhandled to the crest of the Palisades by troops and sailors. It took until nearly 1:00 p.m. to get the cannons up the steep, narrow path from the river.[1]

As the last of his troops reached the top of the Palisades, Cornwallis wasted no time in starting toward Fort Lee. Ensign Glyn recalled that "Lord Cornwallis immediately formed his corps in two columns" and began "a very rapid march." The rebels, the young officer noted with satisfaction, "were completely surprised." But Glyn's claim that the advance was "immediate" may have been a charitable account of events. Von Donop timed the march from the top of the Palisades at about 2:00 p.m., which may indicate that the British had a hard time getting reorganized after their difficult climb.

Donop's account may have been closer to reality. The journal of another Hessian officer, Captain Johann Ewald of the Second Jaeger Company, also recorded a cautious initial advance. The amphibious landing in New Jersey was heavily covered by the Royal Navy, he recalled, and he noted that the first deployments in New Jersey were defensive. "At the top [of the Palisades]," Ewald wrote, the jaegers and light infantry moved to farms in Tenafly where they formed "in a semicircle behind the stone walls and posted sentries by platoon at distances of three hundred paces." There they stayed for the time being, with Fort Lee "two hours away from us on the left."[2] This was not a description of a hard-driving assault column.

The early British delays were providential for the Americans. Once clear of the cliffs, Cornwallis moved quickly, but by then word of his advance had spread. Warned that the British had landed, Washington rode to Liberty Pole, where he learned that the enemy had temporarily halted after advancing to a hill about two miles north of the village. He decided to stay at Liberty Pole to meet the retreating garrison from Fort Lee and lead them to Hackensack.

While waiting at Liberty Pole, Washington tried to inform General Lee of the developing situation. He instructed one of his aides, Lieutenant Colonel William Grayson, to return to Hackensack and send a dispatch to Lee

---

[1]Glyn, "Journal," 28; von Donop to von Heister, November 19, 1776, Lidgerwood Collection; "Journal of Lieutenant General von Heister's Corps, January 1776 to June 1777," Letter H, Lidgerwood Collection.

[2]Joseph P. Tustin, trans. and ed., *Diary of the American War: Diary of Captain Johann Ewald* (New Haven and London: Yale University Press, 1979),. 17. Ewald had no political stake in the war, and his opinions were generally impartial and honest.

with details of the British invasion. Washington told Grayson to have Lee move his corps across the Hudson River. The Commander-in-Chief assumed that Lee would quickly respond, for such was the plan Washington had adopted before leaving North Castle.[1]

After being warned of the British advance, the first reaction of the garrison was, incredibly, to eat a hasty breakfast. Then, with growing disorder fueled by rumors, they streamed off, abandoning their fort and moving westward down Fort Lee Road (a military road built by the army). They passed quickly over Red Hill Road and through English Neighborhood to the Kings Highway (modern Grand Avenue, Leonia), where they turned north. Their route then took them west towards the crossroads of Liberty Pole where Washington, Putnam, and a few aides anxiously awaited them.

The retreating Fort Lee garrison was composed mostly of the poorly trained troops of the Flying Camp. They amounted to about two thousand officers and men.[2] Even with Washington in command, they were no match for the pursuing enemy column.

Washington led the retreat west from Liberty Pole along Liberty Road to New Bridge Road, and then over the Hackensack River at the New Bridge. The retreat became tumultuous. As news of the enemy advance spread, the poorly disciplined Fort Lee garrison came close to panic. Some of the retreating Americans broke away from the main column and went south through English Neighborhood and modern Ridgefield. This group crossed the Hackensack River at Little Ferry and made their way to Hackensack along

---

[1]Grayson's dispatch to Lee, dated Hackensack, Nov. 20, was detailed and alarming. It reached Lee only a few hours after Cornwallis came ashore. "They landed this morning between Dobbs's Ferry and Fort Lee," Grayson wrote, "as it is imagined, at a place called Closter Dock, nearly opposite to Philips's house, and (as the General has been informed) in great numbers, and an advanced party of them have proceeded as far as a hill two miles above the liberty pole, about a mile and an half above General Greene's quarters where I left his Excellency." The roads to the interior of New Jersey were still open, he noted, and retreat was still possible. British intentions were unclear, "but it is imagined the getting possession of Fort Lee is one part of their design; however, it is possible, and perhaps probable, they may have other and more capital views." Grayson then conveyed Washington's advice to move his command to the New Jersey side of the Hudson and "there wait for further orders." Force, ed., *American Archives*, Fifth Ser., III: 780.

[2]There is no reliable count of the troops at Fort Lee. A return of November 13, 1776 listed 2,667 officers and men "fit for duty"; but after the dispatch of last-minute reinforcements to Fort Washington, the Fort Lee garrison on Nov. 20 was probably about 2,000. "Return of the Forces encamped on the Jersey Shore, commanded by Major-General Greene, November 13, 1776," Force, ed., *American Archives*, Fifth Ser., III: 663-664.

what is now Hudson Street. Discipline was no better in the main body. The men abandoned artillery on the road and littered the retreat route with equipment and provisions as they hastened toward the safety of New Bridge.[1] Some six miles separated Fort Lee from New Bridge, no small distance when running from a vastly superior army.

In the commotion, some of the men broke into the liquor supply of the camp sutlers and got drunk. General Greene rode back to Fort Lee two hours after the evacuation and collected several hundred of these drunken stragglers, but he estimated that nearly a hundred more remained hidden in the woods.[2]

Despite Washington's trepidation, Lord Cornwallis made no attempt to seize New Bridge. Nor did his corps chase the retreating garrison.[3] Once

---

[1]Force, ed., *American Archives*, Fifth Ser., III: 1058.

[2]Force, ed., *American Archives*, Fifth Ser., III:., 1071. The British took over a hundred prisoners in the vicinity of Fort Lee, some of whom were probably among the drunken stragglers. See Donald Londahl-Smidt, "British and Hessian Accounts of the Invasion of Bergen County, 1776," *Bergen County History*, 1976 Annual, 50. Captain Johann Ewald also made contact with the column of troops that Greene had gone back to recover. He skirmished with them and called for reinforcements; instead, Ewald received orders from Lord Cornwallis to withdraw. "Let them go, my dear Ewald," Cornwallis told him, "and stay here. We do not want to lose any men. One jager is worth more than ten rebels." Tustin, ed., *Ewald Diary*, 18.

[3]The myth of a race between the Americans and the British for New Bridge can be attributed in part to George Washington's own belief at the time that the British were headed for the bridge. Writing to Governor William Livingston the day after the retreat from Fort Lee, he noted that "Their intent evidently was to form a line across, from the place of their landing to Hackensack Bridge, and thereby hem in the whole Garrison between the North and Hackensack Rivers. However, we were lucky enough to gain the Bridge before them; by which means we saved all our men." Fitzpatrick, ed., *Writings of Washington*, 6: 302. Another source for the story was General Heath, who later wrote that an express rider arrived from Hackensack "with a most alarming account of what he had seen with his own eyes, viz. that the Americans were rapidly retreating, and the British as rapidly pursuing." Heath, *Memoirs*, 88.

It is possible that Cornwallis did not know the New Jersey terrain; and local opinion often attributed the British failure to seize New Bridge to ignorance of the countryside. Some historians have agreed, pointing to an inaccurate map (a hand-drawn chart by British cartographer Claude Joseph Sauthier) which shows New Bridge south of Hackensack. See, for example, Douglas W. Marshall and Howard H. Peckham, *Campaigns of the American Revolution* (Ann Arbor: University of Michigan Press, 1976), 27. But this argument is flawed, as the Sauthier map was drawn after the New Jersey invasion. The fact is that Cornwallis was clearly led by Loyalists who were very familiar with the area. How else did he find a remote and unguarded landing site along the Palisades? Cornwallis knew the terrain well enough, but his objective was to seize Fort Lee and not Washington's army.

Cornwallis had assembled his force on the crest of the Palisades, he advanced deliberately into the interior on a farm road bordering the property of John Ackerson. Ackerson was a Loyalist and may have been one of Cornwallis's guides.[1] As the Crown forces moved inland, they found themselves marching through beautiful farm country. The Germans, in particular, were impressed. One Hessian officer wrote home that "I prefer this province to any other I have seen in America so far. It is not very mountainous; the coast is [not] high and steep except near the North River. It is well cultivated and I find excellent fruits everywhere and very many cattle."[2] It was war; but for some of the confident attacking army, it was also a walk in the country.

The first British troops descended on Fort Lee at dusk. As one British officer recalled, the rebels left a mess behind them. "They have left some poor pork," he wrote, "a few greasy proclamations and some of that scoundrel Common Sense man's letters."[3] The fellow obviously took a dim view of Thomas Paine. However, the Americans had left much more than "greasy proclamations" in their hasty retreat. In and around the post, the royal troops swept all of the former garrison's artillery, a huge supply of forage, and a stockpile of provisions. Every rebel entrenching tool and stacks of tents also fell into British hands. The booty included a herd of over two thousand cattle. Von Donop was amazed at the extent of the haul. "At the foot of the mountain was an important storehouse for corn," he reported, "and in almost every house there were stored large quantities of provisions. At the summit of the forts themselves were huts and tents for more than 6,000 men and quantities of all sorts of provisions and a large amount of ammunition." The Hessian colonel also noted the capture of the gun batteries on the Hudson River, where the

---

In this regard, Bergen County historian Kevin Wright has offered another interesting theory. Wright points out that the Americans had defended Fort Washington just a few days earlier instead of abandoning it. In fact, they had reinforced Fort Washington just before the British assault. Cornwallis may have believed that the Fort Lee garrison would make a similar stand, and he could not have accurately predicted or planned on their hasty retreat.

[1]John Ackerson's land was confiscated in 1784 and purchased by Captain John Huyler. The modern Palisades Parkway, the Greenbrook Nature Sanctuary, and Tammy Brook Country Club have eliminated all traces of the farm road that Cornwallis traveled from the crest of the Palisades.

[2]Item Z, Lidgerwood Collection.

[3]Quoted in Frank Moore, *The Diary of the Revolution* (Hartford: J.R. Burr Publishing Co., 1875), 350.

delighted British found "several 32 pounders together with 2 middle sized and one extraordinarily heavy iron mortar."[1] That night, Cornwallis and his men feasted on the captured food and then slept in the tents of the rebel garrison.[2]

General Charles Cornwallis had performed well, but not brilliantly. He reached New Jersey without detection, but his corps took too long to form on the crest of the Palisades and lost the element of surprise. His landing place was too far from Fort Lee to reach it without the rebels having some warning. Perhaps, as historian Kevin Wright believes, Cornwallis was convinced that the Fort Lee garrison would defend their post, and surprise was not his real concern. In any event, Cornwallis took the fort but missed the rebel army.

That army was in a sorry state. The night of November 20 found the

---

[1]Item A, Lidgerwood Collection. An undated report by Samuel Cleaveland, Brigadier-General, Royal Artillery, "Return of Ordnance and Stores taken by his Majesty's Troops in the Redoubts and Lines of the Enemy, from their landing at Frog-Neck, West-Chester County, from the 8th of October to the 20th of November, 1776," offered a more detailed list of ordnance captured at Fort Lee. The list was extensive: "Fort Lee: The Rock, Redoubt, and Batteries in the Jerseys: Iron Ordnance: 5 thirty-two pounders, 3 twenty-four ditto, 2 six ditto, 2 three ditto, 1 thirteen-inch brass mortar, 1 ten-inch ditto; 2 thirteen-inch iron mortars, 1 ten-inch ditto, 1 eight-inch ditto." Force, ed., *American Archives*, Fifth Ser., III: 1058.

The brass mortar on Cleavland's list had an interesting history. It was part of the cargo of the British ordnance brig *Nancy,* captured at the entrance to Boston harbor in 1775. The Americans named the mortar "Congress" and used it in the siege of Boston. Ward, *War of the Revolution,* 1: 114. Legend says that to celebrate the British evacuation of Boston in March 1776, the rebels filled "Congress" with liquor and used it as a giant punch bowl. The mortar was moved from Boston to a gun battery in New York City in 1776 and later to Fort Lee, where it was recaptured. In his narrative of the New Jersey operation, Captain Andrew Snape Hamond, of HMS *Roebuck,* claimed that the mortar was the same piece of ordnance taken by the Americans from *Nancy.* William James Morgan, ed., *Naval Documents of the American Revolution* (Washington: Government Printing Office, 1976), 7: 266.

[2]Francis, Lord Rawdon, wrote to Robert Auchmuty on November 25, 1776 and recorded some wonderful, but perhaps questionable, details on the capture of Fort Lee. Rawdon did not participate in the attack and his information was second-hand. But his letter has the ring of truth and generally agrees with the fully-confirmed accounts of other British witnesses. "His Lordship [Cornwallis] immediately marched to attack" Fort Lee, Rawdon said, but upon reaching it found that the rebels had fled "so precipitately that the pots were left absolutely boiling on the fire, and the tables spread for dinner of some of their officers. In the fort they found but twelve men, who were all dead drunk. There were forty or fifty pieces of cannon found loaded, with two large iron sea mortars and one brass one, with a vast quantity of ammunition, provision and stores, with all their tents standing." Quoted in Henry Steele Commager and Richard B. Morris, eds., *The Spirit of Seventy-Six* (New York: Harper & Row, 1975), 496.

rebel troops, including the Fort Lee garrison, without tents and cramped into houses and barns along the main road from New Bridge to the Hackensack village green. The British sent patrols forward to the Hackensack River to observe the rebel-held town, but there was no action.

The night was illuminated by huge campfires which lit both sides of the Hackensack River. On the eastern shore, Cornwallis' justly happy men were celebrating their victory. During the night, British and Hessian soldiers plundered the local farms.[1] On the western shore, the dejected patriot army lay exhausted and solemnly inventoried its remaining materials. Depleted units were getting ready for what some believed would be the last gasps of the American Revolution. Under cover of darkness, scores of disheartened American soldiers silently deserted their posts and began the trek back to their homes.

---

[1]Ensign Thomas Glyn's "Journal" says that General Cornwallis issued an order on November 20 warning his troops not to plunder. Apparently, the order was ineffective. Captain Ewald noted that "during the night all the plantations in the vicinity were plundered, and whatever the soldiers found in the houses was declared booty." Tustin, ed., *Ewald Diary*, 18.

CHAPTER FOUR

Hackensack

I must leave a very fine Country open to their Ravages.
—Washington to Charles Lee, November 21, 1776

The fleeing remnants of the Continental establishment began stumbling into Hackensack at dusk on November 20. A village resident described the wretched scene: "The night was dark, cold and rainy, but I had a fair view of Greene's troops from the light of the windows as they passed on our side of the street. They marched two abreast, looked ragged, some without a shoe to their feet and most of them wrapped in their blankets."[1]

The troops found whatever shelter they could and lay down to sleep. As bad as things were, the men perhaps felt lucky that at least they did not share the fate of the troops of Fort Washington, who were imprisoned in New York. Washington could scarcely count four thousand men fit for duty.[2] The rebels' material losses were staggering. The garrison had managed to save only

---

[1]Quoted in Leiby, *Revolutionary War in the Hackensack Valley*, 72.

[2]William S. Stryker, *The Battles of Trenton and Princeton* (Boston: The Riverside Press, 1898), 3.

two field pieces; all other artillery at Fort Lee had been lost. Also, nine hundred tents and every entrenching tool the army owned had been abandoned. Only the narrow Hackensack River divided the two armies. The next morning, Washington faced the difficult task of informing the Congress of what had happened at Fort Lee. "The unhappy affair of the 16th," he began sadly, "has been succeeded by further misfortunes." He then proceeded to tell his civilian bosses of the new setbacks and his precarious situation at Hackensack.[1]

Looking back, Washington had predicted the British invasion of New Jersey for its bountiful food, wood for fuel, and feed for animals. But his good judgment in moving a portion of his army to New Jersey was forgotten in the desperate military situation that followed the loss of Fort Lee. Washington had marched into the state only those troops whose homes were south of New England—about three thousand men. He anticipated that this small force would be increased by the garrisons at Forts Lee and Washington, as well as by the Flying Camp and New Jersey militia. He was wrong on every count. Washington's first shock was the Fort Lee garrison. Arriving at Fort Lee on November 13, he was stunned to learn from Greene that the garrison consisted of untrained and poorly disciplined troops from the Flying Camp. They were far less numerous than expected, especially after Greene had clandestinely drawn many away at the last moment to help defend Fort Washington.[2] The Fort Washington garrison included some of the best troops in the Continental Army, all of which were lost in the staggering defeat of November 16.

Then there was the continuing disappointment of the New Jersey militia. The general usually was able to count on the short-term service of militia to augment his army, and had expected to do so in New Jersey.[3] But

---

[1]Fitzpatrick, ed., *Writings of Washington*, VI: 295-296.

[2]In a letter to Congress of Nov. 19, Washington identified the Fort Lee troops as the Maryland militia brigade of Brig. General Reazin Beall, the New Jersey militia with Brig. General Nathaniel Heard, and the Pennsylvania militia under Brig. General James Ewing. In this same letter, he named the only other American troops in New Jersey as "Hand's Hazlet's; the Regiments from Virginia." Fitzpatrick, ed., *Writings of Washington*, VI: 293-294. These brigades were all part of the Flying Camp commanded by General Hugh Mercer. Ernest Kipping and Samuel Stelle Smith, *At General Howe's Side* (Monmouth Beach, NJ: Philip Freneau Press, 1974), 56, fn 9.

[3]Washington calculated on adding at least 5,000 men to his army from the Flying Camp and New Jersey militia before he left North Castle for New Jersey. Washington to John Augustine Washington, Dec. 18, 1776, Fitzpatrick, ed., *Writings of Washington*, VI: 397.

the troops of the New Jersey militia failed to respond to orders or entreaties to turn out and defend their state. As the crisis built, the citizen-soldiers were reluctant to leave homes and families exposed, and they seldom rallied in appreciable numbers.

Washington also had to cope with other invasion threats. He knew that Howe's army might attack at virtually any point along the New Jersey coast. There were any number of good landing places, and Perth Amboy, Elizabethtown, and Woodbridge were particularly vulnerable because they were directly across from British-held Staten Island.[1] A landing at any one of these locations would put the British on a good road system, in easy communication with their base at New York City, and on the shortest route across the state to Philadelphia. Security on the New Jersey coast was a real problem.

Therefore, soon after he arrived in New Jersey Washington felt compelled to deal with the situation. He dispatched eight regiments from his already-meager force to protect the exposed coastline from Amboy to Elizabethtown Point. These were regiments the general could have used with the main army, but the Commander-in-Chief felt he had no choice in the matter. It was essential that he prevent a British strike into the New Jersey interior.

The detached troops served under the command of Lord Stirling, the popular New Jersey general. The soldiers had an ambitious assignment. Their deployment sought to protect as much of the coastal region as possible as well as the most important routes leading inland. On November 18, a few days before the British invaded the state, Stirling wrote Congress that he was at New Brunswick with five regiments, having left three en route to guard the coast near Rahway.[2] His troops were not models of discipline. Some of them found large stores of liquor at New Brunswick and proceeded to get drunk.[3] General Adam Stephen arrived from Virginia after a long march with three Virginia regiments, which were ordered to remain at Perth Amboy. Colonel

---

[1]As Douglas Freeman pointed out, the correspondence of most Americans failed to make distinctions between the place names of Amboy, Perth Amboy, or South Amboy. Most references to these names, unless very specific, usually meant the general area of Raritan Bay. Freeman, *George Washington,* IV: 303.

[2]Force, ed., *American Archives,* Fifth Series, III: 750.

[3]"Diary of Lieutenant James McMichael," *The Pennsylvania Magazine of History and Biography,* XVI, No. 2 (1892): 139.

Hand had an additional 1,200 troops stationed between Elizabethtown and Woodbridge to guard the coast.[1]

Washington's situation would have been much improved if he still had the 2,900 troops from Fort Washington. Why did he stick by Greene after the disaster at Fort Washington? The answer lies in Greene's gift for organization and administrative detail. Greene proved one of the most capable American officers in the Revolution. He was a good combat officer, but his real talent was for organization.[2] Greene displayed these skills on October 29, 1776, when he submitted a plan to Washington for establishing supply depots across New Jersey. He proposed moving valuable stores from coastal areas to more secure inland depots, which was only logical. If an invasion of New Jersey took place, Greene anticipated an American retreat into the interior, and perhaps all the way to Philadelphia. His plan was to deposit provisions in a prearranged retreat route: Hackensack, Acquackanonk, Elizabethtown, Newark, Springfield, Bound Brook, Princeton and Trenton. Greene's plan was entitled "An Estimate of the Magazines To Be Laid In At the Following Posts for the Subsistence of the Troops and for the Horses In Waggons and Artillery" and was put into action by early November.[3]

While the British captured a staggering amount of foodstuffs and

---

[1]Stephen's brigade was composed of the 4th, 5th and 6th Virginia regiments. These troops started north from Virginia to reinforce Washington in September, 1776. The brigade was in Princeton, New Jersey, on November 8 and Washington ordered it to Fort Lee. This order was countermanded, and the brigade went instead to Perth Amboy, where Stephen replaced General Mercer. John Sellers, *The Virginia Continental Line, 1775-1780* (Ph.D. diss., Tulane University, 1968), 181-182. On Hand's men, see Clement Biddle to the President of Congress, Nov. 17, 1776, Force, ed., *American Archives*, Fifth Series, III: 740.

[2]Historian Christopher Ward commented that "with inexplicable infatuation," Greene "made the grand mistake of his whole military career" in holding Fort Washington. *The Delaware Continentals*, 93.

[3]On November 7, Washington wrote Greene with the news that he was going to send part of his army to New Jersey. Washington was also thinking where to place military depots. He wrote Greene: "They can have no capital Object in view, unless it is Philadelphia...I am of Opinion, that if your Magazines at Princeton were increased and those in the vicinity of New York lessened, it would be better. We find great risque and inconvenience arising from having Stores near Navigation, perhaps a Magazine at Brunswick might not be amiss." George Washington to Nathanael Greene, White Plains, November 7, 1776. Fitzpatrick, ed., *Writings of Washington*, VI: 253-254. For Greene's plan for magazines in New Jersey, see Showman, ed., *Greene Papers*, 1: 327.

equipment at Fort Lee, still larger quantities had been removed to the interior of New Jersey before the attack. Ammunition, in particular, had been moved to safety. During their subsequent retreat through New Jersey, the rebels never faced critical shortages of ammunition or food. This can only be attributed to the genius of Greene in organizing depots and the good sense of Washington in looking beyond Greene's bad judgment at Fort Washington to recognize his great talent for organization.[1]

On November 21, the intentions of General Lee were paramount among Washington's concerns. Washington wrote to Lee describing the events of the day before, and again emphasized the need for Lee to bring his command across the Hudson River and into New Jersey. The letter was diplomatic: like many other colonials, Washington remained impressed by the former British colonel. "It must be painful to you as well as to us to have no news to send you," he wrote, "but of a melancholy nature." Washington related the British landing and advance, and the retreat of the Fort Lee garrison. "We have no Account of their movements this Morning," he continued somberly, but noted that the situation was grim. He had "not above 3,000 Men" with him, and material losses and shock had left them "broken and dispirited." Under the circumstances, an offensive was impossible. "I have resolved to avoid any Attack," he wrote, "tho' by so doing I must leave a very fine country open to their Ravages." New Jersey was crucial to patriot fortunes. It was a source of food and supplies, he observed, and thus he wanted Lee's corps in the state. But Washington's respect for Lee inhibited him from sending a direct or preemptory order. Instead, he was circumspect. "Upon the whole therefore, I am of Opinion, and the Gentlemen about me concur in it, that the publick Interest requires your coming over to this side, with the Continental Troops." The Commander-in-Chief explained that "My reasons for this measure and which I think must have weight with you, are, that the Enemy are evidently changing the Seat of the War to this side of the North River" and "It is therefore of the utmost Importance, that at least an

---

[1]Most accounts of the 1776 retreat did not mention food shortages, although the narrative of Sergeant Joseph White, of Colonel Henry Knox's artillery regiment, was an exception. "The privations and sufferings we endured," he wrote years later, "is beyond description--no tent to cover us at night--exposed to cold and rains day and night -- no food of any kind but a little raw flour." Other contemporary sources corroborated the lack of tents and the bad weather—hardly insignificant problems—but White's account stands alone regarding the lack of food. Perhaps this old and revered veteran exaggerated his sufferings to impress his young readers. Joseph White, *A Narrative of Events...* (Charlestown, MA, 1833). Reprinted in *American Heritage*, No. 4, June 1956.

Appearance of Force should be made, to keep this Province in the Connection with the others."[1]

The deference in Washington's letter was puzzling. The general may have felt humiliated by his repeated errors in judgment during 1776, including his mistake in trying to defend New York City and failing to abandon Fort Washington while there was still time. He apparently felt obligated to convince his second-in-command of the necessity for the action he advocated.

When Washington finished his letter to Lee, he called for an express rider to carry it to Lee's camp at North Castle. However, while Washington's back was turned, another letter to Lee was quietly slipped into the horseman's dispatch case. The second letter carried to General Lee was from the cultured and successful Philadelphia lawyer, Joseph Reed (1741-1785), who was the most important member of Washington's military circle at the time and the commander-in-chief's closest counselor.

Reed would play an interesting role in unfolding events. Washington delighted in having bright, educated, politically-connected men in his military family. They served as aides and secretaries, often composing or redrafting his correspondence, orders and other official documents. Washington had grown up in moderate wealth, but had little formal education. He spoke no foreign language and had never traveled to Europe. What he knew, he had learned from books and his association with educated people. He liked the company of rich, young men of education and social grace. Of all who served close to him throughout the Revolution, Washington most admired Reed. Reed was the son of a wealthy Trenton merchant. He had obtained a good education in London and returned to the colonies to pursue a successful career as a lawyer and businessman in Philadelphia. Reed was everything that Washington dreamed of being in his youth: intellectual, sophisticated, charming and rich. By the outbreak of the Revolution, Reed already had joined the rebel cause and served on several important committees.

Although he had no training or experience as a soldier, Reed agreed to join Washington's staff as an aide with the rank of lieutenant colonel. He proved temperamental, but was prized by Washington as a first-rate expediter and troubleshooter. As an attorney, Reed knew about law and public affairs. He was also a brilliant writer. By late 1776, Reed was the army's adjutant general (that is, its administrative head) and Washington's trusted friend.

Soon after joining the army, Reed came to despise the amateur

---

[2]Fitzpatrick, ed., *Writings of Washington*, VI: 297-300.

officers who then were Washington's favorites. He was particularly put off with Greene, the son of a Rhode Island blacksmith, and Henry Knox, the fat Boston bookseller and self-taught artillerist. Reed blamed them for influencing Washington to defend New York City instead of burning it, and for holding Fort Washington when it should have been abandoned. Besides the actual loss of Fort Washington, Reed was angry because the fort was defended by many fellow Pennsylvanians, including some close friends, who now were dead or captive in New York. Reed was drawn to the cosmopolitan and intellectual Lee, whom he saw as a savior of the American cause.

Reed had his enemies. The influential Joseph Trumbull, who was commissary general of the Continental Army and the son of the Governor of Connecticut, had this to say about him: "he has done more to raise and keep up a jealousy between the New-England and other troops than all the men in the Army beside. Indeed, his stinking pride, as General George Clinton expresses it, has gone so far that I expect every day to hear he is called to account by some officer or other; indeed, he is universally hated and dispised; and it is high time he was displaced."[1]

It was Reed who quietly dropped a second letter into the pouch of the dispatch rider sent off to Lee. Reed knew the contents of Washington's letter, since the Commander-in-Chief had dictated it to him.[2] In his own letter, Reed concurred with Washington's appraisal of the situation, but added that "I have some additional reasons for wishing most earnestly to have you where the principal scene of action is laid. I do not mean to flatter or praise you at the expense of any other," he told Lee, "but I confess I do think it is entirely owing to you that this army, and the liberties of America, so far as they are dependent on it, are not totally cut off. You have decision, a quality often wanted in minds otherwise valuable," and he credited Lee with the survival of the army through the actions around New York and White Plains. He also thought that Lee might have prevented the disaster at Fort Washington. Officers and men looked to him with confidence, Reed insisted, and even the enemy worried about him and seemed "to be less confident when you are present."[3]

---

[1]Joseph Trumbull to William Williams, North Castle, New York, Nov. 18, 1776. Force, ed., *American Archives*, Fifth Ser., III: 1497-1498.

[2]The draft of Washington's letter to Lee was in Joseph Reed's handwriting.

[3]Reed to Lee, Nov. 21, 1776, William B. Reed, *Life and Correspondence of Joseph Reed* (Philadelphia: Lindsay and Blakiston, 1847), I: 255-257.

Reed's flattering dispatch went on to blame Greene for influencing the Commander-in-Chief to hold Fort Washington. Thus Washington vacillated until, as Reed put it, "the blow was struck" and the fort was lost. "Oh! General," wrote Reed, "an indecisive mind is one of the greatest misfortunes that can befall an army; how often have I lamented it this campaign. All circumstances considered, we are in a very awful and alarming situation, one that requires the utmost wisdom and firmness of mind." As soon as events allowed, he wanted Lee and others of like mind to visit Congress and present a plan for the reform of the army. Reed concluded with a final assertion of Lee's importance to the cause.[1] It was an extraordinary letter, calculated to flatter the colossal ego of a general already the rallying point for critics of the Commander-in-Chief.

Reed's imprudent communication was not the limit of his mischief. According to Heath's memoirs, Reed also had sent Lee an earlier message, written on November 20. Heath recalled sending a cavalryman to Washington in Hackensack, who arrived at Washington's headquarters and learned that the British had landed in New Jersey and that the Fort Lee garrison was rapidly retreating towards Hackensack. "The Adjutant-General [Reed] wished to write to Gen. Lee," Heath recalled; "but he had neither pen, ink, nor paper with him." The messenger had "a rough piece of wrapping-paper in his pocket" and Reed had a pencil; but after writing to Lee that "we are flying before the British. I pray," the pencil broke. Reed "then told the light-horseman to carry the paper to Gen. Lee, and tell him that he was verbally ordered to add, after I pray, you to push and join us."[2] The rider returned to Heath, relating everything he had seen, and, although fatigued and wet, insisted on pushing on to Lee's headquarters to deliver Reed's message.

The village of Hackensack lay in level, open country between the Hackensack and Passaic Rivers. On the morning of November 21, the New Bridge across the Hackensack River was intact and defended by American skirmishers who had barricaded themselves into several buildings. The eastern approach to the bridge was well suited for defense; it was at the end of a long, narrow spit of land jutting out from the shoreline and surrounded by swamps. Hard by the bridge stood the sturdy, stone Hoogland Tavern, built in 1767. There were a few other buildings nearby, but the tavern was the best position from which to defend the bridge.

---

[1] Reed to Lee, Nov. 21, 1776, Reed, *Joseph Reed*, I: 255-257.

[2] Heath, *Memoirs of the American War*, 88.

On the morning of November 21, British light infantry, grenadiers, and a company of jaegers approached the New Bridge from the east under the command of Major General John Vaughan.[1] As Vaughan's force advanced, the rebel defenders set fire to their stores and some of the houses. "The Americans had occupied the houses on both sides of the bridge and defended themselves very well," Ewald noted, but "the post was forced and the greater part were killed, wounded or captured."[2] The British captured the bridge intact, although Cornwallis did not push on to Hackensack until the following morning. By the afternoon of November 22, one resident reported, "the church green was covered with Hessians, a horrid, frightful sight with their whiskers, brass caps and kettles or brass drums."[3] With Hackensack secured, New Jersey Loyalists emerged from their silent watching to congratulate Lord Cornwallis and offer their services. Probably no one was happier than Dr. Abraham Van Buskirk, whose elegant home stood near New Bridge. Van Buskirk, a surgeon, had been secretly raising a Loyalist regiment in anticipation of a British invasion. Now he openly enlisted men for his regiment, which was designated the 4th Battalion, New Jersey Volunteers.[4]

By the time the British reached Hackensack, Washington was gone. The general knew his position at Hackensack was untenable, and that he needed to retreat in order to consolidate his forces, rally the New Jersey militia, and await the arrival of Lee with the best part of the army. The Commander-in-Chief abandoned Hackensack on November 21, having already decided to

---

[1]Howe to Germain, Nov. 21, 1776, *Bergen County History*, 49.

[2]Stirke, *Bergen County History*, 54; Ewald, *Diary of the American War*, 18-19.

[3]Leiby, *The Revolutionary War in the Hackensack Valley*, 77.

[4]On July 1, 1776, Howe authorized the former Attorney General of the Province of New Jersey, Cortlandt Skinner (1728-1799) to raise a provincial regiment to be called the New Jersey Volunteers. On paper, the Volunteers had five battalions, each of 500 men. A sixth battalion was later authorized. Abraham Van Buskirk was secretly commissioned by Skinner as a colonel and commander of the 4th Battalion. Van Buskirk in turn, clandestinely recruited men for his regiment while Bergen County was still under control of the rebel army. William Bayard was another Loyalist suspected of recruiting for the Volunteers prior to the British invasion of New Jersey. Bayard operated the ferry that ran between New York City and Hoboken. The Volunteers, like other provincial regiments, were armed, paid, fed and clothed by the British government. Provincial troops were subject to the same discipline as regular British army troops and were obligated to serve anywhere they were ordered. Troops of the New Jersey Volunteers probably accompanied the Crown forces as they advanced through New Jersey in pursuit of Washington.

head for the town of New Brunswick on the western bank of the Raritan River. Washington retreated from Hackensack and marched his army west to the Passaic River and the little port village of Acquackanonk Landing (modern Passaic), on the river's west bank. The village had numerous wharves and landings to load shipments of local produce and lumber, which were sent down the Passaic to Newark, Perth Amboy, or New York City.[1]

Only one bridge crossed the Passaic, a frail wooden structure close to the village. Washington ordered it destroyed as soon as his army was safely across. He occupied the Blanchard House during his tense overnight stay in Acquackanonk.[2] Probably from there, Washington wrote Governor Livingston to call out the New Jersey militia. He believed its members surely would respond, now that their state had been invaded.

As Washington scurried out of Hackensack, General Howe journeyed from New York City to inspect Fort Lee and congratulate Cornwallis. Howe's invasion had limited objectives; he wanted Fort Lee in order to secure the Hudson River, and then to use this foothold as a "ready road to penetrate into Jersey." The British commander was heartened by reports that the road between Fort Lee and Hackensack was littered with rebel muskets and equipment; and British light infantry also found twelve pieces of abandoned American artillery.[3] The operation had done well.

The quick success of Cornwallis and the news that Washington's army was in tatters led Howe to authorize a deeper drive into New Jersey. However, the British commander was still thinking in limited terms: quarters and food for his army during the coming winter and using New Jersey as a base for an offensive against Philadelphia in the spring. It was more militant officers who talked about conquering New Jersey and pushing all the way to Philadelphia by the end of the year. And Cornwallis was just the tough

---

[1]Washington to William Livingston, Nov. 21, 1776, Fitzpatrick. ed., *Writings of Washington*, VI: 302. Washington wrote that he would link up with troops under Lord Stirling near New Brunswick. On Passaic, see Wheaton Lane, *From Indian Trail to Iron Horse*, (Princeton: Princeton University Press, 1939), 63.

[2]Albert H. Heusser, *In the Footsteps of Washington* (Paterson, NJ: privately printed, 1921), 260.

[3]General Sir William Howe to Lord George Germain, Nov. 30, 1776, Force, ed., *American Archives*, Fifth Ser., III: 925; "Return of Ordnance and Stores taken by his Majesty's Troops in the Redoubts and Lines of the Enemy, from their landing at Frog-Neck...to the 20th of November, 1776," *ibid.*, 1058.

combat officer to lead them. As one British officer wrote, Cornwallis's "face seems to be set towards Philadelphia."[1] As Cornwallis prepared to resume his attack, Howe quickly reinforced him with troops from New York, including the 16th Dragoons under the command of Colonel William Harcourt.[2] But the weather suddenly turned cold and rainy, and by the time Cornwallis got his army into motion Washington had fled Hackensack and crossed the Passaic River. Advanced elements of Cornwallis' army arrived at the Passaic to find the bridge destroyed and the rebels encamped on the far shore.

---

[1]Rawdon to Robert Auchmuty, Nov. 25, 1776, in Commager and Morris, ed., *The Spirit of 76*, 497.

[2]On November 21, Ensign Henry Stirke wrote in his diary that "This day a body of Light Dragoons landed and joined us." Light dragoons were elite troops who rode and fought on horseback. They were used for scouting and raids deep into enemy territory. The term "heavy horse" or simply "dragoons" specified men who used horses to get to a battle but fought on foot. Heavy horse and dragoons were more heavily armed and rode bigger horses than the light dragoons. Two British regiments of light dragoons participated in the American Revolution, the 16th and 17th. They were the only British cavalry to serve in the war. The Americans developed an equivalent to the light dragoons later in the Revolution, which they called "light horse."

CHAPTER FIVE

Newark

It is difficult to determine how Washington's army could have been saved, if General Howe had not limited Cornwallis by exact orders.
— Historian Henry Carrington, 1877[1]

At dawn on Friday, November 22, Washington and his battered little army pulled out of Acquackanonk and marched south along the narrow farm road on the west bank of the winding Passaic River. The weather turned cold and it started to rain, turning the roads to mud as the rebels retreated south.[2] In late afternoon, the exhausted and sodden vanguard of the Grand Army arrived in Newark. The rest of the army, under Washington, halted in the village of Belleville that night and entered Newark in the morning. Many were

---

[1]Henry Carrington, *Battles of the American Revolution* (New York: A.S. Barnes & Company, 1877), 258.

[2]Weather conditions in the New York area were noted in the *Journals of Lieut.-Col. Stephen Kemble* (New York: New York Historical Society, 1883) I: 101; *Diary of Frederick Mackenzie* (Cambridge: Harvard University Press, 1930) I: 114; and Edward Tatum Jr., ed., *The American Journal of Ambrose Serle* (San Marino, California: The Huntington Library, 1940), 145. The muddy roads were reported in the "Diary of Andrew Hunter," Nov. 21, 1776, Firestone Library, Special Collections, Princeton University, Princeton, New Jersey.

sick; some were sent to Morristown and others were cared for in the town's churches, which were turned into makeshift hospitals. All of Lord Stirling's troops at New Brunswick began the march towards Newark to reinforce Washington's meager corps.[1]

Marching with Washington's army was the middle-aged Thomas Paine, who accompanied the column as a civilian. He had become famous as the author of the pamphlet *Common Sense*, even though it had been published anonymously in January 1776. Paine accepted a political appointment as General Greene's secretary and was with Greene at Fort Lee when the British attacked. Paine witnessed everything that had happened since the evacuation of Fort Lee and began to write about it when he got to Newark with the retreating American army. Legend says that Paine used the head of a drum as a desk when he began writing his justly famous *The American Crisis--Number One*. Paine's essay vividly captured the moment: the times were indeed such as to "try men's souls."[2]

---

[1]Sergeant Thomas McCarty was with Stirling's (Alexander's) brigade. His journal entry for Sunday, November 23, 1776 included orders "to march back to stop the enemy, as they were expected to be now marching towards Elizabethtown." He identified the regiments with him on the march as "the Delaware Battalion [Colonel Haslet's First Delaware Regiment] in front, the 3rd Virginia in the center, and the 1st Virginia Regiment in the rear." The riflemen followed the baggage. McCarty did not advance beyond Elizabethtown; nor did he say that any of Stirling's other regiments went further than Elizabethtown. From this account, it appears that Stirling had orders to bring up his brigade from the New Brunswick area to reinforce the Grand Army at Newark. However, he stopped at Elizabethtown, probably ordered to wait because Washington was planning to retreat to New Brunswick and would pick up Stirling's troops en route. Jared C. Lobdell, ed., "The Revolutionary War Journal of Sergeant Thomas McCarty," *Proceedings of the New Jersey Historical Society*, 82 (1964); guide to the Draper Manuscripts, Wisconsin Historical Society, Madison, Wisconsin. The start of the march on November 23 is noted in the "Diary of Lieutenant James McMichael," *Pennsylvania Magazine of History and Biography*, 16 (1892).

[2]Paine immigrated from England in 1774. He was one of the group of wandering misfits and idealists attracted to the unrest in America. (Charles Lee belonged to this same group.) In July 1776, following the publication of *Common Sense*, Paine marched to Perth Amboy with the newly formed Pennsylvania Flying Camp commanded by General Roberdeau. There was no provision for a secretary to Roberdeau, and Paine served as a volunteer, asking only that his expenses be paid. From Perth Amboy, Paine went to Fort Lee, and about September 19, General Greene appointed him an aide-de-camp. Historian Richard Ketchum believes that Paine wrote much of the first *Crisis* in Newark, added to it over the next few days, and then hastened to Philadelphia where the essay came out on Dec. 19, 1776 in the *Pennsylvania Journal*. Richard Ketchum, *The Winter Soldiers* (Garden City: Doubleday &

Without knowing it, a British officer fully corroborated Paine's observations of the American situation. Writing of the American army, he recorded his belief that "no nation ever saw such a set of tatterdemalions. There were but few coats among them but what are out...are mostly gone."[1] Samuel Blatchley Webb (1753-1807), an aide-de-camp and secretary to Washington, wrote from Newark on November 24 that "Fatal necessity has obliged us to give up to the Enemy much of a fine country, well Wooded, Watered & Stock'd; not only that, but our Cannon, Mortars, Ordinance Stores &c are mostly gone."[2]

The first rumors of the capture of Fort Lee reached members of the Continental Congress in Philadelphia on November 22. Confirmation of the disaster came a day later, when Washington's letter to President John Hancock, dated November 21, was read aloud to the delegates. Alarmed by this latest setback, Congress appointed a delegation of three members (John Witherspoon, William Paca, and George Ross) to immediately travel to New Jersey to consult with Washington. John Hancock informed the general of the

---

Co., 1973), 211.

[1] This quote is attributed to an "English Officer" (perhaps Major John Andre) and appears in T.N. Glover, *The Retreat of '76 Across Bergen County* [abstract of a paper read on Nov. 20, 1905] (Hackensack: Bergen County Historical Society, 1905), 22.

[2] Samuel Blatchley Webb, *Correspondence and Journals of Samuel Blachley Webb* (New York: Wickersham Press, 1893), I: 172. This quote is from a letter Webb wrote to his friend Joseph Trumbull (Commissary General of the Continental Army). Webb was a wealthy and educated young man serving in Washington's military family. While Webb's fiery comments seem too spirited for the circumstances, he made some valid points. Washington's weakened army was still a dangerous fighting force. To give "a true Account of our Situation," Webb wrote, was "next to Impossible." No troops, he assured Trumbull , were more active on a retreat; "Our Soldiers are the best fellows in the World at this Business." The entire army had numbered under two thousand men when the British struck, he noted, and a stand was impossible. But at Newark, the rebel army had regrouped; they were ready to fight, and the British knew it. It was "a sacred truth they never yet have ventured to Attack Us but with great Advantages; they pursue no faster than their heavy Artillery can be brought up. With this they Scour every piece of Wood, Stone Walls, &c, before they approach. If they come on soon we shall I trust give a good acct to our Country." They had to, as many rebel enlistments were up on Dec. 1, and Webb feared that much of the army would go home.

delegation in a November 24 letter, which also authorized Washington to order troops from the Northern Department to come to his aid.[1]

Washington wrote Congress soon after his arrival in Newark. "The situation of our Affairs is truly critical," he admitted, "and such as requires uncommon exertions on our part. From the movements of the Enemy and the information we have received, they certainly will make a push to possess themselves of this part of the Jerseys." Desperate for help, Washington wrote in the same letter that he was sending the influential General Mifflin back to his home city of Philadelphia to report to the Congress, "In order that you may be fully apprized of our Weakness and of the necessity there is of our obtaining early Succours."[2]

Looking everywhere for help, Washington dispatched the urbane Reed on a similar mission to Burlington to confer with Governor Livingston and the New Jersey legislature.[3] Of course, Washington had no idea that Reed had written Lee from Hackensack a few days earlier.

There is a sketch in David Ramsay's 1793 *The History of the American Revolution* in which Washington confers at Newark with his confidant, Reed. According to Ramsay, Washington asked Reed, "Should we retreat to the back parts of Pennsylvania, will the Pennsylvanians support us?" Reed replied, "[I]f the lower counties are subdued and give up, the back counties will do the same." The general said, "[W]e must retire to Augusta county, in Virginia. Numbers will be obliged to repair to us for safety, and we

---

[1]Smith, ed., *Letters of Delegates to Congress*, V: 528, 534. A few days following the staggering manpower losses at Fort Washington, the general was already looking towards the Northern Army as a source for badly needed reinforcements. On November 20, 1776, just four days after the fall of Fort Washington (and the same day the British attacked Fort Lee), he wrote to General Schuyler, commanding the Northern Army, asking Schuyler to send his Pennsylvania and New Jersey regiments. The enlistments of these regiments were expiring but Washngton hoped that they would continue to serve or reenlist. Robert Harrison to William Schuyler, Nov. 20, 1776, Force, ed., *American Archives*, Fifth Ser., III: 780-781.

[2]Fitzpatrick, ed., *The Writings of George Washington*, VI: 303.

[3]Reed's mission was to assist Livingston to raise four New Jersey regiments that would serve until April 1, 1777. Freeman, *George Washington*, IV: 267. The dispatch of these two competent officers is summed up in a postscript from Webb to Trumbull: "Mifflin gone for Philadelphia. Reed to Brunswick, Burlington &c." Webb, *Journals*, I: 173.

must try what we can do in carrying on a predatory war, and if overpowered, we must cross the Allegany mountains."[1]

In 1776, Newark was a farming center of three thousand people on the west bank of the Passaic River. An English traveler, passing through Newark in September, 1776, called it "Nothing more than a Village." It had about one hundred forty dwellings scattered irregularly over some two miles.[2] All accounts agree that the land around Newark was very fertile and the farms prosperous. Some inhabitants were fishermen, and the brackish Passaic River was known for its excellent clam and mussel beds.

Washington probably occupied the Eagle Tavern in Newark as his headquarters near the modern intersection of Broad and William Streets.[3] The village was too small to shelter much of the army, and the majority of the soldiers camped in open farmland behind the village.[4] Today this area is called High Street Ridge. The soldiers were in wretched condition; having lost all their tents in the flight from Fort Lee, they had to sleep on the ground and improvise protection from the wet and cold. Blankets were scarce and the

---

[1] David Ramsay, *The History of the American Revolution* (Philadephia, 1793), I: 291. This same story appears in Washington Irving's biography of Washington. In the Irving version, George Washington is conferring with General Hugh Mercer in early December 1776. ."What think you," said Irving's Washington, "if we should retreat to the back parts of Pennsylvania, would the Pennsylvanians support us?" "If the lower counties give up, the back counties will do the same," was the discouraging reply. "We must then retire to Augusta County in Virginia," said Washington. "Numbers will repair to us for safety, and we will try a predatory war. If overpowered, we must cross the Alleganies." Irving, *Life of Washington*, II: 448. There is a third variation of the story, which appears in William Gordon's *History of the Independence of the United States*, II, 141, in which Washington has his exchange with adjutant Reed and then passes his hand over his throat, and remarks, "My neck does not feel as though it was made for a halter. We must retire to Augusta county in Virginia."

[2] *The Journal of Nicholas Cressell* (New York: Dial Press, 1924), 157; Burnaby, *Travels Through America*, 105.

[3] In 1921, Albert H. Heusser privately published a Washington travelogue, *In the Footsteps of Washington* (Paterson: NJ). "Some historians maintain that Washington ate and slept at the ancient Eagle Tavern," he wrote, "while others insisted on alternate sites; but the evidence was too vague to substantiate any claim." Heusser identified present-day Military Park, in the center of modern Newark, as the site of the army's encampment. See pages 262-263.

[4] Frank J. UrQuhart, *History of The City of Newark* (Newark: Lewis Historical Publishing Co., 1913).

ground was freezing. It was as if a legion of beggars had descended on a gentle village of small farmers. The civilians in Newark were scared. According to diarist Andrew Hunter, they were "engaged in carrying off their goods to places of security."[1]

Washington knew that the narrow Passaic River was a minor obstacle and would only briefly delay Cornwallis. The rebels needed to retire to a defensive position where they could recover and recruit a new army. The village of Morristown was an ideal place for that purpose, and it was only a short journey west from Newark. Morristown sat on a fertile plateau surrounded by the rugged Newark Mountains (today called the Watchung Mountains). Few roads ran into Morristown, and each was easily defended, especially in the winter, when deep snow made the area difficult to penetrate. In addition, the local farmers were friendly to the rebellion. Washington was aware of the advantages of Morristown because the village had become the rallying point for the New Jersey militia. During a council of war held at Newark, several of his officers urged a move to Morristown.[2] But Washington was convinced the enemy's objective was the rebel capital of Philadelphia, and he felt duty-bound to keep his army, no matter how frail, between it and the Crown's forces. Under this strategy, Washington had no option but to march his army southwest from Newark, to the town of New Brunswick on the Raritan River.

New Brunswick lay in the middle of New Jersey and along the best road between New York and Philadelphia. At New Brunswick, the Americans would have the advantage of having the Raritan between them and the enemy. In addition, Washington had a supply depot at New Brunswick and hoped to find many New Jersey militiamen waiting for him there.

It is impossible to appreciate the danger of Washington's decision to retreat to New Brunswick instead of Morristown without analyzing the network of roads and navigable rivers in central New Jersey at the time of the Revolution. New York City and Philadelphia, the most important commercial

---

[1]Andrew Hunter, "Diary, 1776-1779," bound manuscript, Special Collections, Princeton University. This entry is dated Nov. 24, 1776, when Hunter was at Newark. Hunter was a Princeton graduate, Class of 1772, and a chaplain to the New Jersey troops.

[2]Washington Irving, *Life of George Washington* (New York: G.P. Putnam & Co., 1855-1859), II: 440.

centers of the colonies, were ninety miles apart and separated by New Jersey. It took at least one and a half days by fast stage to make the trip.[1] Although crude by European standards of the time, New Jersey had the best transportation system in the colonies. The early routes between New York and Philadelphia were by ferry to Staten Island and then across Staten Island to the old Blazing Star Ferry at Travis (modern Rossville) on the Arthur Kill. This ferry took freight wagons and coaches to Woodbridge, New Jersey, from which a road went to New Brunswick.[2] A variation of this route was across Staten Island to the ferry at Captain Billop's Landing to Perth Amboy, New Jersey, connected by road to New Brunswick. Still another alternate route: a boat to Bergen Point (modern Bayonne, New Jersey) and follow a decent road north along Bergen Neck to Newark. From Newark, there was a tolerable road southwest, which picked up traffic from the ferry crossings at Elizabethtown Point and Woodbridge and ran west to New Brunswick.

From New Brunswick, all traffic went through the college town of Princeton and into Trenton on the eastern bank of the Delaware River. At Trenton, an active river port, goods and passengers were transferred to boats for shipment downstream to Philadelphia. Two busy ferries at Trenton also took traffic across the river to Pennsylvania. On that side, a good road ran to Philadelphia via the town of Bristol.

---

[1]The stage wagon was a lightweight vehicle with a flat top, pulled by four or six horses, and had leather or woolen side curtains and large wheels set on crude springs. Luggage was stowed under the seats; heavier baggage was fastened on the rear. The passengers sat on four rows of seats; twelve people, including the driver, were considered a full load. In 1771, Abraham Skillman advertised that his stage would travel between New York and Philadelphia in a day and a half. More typically stage wagons made the journey in two days. John Mercereau advertised that his coach, the "Flying Machine," would run between Paulus Hook Ferry and the Indian Queen Tavern, Philadelphia, in two days' time. Passengers stayed overnight in Princeton, New Jersey, halfway between the two cities. In addition, there was the travel time by ferry between Paulus Hook, New Jersey and New York City. The advertisement for the "Flying Machine" noted that "As the Machines set off from Powles-hook early in the morning, passengers should cross the ferry the evening before." Patrick M'Robert, *A Tour Through Part of the North Provinces of America* (Edinburgh, 1776), 41. In the snow, sleighs or sledges replaced wheeled vehicles. More elaborate and costly coaches had come into use just prior to the Revolution.

[2]By the eve of the American Revolution, the New Blazing Star tavern and ferry crossing was in operation a few miles north of the original Blazing Star. The New Blazing Star ferry provided service from Staten Island to either Woodbridge or Elizabethtown Point. There was a second crossing from Staten Island to Bergen Neck, to the east of Decker's Ferry known as Ryerson's Ferry.

Another early route across New Jersey was the Old York Road. It followed a route from Elizabethtown, Scotch Plains, Bound Brook and Ringoes to a ferry across the Delaware River at Lambertville, New Jersey. The road continued on to Philadelphia. Then there was Lawrie's Road, running east-west across New Jersey from Perth Amboy to Burlington, unpopular because it passed through a "barren Country" and bypassed many of New Jersey's important commercial centers.[1] It also was possible to take an all-water route from New York harbor to the mouth of the Delaware River, then up the Delaware to Philadelphia.

Fast travel times were as big an obsession in colonial America as they are today. The New Jersey stage wagon was one way to reduce travel time between New York City and Philadelphia, but a big improvement arrived in 1764 with Cornelius Van Vorst's new ferry service from the bottom of Cortlandt Street in New York City to Paulus Hook Island, New Jersey.[2] From Paulus Hook Island, a new road and ferries brought passengers and freight across the wetlands and hills of Bergen County to Newark. There already was a good road between Newark and Philadelphia via Woodbridge, New Brunswick, Princeton and Trenton. The entire route was flat, making the trip faster. The new ferry and road connecting Paulus Hook to Newark were great successes, and caused a shift in New York City-Philadelphia traffic from the older routes. This made Newark an important commercial and travel center.

At the outbreak of the War for Independence, the New York-Newark-New Brunswick-Trenton-Philadelphia route was the most popular and busiest transportation system in America. From Elizabethtown south, it was originally named the Assanpink Trail, then the Old Dutch Road and the Upper Road by the time of the Revolution. A traveler took the busy New York-Paulus Hook ferry-Newark-Philadelphia route sometime during 1774-1775 and wrote down the distances from New York City in his journal, including: 9 miles to Newark; 15 miles to "Elizabeth-town"; 35 miles to Brunswick; 52 miles to "Prince-town"; 65 miles to Trenton; and 95 miles to Philadelphia.

---

[1]Lane, *From Indian Trail to Iron Horse*, 104.

[2]Paulus Hook was a low-lying point of sand protruding into the Hudson River, partially surrounded by a salt marsh. The Hook was two miles east of the village of Bergen. Both Paulus Hook and Bergen are now unidentifiable, and are parts of modern Jersey City.

The Revolutionary War armies used the Upper Road as they maneuvered south from Newark. The route played a central role in the campaign.[1]

Washington and his army arrived in Newark using the secondary roads that served northern New Jersey. Then, at Newark, he joined the road that bore the heavy traffic between New York and Philadelphia. The Upper Road would allow his army to move faster, but Loyalists told the British about this route and all the alternate roads across New Jersey. With this knowledge, the Crown's forces could outflank Washington's retreating army.

The general had much to ponder while his army was at Newark. His men faced the threat of the British outflanking them by landing troops at Perth Amboy and cutting off any retreat along the Upper Road to New Brunswick. The Americans would be caught on the flat, defenseless plains of central New Jersey, trapped between Cornwallis' six thousand men moving south from Hackensack and a second British force moving north from Perth Amboy. If this happened, the only direction open to Washington would be west towards Springfield and Morristown. This would save his army, but leave the Upper Road wide open to Philadelphia. Washington knew the possibility of a landing at Perth Amboy was real because spies in New York City had warned him of a British fleet of warships and transports with seven thousand troops, supposedly preparing to embark on a secret mission. This fleet could sail to Perth Amboy in a day.

Washington worried constantly about this British task force while he waited in Newark for the New Jersey militia and Lee to arrive. "The frequent advices," he informed Congress, "that the Enemy were embarking or about to embark another detachment for Staten Island, with a view of Landing at Amboy to co-operate with this, which seemed to be confirmed by the information of some persons who came from the [Staten] Island."[2] Another lethal scenario had Cornwallis maintaining pressure on Washington in New Jersey while British troops at New York sailed for the Delaware River, and

---

[1]M'Robert, *A Tour Through Part of the North Provinces of America*, 43. The Upper Road actually started at Elizabethtown Point, where there was a ferry from Staten Island. The Upper Road is today's New Jersey Highway 27 from Elizabeth to Princeton, and then New Jersey Highway 202 from Princeton to Trenton.

[2]Washington to the President of Congress, Nov. 30, 1776, Fitzpatrick, ed., *Writings of Washington*, VI: 314-315. Another warning of a landing at Perth Amboy came in a letter from Lee to Washington of Nov. 26. "Several deserters come out today," Lee wrote, "inform us that a considerable embarkation is made for Amboy." *Lee Papers*, II: 316.

then on to capture Philadelphia. This mystery fleet and its seven thousand troops were no subterfuge, and will enter into this narrative later.

The Commander-in-Chief faced other serious questions as well. Manpower problems were acute. On November 23, he reported to Congress that he had 5,410 troops with him in and near Newark. Of these, more than 2,000 had the right to leave on December 1, when their enlistments expired. An additional 1,000 men could leave on January 1.[1] In urgent need of reinforcements, Washington quickly acted on the wishes of Congress and instructed General Philip Schuyler, the commander of the Northern Department, to immediately send part of his force south to New Jersey. Schuyler's corps was in wretched shape at Fort Ticonderoga, New York, but Schuyler responded promptly and ordered eight regiments of New England troops, amounting to 1,200 men, to move south under the command of General Horatio Gates.[2] Washington gave New Brunswick as the probable meeting

---

[1]Force, ed., *American Archives*, Fifth Ser. III: 821-822.

[2]After an auspicious start in 1775, an effort to conquer British-held Canada ended disastrously in 1776. By December 1776, the Northern Army had retreated south to Fort Ticonderoga, where it reported having 5,000 men. But this was only on paper. Its actual numbers had been vastly reduced by expired enlistments, smallpox, malaria, dysentery, and desertions. A return of the forces at Fort Ticonderoga, dated November 29, 1776, noted only 1,413 men fit for duty. Force, ed., *American Archives*, Fifth Ser., III: 1589. An additional, and more detailed, return is in Charles H. Lesser, ed., *The Sinews of Independence*, (Chicago: The University of Chicago Press, 1976), 41.

Gates said that eight regiments were en route to Albany, where they would spend the winter or reinforce Washington; but Gates named only seven regiments: "Bond's, Porter's, Bedel's, Stark's, Poor's, Greaton's, and Patterson's." On Nov. 27, Schuyler ordered these regiments to Washington in New Jersey. Gates to the President of Congress, Nov. 27, 1776, Force, ed., *American Archives*, Fifth Ser., III: 874. The brigades sent as reinforcements from the Northern Department were Vose's, consisting of Greaton's 24th Continentals (Massachusetts)and Bond's 25th Continentals (Massachusetts), and Porter's Massachusetts regiment; a brigade commanded by General Gates; and brigades commanded by Reed (2nd Continental Regiment, formerly the 3rd, New Hampshire), Stark (5th Continental Regiment, formerly the 1st New Hampshire), Poor (8th Continental Regiment, formerly the 2nd New Hampshire), Paterson (15th Continentals, Massachusetts). See "State of Troops at Tyonderoga, 17 November, 1776," Force, ed., *American Archives*, Fifth Ser., III: 743-744; Lesser. ed., *The Sinews of Independence*, 38; regimental histories in Wright, *The Continental Army*, 197-199, 203, 205, 214, 219-220; and Stryker, *Battle of Trenton*, 354, which gives the lineage of Stark's, Poor's, Reed's and Paterson's regiments. Some 1,200 troops probably embarked from Albany to reinforce Washington.

Getting reinforcements from the Northern Department was a sound idea. Troops from the north quickly reached lower New York state by sailing down the Hudson River from Albany. Gates' regiments then sailed to the river town of Esopus (Kingston) New York.

place. Fort Ticonderoga was a long way from New Jersey and there was little hope that these reinforcements would arrive in time to make a difference.

Adding to Washington's problems was a Tory uprising in Monmouth County, New Jersey. Encouraged by the entry of the British army into New Jersey, pro-British factions in Monmouth were becoming more aggressive. Washington dispatched the New Jersey State Regiment, commanded by Colonel David Forman, to put down the uprising.[1]

Washington learned from scouts and parties of riflemen that Cornwallis was still near Hackensack and had not yet crossed the Passaic River. The Commander-in-Chief was desperate for reinforcements and risked stopping at Newark in hopes that the militia, called out by Livingston, would rally to him.[2] The Grand Army had to stay in one place long enough for the militia to learn where it was and march to its aid. But the militia never formed, save for a few hundred men who gathered at Morristown. However, Washington and his officers remained confident because Lee soon would be arriving with his seven thousand troops. After all, Washington's directive to Lee had been clear before he left Westchester: "If the Enemy should remove the whole, or the greatest part of their force, to the West side of Hudson's River, I have no doubt of your following, with all possible dispatch."[3]

This voyage took two days. *Diary of Chaplain David Avery*, microfilm edition of manuscript, Princeton Theological Seminary, Princeton, New Jersey.

After Schuyler dispatched reinforcements to Washington and allowed regiments whose enlistments had expired to march off, he was left with six regiments at Fort Ticonderoga, one of which was the 3rd New Jersey Regiment, commanded by Elias Dayton. Lesser, ed., *The Sinews of Independence*, 41.

[1]The New Jersey State Regiment was raised for limited service during the New York campaign and disbanded by the end of 1776. In early November 1776, the regiment reported 253 officers and enlisted men present and fit for duty. It was part of Colonel Nathaniel Heard's Flying Camp brigade. Lesser, *Sinews of Independence*, 37.

[2]On November 25, Livingston wrote General Matthias Williamson from Burlington: "By Intelligence just received of the Enemy's having made a Descent into this State who will doubtless take Encouragement from not meeting with the opposition which it is in our Power to give to ravage the Country I think it necessary that you should immediately call out the whole militia of this State & march them towards Newark as fast as they are raised taking their orders in their march from General Washington." Carl E. Prince, ed., *The Papers of William Livingston* (Trenton: The New Jersey Historical Commission), I: 188.

[3]Fitzpatrick, ed., *Writings of Washington*, VI: 266.

On November 21, Lee received the first appeal for help from Washington and got busy immediately. But instead of breaking his camp and marching to reinforce Washington in New Jersey, Lee used the news to write several letters, one of which was to James Bowdoin, the influential president of the Council of Massachusetts. In this letter, Lee suddenly created two American armies, "that on the east and that on the west side of North River," telling Bowdoin they should operate independently of each other and that the idea of reinforcing from one side to the other, on every motion of the enemy, was chimerical. Lee proceeded to play on the fears of the New Englanders by reminding them that even though the enemy had invaded New Jersey, a British attack north of New York was still possible; the enemy might "alter the present direction of their operations, and attempt to open the passage of the Highlands, or enter New England." Pressing his point, Lee told the fearful Massachusetts men that once his army was in New Jersey with Washington, there would be no chance of returning to defend New England. "We must depend on ourselves," Lee concluded.[1]

The same day Lee received Washington's "request" to cross the Hudson, he sent a letter to Major General William Heath. Heath commanded the four thousand troops Washington had left at Peekskill, New York, to guard the Hudson River. He was from Roxbury, Massachusetts, where he was active in politics and the local militia before the war. His high rank in the Continental Army was part of the price for Massachusetts' support of the Revolution. Enthusiastic and loyal, his talents were limited; commanding the small garrison at Peekskill was typical of the assignments Washington gave mediocre but politically important generals.

Yet Heath thought he knew Washington's mind in late November, and thus he was taken aback by Lee's letter. Lee told Heath that he had just received, "a recommendation, not a positive order, from the General, to move the corps under my command to the other side of the River." Lee gave excuses why he could not comply and told Heath to send two thousand men from his command across the Hudson. Lee promised he would replace Heath's detachment with troops from his own corps. Heath replied instantly (on the night of November 21), writing that he would not comply with Lee's request. He quoted his orders from Washington to stay at Peekskill with his corps and guard the Hudson River. Under the circumstances, Heath protested that it "would be very improper in me to order any of the troops from posts to which

---

[1] Lee to James Bowdoin, Nov. 21, 1776, *Lee Papers*, II: 291-292.

they are so expressly assigned, and from business which in his Excellency's view is so very important."[1]

But Heath was no literary match for Lee. Lee's response was a classic of superciliousness: "Sir, I perceive that you have formed an opinion to yourself that shou'd General Washington remove to the streights of Magellan, the instructions he left with you upon a particular occasion, have to all intents and purposes invested you with a command separate from and independent of any other superior. That General Heath and General Lee are merely two Major Generals, who perhaps ought to hold a friendly intercourse with each other, and when this humour or fancied Interests prompts, may afford mutual assistance; but that General Heath is by no means to consider himself obliged to obey any orders of the Second-in-Command--this Idea of yours, sir, may not only be prejudicial to yourself but to the Public." Lee concluded: "If any misfortune shou'd happen from this refusal, you must answer for it."[2]

Lee was distancing himself from the American defeats at Forts Washington and Lee and using them to advance his own career. However, he was still subordinate to Washington and had to respond to instructions to cross the Hudson. Luck had given Lee an independent command, the most powerful left to the rebels, and he would not throw away this opportunity by having his corps absorbed into Washington's retreating army. He apparently believed that if he could bring off some dramatic stroke, it would prove his military genius and his superiority to Washington as a commander.

But all of Lee's actions were unknown to Washington when an express rider rode into Newark on Sunday, November 24. The courier bore a letter from Lee, dated November 21 and addressed to Reed. Lee's dispatch was full of excuses, saying that he had no easy means of crossing the Hudson River and, "we cou'd not be there in time to answer any purpose--I have therefore order'd General Heath who is close to the only Ferry which can be pass'd, to detach two thousand men...a mode which I flatter myself will answer better what I conceive to be the spirit of the orders."[3]

Washington maintained his composure, but his response revealed his

---

[1]*Ibid.*, 291; Heath to Lee, Nov. 21, 1776, *ibid.*, 299.

[2]Lee to Heath, Nov. 26, 1776, *Lee Papers*, II: 313-314. Lee's response to Heath is included here to give this interesting confrontation continuity. There would be further efforts by Lee to pry troops from Heath.

[3]Lee to Reed, Nov. 21, 1776, *ibid.*, II: 301.

first signs of irritation with Lee. "You seem to have mistaken my views intirely in ordering Troops from Genl Heath to cross Hudson's River to this side," the general wrote. "The importance of the posts and passes thro' the High Lands, is so infinitely great, that I never thought there should be the least possible risk of loosing 'em." The Commander-in-Chief then came to the point. It is "your division I want to have over," he reminded Lee. Satisfied that his letter would eliminate any confusion and quickly bring Lee to New Jersey, Washington sent him a second dispatch later that day, warning that he had intelligence that the British were trying to intercept his march.[1]

But Lee's game continued. On the night of November 26, another dispatch arrived from Lee, who had not budged from North Castle. Washington fired back a reply the following morning, now clearly losing his patience and desperate for Lee's reinforcements. "My former Letters were so full and explicit, as to the necessity of your marching as early as possible, that it is unnecessary to add more on that Head. I confess I expected you would have been sooner in motion," he wrote.[2]

Dispatches continued to fly. Another note from General Lee arrived in Newark, this one dated November 26. He complained that Heath should have obeyed him and sent two thousand men across the Hudson, adding that he could not move his own units because of enemy activity in Westchester and the need to provide security for the area. Lee added that judging by the British activity in Westchester, "we conceived the numbers transported to the Jerseys not near so great as you were taught to think." Continuing his excuses, Lee said he had no shoes or blankets for his men, and was waiting for militia to arrive to take over the defense of Westchester County before he could cross the Hudson. He closed by saying that he would "take care to obey yr Excellency's orders in regard to my march as exactly as possible."[3]

---

[1]Fitzpatrick, ed., *Writings of Washington*, VI: 306. Douglas Southall Freeman feels that Washington thought Lee "merely had misunderstood or had misinterpreted orders"; *George Washington*, IV: 264-265.

[2]The letter arriving on November 26 was written by Lee the day before. Its contents have been lost; but we can surmise from Washington's reply that Lee said his men were unable to march. Washington's reply is in Twohig, ed., *The Papers of George Washington*, VII: 224. The editors of Washington's papers believe he may have been responding to Lee's letter of November 24, which he inadvertently referred to as having been dated November 25.

[3]*Lee Papers*, II: 315.

Washington remained in jeopardy, but if he had known what the British commanders were thinking and doing after their Fort Lee victory, he might not have been so worried. By failing to pursue the rebels quickly after capturing Fort Lee, the enemy lost a potentially decisive opportunity. The British, however, never seemed to have grasped this fact.

On November 21, the 16th Light Dragoons arrived in New Jersey to join Cornwallis, giving him the added advantage of cavalry. The next day, the dragoons and some light infantry "scoured the country as far as the Passaic River, and," as Howe reported, "found the enemy had abandoned all the intermediate country"[1] Only a few miles separated the two armies, but there was no movement from Cornwallis's corps; it remained incomprehensibly quiet in camps along the banks of the Hackensack River. American scouts and riflemen were operating in the no-man's-land between the armies. But they could have done little to stop Cornwallis if he made a lunge at Washington's battered troops.[2] The British never hinted at making any such movement.

In fact, Cornwallis was in no hurry. It rained heavily on the night of November 23, but the 24th and 25th were, "soft, warm days".[3] Lord Cornwallis did not take advantage of this fine weather to pursue the rebels further. His failure to quickly follow up on his victory at Fort Lee seems a mystery, especially with Cornwallis' aggressive reputation. But the British general's leisurely pursuit of Washington makes sense in light of a meeting he had with Howe at Fort Lee on November 22. Howe visited the fort two days after the British captured it.[4] Cornwallis and Howe surely discussed the military situation. The seizure of Fort Lee had been the purpose of the British assault on New Jersey. But success had emboldened Cornwallis. He asked his commander to let him advance further into New Jersey to try to catch

---

[1]*Diary of Lieutenant Stirke*, Nov. 21, 1776. Stirke, an officer in the light infantry company of the 10th Regiment of Foot, witnessed the arrival of the dragoons. Force, ed., *American Archives*, Fifth Ser., III: 925.

[2]Ewald, *Diary of the American War*, 20-21.

[3]*Diary of Frederick Mackenzie*, I: 114-115.

[4]*Kemble's Journal*, 101. Kemble's entry for November 22 noted that "the General went to Jersey; return'd about 11 at Night." Captain von Muenchhausen, an aide to Howe, corroborates Howe's presence at Fort Lee on November 22. "I had just arrived at the headquarters in New York," he wrote, "when my General departed for the Hudson River by a big detour, and from there crossed to Jersey with two of his aides." Muenchhausen, *Diary*, 5.

Washington's crippled army. Further operations seemed promising, he suggested, and cited Tory reports that the American forces were weak and demoralized. A vigorous push might finish the patriots.

Confronted with changing and apparently favorable circumstances, Howe assented. Still, he imposed limits on any new advance. He gave Cornwallis orders to move only as far as New Brunswick, which would give the British control of much of "east Jersey" and ample fertile country in which to find foodstuffs and towns for winter quarters. Then Howe said Cornwallis should have reinforcements before he advanced. It was the time lost in waiting for reinforcements that accounts for the delay in pursuing Washington's army.

The reinforcements arrived quickly as troops moved steadily across the Hudson. The English Brigade arrived at Fort Lee on November 25, followed the same day by the 2nd and 4th British brigades. By December 1, Cornwallis probably had a force of around ten thousand men in New Jersey. In anticipation of an advance, he had been sending out scouting parties and patrols; but with his new units ready, Cornwallis felt he could advance in strength. On November 26, he finally moved his reinforced corps out of Hackensack to capture rebel-held Acquackanonck on the Passaic.[1]

Unfortunately for the British, the dry weather of the past two days turned to rain. In poor conditions, Cornwallis moved cautiously, sending his right column across the Passaic about 4:00 a.m.; covering the move, British artillery fired into the opposite woods to "prevent ye lurking Scoundrels, from annoying us in Crossing."[2] The left column, under Brigadier General Mathews, included the Brigade of Guards, the Hessian grenadiers and thirty jaegers. It was a strong force. These troops began their march an hour behind Cornwallis, moving along the main road to the decrepit bridge that crossed the Passaic. Once there, Ensign Glyn reported, they "found the Bridge demolished" and the rebels in sight "on the Heights above the Town."[3] But the

---

[1]Samuel Steele Smith, *The Battle of Trenton* (Monmouth Beach, N.J.: Philip Freneau Press, 1965), 5-6; Letter FZ, Lidgerwood Collection, Morristown National Historical Park, "Short Description of the Journey of the Hon. Hessian Troops from Bremerlehe to America under the Command of His Excellency Lieutenant-General Von Heister," Nov. 25, 1776; "Journal of Lieutenant General von Heister's Corps, January 1776 to June 1777," Lidgerwood Collection.

[2]*Diary of Lieutenant Stirke*, Nov. 26, 1776; "Glyn Diary," Nov. 26, 1776; *Mackenzie's Diary*, I: 115.

[3]"Glyn Diary," Nov. 26, 1776.

Americans retreated from Acquackanonk when Cornwallis's column suddenly appeared. Cornwallis had waded the Passaic a mile and a half upstream to surprise the patriots, and the maneuver had worked.

Having secured the village, the British seized a sloop to bring Mathews's corps over. This occurred without American opposition. That night, the successful but tired British camped at Acquackanonk, only nine miles from Newark.[1] Their day had gone very well indeed.

The following morning, November 27, the advance continued. Leading the way, the 16th Light Dragoons, and the 1st and 2nd Battalions of Light Infantry, reached to the village of Second River (modern Belleville) on the road to Newark. The rest of Cornwallis' men waited at Acquackanonk in what Baurmeister called a "day of rest." They had earned it. Other units, however, remained active. The 4th Brigade under General Grant moved up to join Cornwallis. The following day, three additional regiments of Hessians arrived from New York under the command of an arrogant officer with 35 years of soldiering, Colonel Johann Gottlieb Rall.[2]

On November 28, Cornwallis broke camp at Acquackanonk and advanced in two columns against Washington at Newark. The right column, commanded by von Donop, included the Hessian grenadiers, two British regiments, the two companies of jaegers, and two six-pound field pieces. This column advanced on the town from the west and "marched into quarters at a village to the right of Newark." Cornwallis commanded the left flank, and his column was solely British troops with the army's baggage. Cornwallis remained in close contact with his superiors in New York as he advanced.[3]

The British moved through prosperous farms, and looting became a serious problem among the troops. The general was unable to restrain them, wrote Kemble, and their plundering "carried to a most unjustifiable length."

---

[1]Baurmeister, *War in America*, 73; the entry for November 26 noted that "General Cornwallis forded the Passaic with his entire corps and remained during the night without tents near the village of Acquackanonk."

[2]"Glyn Diary," Nov. 27, 1776.

[3]Letter FZ, Lidgerwood Collection, Morristown Historical Park, "Short Description of the Journey of the Hon. Hessian Troops from Bremerlehe to America under the Command of His Excellency Lieutenant-General Von Heister," 40. The "Glyn Diary," Nov. 28, 1776, indicates that "the parish" was Mountain Meeting House, now Orange, New Jersey. Baurmeister, *War in America*," 73, called the area the "Newark Mountains." on page 73. Muenchhausen, *Diary*, 5; his entry for Nov. 28 recorded the arrival of two couriers from Cornwallis at New York headquarters.

Ewald wrote that the residents had fled, and their houses were robbed and destroyed by the troops.[1] Historian Leonard Lundin summed up the situation: "Upon crossing the Passaic River, the invaders found themselves in a promised land, where everything they could desire was theirs for the taking." The lists of depredations compiled after the war were astonishing. However briefly, the British officers lost control of their men, who simply took what they wanted and destroyed much of what they could not take.[2]

Cornwallis had expected Washington to stand and fight at Newark. However, the British arrived about 1:00 p.m. to find the village deserted.[3] The Americans, obviously well-informed of the British advance, easily slipped away during the morning and retreated further south towards Elizabethtown, Woodbridge, and New Brunswick.

A future president of the United States, James Monroe, was with Washington in Newark. Monroe was a young lieutenant in the 3rd Virginia Regiment. He drafted pieces of his autobiography from 1827 to 1830, after retiring from public life. But he was proud to have fought with the venerated Washington: "I saw him in my earliest youth," he recalled, "in the retreat through Jersey, at the head of a small band, or rather, in its rear, for he was always near the enemy, and his countenance and manner made an impression on me which time can never efface." While "on the rear guard at Newark," Monroe counted the troops who passed him, which he reckoned at "less than 3,000 men." Yet the general was unshaken. "A deportment so firm, so dignified, so exalted, but yet so modest and composed," the former lieutenant wrote, "I have never seen in any other person."[4] Monroe died on July 4, 1831.

The British never came close to capturing Washington's army at Newark. The belief among some historians in a narrow rebel escape is based

---

[1] *Kemble Papers*, 101-102; Ewald, *Diary*, 22. Ewald noted the army marching in only one column to Newark. However, every other eyewitness source is clear that there were two columns. Ewald would have been with von Donop in the column on the right flank. The Glyn diary, in particular, supports the idea that there were two columns advancing south from Acquackanonk.

[2] Leonard Lundin, *Cockpit of the Revolution* (Princeton: Princeton University Press, 1940), 173.

[3] Archibald Robertson, *His Diaries and Sketches in America* (New York: The New York Public Library, 1930), 114.

[4] *The Autobiography of James Monroe* (Syracuse, 1959), 24.

in large part on a letter Washington wrote to Congress on November 30. While in New Brunswick, the Commander-in-Chief informed the delegates that he quit Newark "as our force was by no means sufficient to make a stand against the Enemy, much superior in number, with the least probability of success, and whose advanced Guards were entering the Town by the time our Rear got out."[1] The vigilant rear guard of the American army was composed of riflemen and other combat-hardened troops, and the British never got close enough to press them. Washington's main army was safely gone by the time the vanguard of Cornwallis' army reached the outskirts of Newark. A few hours after arriving safely in New Brunswick, it was a somewhat relieved Washington who wrote to General Heath that all was well: "The Enemy gave us not the least Interruption upon our March."[2] The Americans had retreated again, but things could have been much worse.

---

[1]Twohig, ed., *Papers of George Washington*, VI: 232-233.

[2]Fitzpatrick, ed., *Writings of George Washington*, VI: 310-311. Benson Lossing referenced a similar story. "Often the music of the pursued and the pursuers," Lossing wrote, "would be heard by each other, yet no action occurred." Benson Lossing, *Pictorial Field Book of the Revolution* (New York: Harper & Brothers, 1855), II: 15. William Stryker fueled the myth of the near-capture of Washington's army at Newark when he wrote "the enemy's advance guard entered Newark, November 28th, as the American army left that city." Stryker, *Battles of Trenton and Princeton*, 9.

CHAPTER SIX

New Brunswick

This retreat into, and through New-Jersey, was attended with almost every circumstance that could occasion embarrassment, and depression of spirits.
—Historian David Ramsay, 1789[1]

New Brunswick, wrote traveler Peter Kalm, was "a pretty little town in the province of New Jersey, in a valley on the west side of the river Rareton." The houses had small front porches with benches, "on which the people sat in the evening, in order to enjoy the fresh air, and to have the pleasure of viewing those who passed by." Another visitor described New Brunswick as "a small trading town, situated on Rareaton River, which is navigable to the town for small craft." Yet another thought that the town, along with Philadelphia, had "the handsomest women that I saw in America."[2]

---

[1]David Ramsay, *The History of the American Revolution* (Philadelphia: R. Aitken, 1789), I: 398.

[2]Peter Kalm, *Travels into North America* (Barre, MA: Imprint Society, 1972), 120; *The Journal of Nicholas Cresswell* (New York: The Dial Press, 1924); 157. Andrew Burnaby, *Travels Through The Middle Settlements in North America* (London, 1798), 104.

John Adams passed through New Brunswick in 1774 and said the town had about one hundred fifty houses, three churches and several paved streets. The beauty of the Raritan River impressed him, as did the number of boats there, in front of the town.

By the eve of the Revolution, New Brunswick carried on a brisk trade with New York City. Warehouses and storehouses lined the waterfront. Every day, sloops loaded corn, flour, bread, linseed, meat, and timber for sale in New York. Occasionally, a ship would sail from New Brunswick for the West Indies or England. The town was a popular stop on the Upper Road, and profited from the many travelers who stopped at its numerous taverns and inns. The three best-known taverns were the White Hart, Sign of the Ship, and Indian Queen.[1] New Brunswick's days of peace were numbered, however, for it was about to become a seat of war.

On November 28, 1776, the patriot Grand Army evacuated Newark and retreated south to Elizabethtown, described at the time as "very pleasantly situated" with "about four hundred houses, most very neat brick buildings."[2] Washington passed quickly through Elizabethtown and made no effort to defend it. His destination was New Brunswick. The road from Elizabethtown to New Brunswick, called the Upper Road, or sometimes the Old Dutch Road, passed through Rahway, Woodbridge and Piscataway. Near Woodbridge, it was joined by a road from Perth Amboy on the seacoast.

The vanguard of Cornwallis's force entered Newark from the north as Washington's rear guard abandoned it to the south. Stories already circulated about looting and rape by the Hessians. Some civilians from Newark and Elizabethtown fled west to safety in the rugged Morris County terrain around the villages of Chatham and Morristown. Other frightened refugees loaded families and belongings into wagons, and jammed the rough, rain-soaked road south of Newark along with Washington's ragtag soldiers.

The delegation sent from the Continental Congress found Washington at Elizabethtown. Having taken the Upper Road from Trenton, they saw the terrible condition of their army as they passed the sick and wounded moving ahead of the main force. Congressman George Ross was shocked. "The distress of our Soldiers," he wrote to a friend, "who I have met almost naked and hardly able to walk or rather wade through the mud has given infinite pain

---

[1]Kalm, *Travels into North America*, 121; Lane, *From Indian Trail*, 61, 109.

[2]Patrick M'Robert, *A Tour Through Part of the North Provinces of America* (Edinburgh, Scotland, 1776), 33.

but I shudder to tell you that they fall dead on the road with their packs on their backs or are found accidentally, perishing in hay lofts."[1] The scene was of hurry and confusion as the congressmen reached Washington. The tall Virginian took the delegates out of the stream of humanity and spoke calmly with them by the side of the road. Those close to the general said that the loss of Fort Washington, less than two weeks earlier, had toughened him. It was the sturdy Washington, frontier Indian fighter who had saved the shattered remnants of Braddock's army on the Pennsylvania frontier, who retreated with his soldiers through New Jersey.

Washington told the delegation that he would try to form a defense line at New Brunswick, and said he was convinced that the Royal army meant to push all the way to Philadelphia. Ross stood by the roadside and counted only two thousand dirty and poorly clothed American soldiers. He learned that a second column, of less than two thousand, followed half an hour behind. It shook Ross to see how small and shabby Washington's army was, and to learn that the enlistments of half would expire within days. Meanwhile, they were being pursued by a reported eight thousand enemy soldiers.[2] It was dangerous for the three rebel congressmen to remain so close to the enemy. Having seen enough, they turned back towards Philadelphia to report to the Continental Congress. Washington continued his retreat towards New Brunswick.

The following morning, a tired and mud-spattered post rider with a letter from Lee found Washington nearing New Brunswick. Surrounded by aides and protected by his heavily-armed Life Guard, Washington eagerly tore it open.[3] Here, finally, thought Washington and his staff, was the news that Lee had crossed the Hudson! Lee's letter was dated November 26. Washington was discouraged to find it addressed from "Philipsbourg," New

---

[1]Paul H. Smith, ed., *Letters of Delegates to Congress 1774-1789* (Washington, D.C.: Library of Congress, 1979), V: 547.

[2]George Ross to James Wilson, Nov. 28, 1776, Smith, ed., *Letters of Delegates to Congress*, V: 449-550.

[3]Washington was protected at the time by a bodyguard force of about 50 enlisted men. Carlos Godfrey, *The Commander-In-Chief's Guard* (Washington, D.C.: Stevenson-Smith Company, 1904), 37. The official name of Washington's guard force was "The Commander-in-Chiefs Guard." It was also known popularly by the soldiers during the Revolution as "Washington's Life Guard." The unit was formed in March, 1776, while the American army was still at Cambridge, Massachusetts, and was commanded throughout the war by Captain Caleb Gibbs (1748-1821) of Massachusetts. Little is known about the Guard during 1776 since all the records for the year were destroyed in a fire at the Charlestown Navy Yard in 1815.

York. Lee had not even moved from his camp. Lee began his letter by complaining that Heath would not release his two thousand men to reinforce Washington: "the want of Carriages and this disappointment with respect to Heath...have still detained me here" and, again, he claimed that the British were very active in his district. He enumerated other problems: lack of transportation, bad roads, no militia to defend New York if his army moved out, no blankets, no shoes no money. But the letter ended with the long hoped-for news that "I set out tomorrow."[1] Washington slowly folded the dispatch while he pondered the shock that it would be days before any reinforcements could reach him. Scouts reported that Cornwallis and his legion had stopped in Newark, but now were advancing and not far behind.

On the morning of November 29, the first ragged American soldiers crossed the Raritan River and entered New Brunswick.[2] They had marched 25 miles through continuous rain the previous day. Washington arrived later that day with the main body of the Grand Army. The Raritan River now separated Washington's little army from the Crown's forces. Cornwallis was finally moving fast. His main army left Newark at daybreak on November 29, but had to advance carefully because of the threat of rebel skirmishers and, more important, the corps of the cunning Charles Lee, whose position still was unknown to Cornwallis. Concerned about Lee, Cornwallis ordered Ewald's

---

[1] Lee to Washington, Nov. 26, 1776, *Lee Papers*, II: 315. "Philipsburg" implies anywhere in the large tract of territory in Westchester County, New York, owned by the Philips family.

[2] Stryker said that Washington's army marched in two columns from Newark to New Brunswick. One column reached New Brunswick by way of Elizabethtown and Woodbridge following the main road (the Upper Road) while the other went via Springfield, Scotch Plains, and Quibbletown (part of modern Piscataway). This column arrived at New Brunswick on the afternoon of Nov. 29. While Stryker gives no references for this information, it is probably correct, although the column which marched via Springfield may have been small. Stryker, *Battles of Trenton and Princeton*, 10. Stryker also states that a small body of troops commanded by General Lord Sterling were sent in advance of the main army to guard the Raritan River at New Brunswick. This information would support the story that the Grand Army arrived in New Brunswick to find some soldiers had found a supply of liquor in the town and had gotten drunk. There was no bridge across the Raritan River at New Brunswick in 1776. The first bridge to ford the Raritan at New Brunswick was opened in 1795. There was a ferry at New Brunswick across the Raritan called "Inian Ferry" (Inman Ferry) after John Inman, who started a ferry service there in 1686. The reference to a bridge at New Brunswick during Washington's retreat refers to the Landing Bridge (modern Landing Lane Bridge stands on the same location) at the village of Raritan Landing, which was two miles above New Brunswick.

Jaeger company to patrol towards Springfield.[1]   Arriving at Elizabethtown, Cornwallis ordered a halt for the night. The common soldiers and the women following the corps immediately began to plunder the town. The vanguard of Cornwallis's army, including a battalion of British light infantry and the lst Hessian Jaeger Company under the command of Captain Carl August von Wreden, advanced further along the upper road to Rahway, where they spent the night.[2] The next day, Saturday, November 30, Cornwallis' corps was up early and out of Elizabethtown. Some elite troops moved ahead of the main column and occupied Woodbridge and Perth Amboy, both of which they found deserted. The weather remained miserable: heavy rain and wind. The roads were a sea of mud, which slowed Cornwallis's advance.[3] Cornwallis continued to have serious problems preventing pillaging. Everywhere, British and Hessian soldiers, "women of the army," camp followers and children broke into the hastily evacuated houses and looted valuables.

"Women of the army," camp followers and children were characteristic of all eighteenth-century armies, including the American army during the Revolution. Women of the army were traditionally wives or other female relatives of common soldiers, and authorized to accompany their men wherever the army went. They commonly did laundry and sewing, and occasionally acted as nurses for meager pay. These women were a tough, hard-working lot. Camp followers, on the other hand, were considered "loose women," prostitutes who usually stayed with the sutlers. Some children were often part of this curious entourage behind an 18th Century army. A typical sight in central New Jersey at the time was a group of women of the army or camp followers at a roadside, guarding a hastily-assembled pile of household goods. British or Hessians would break into an empty house and carry out anything from furniture to frying pans. They would heap these by the road and

---

[1]Ewald, *Diary of the American War*, 22;   Bernard Uhlendorf, ed. and trans., *Revolution in America*, (New Brunswick: Rutgers University Press, 1957), 73; "Glyn Diary."   Ewald made his headquarters at Liberty Hall, the manor of Governor William Livingston, on the road between Elizabethtown and Springfield. Ewald said he did not permit Livingston's house to be looted, even though it was the home of "one of the first and most fiery rebels."

[2]Baurmeister, *Revolution in America*, 73.

[3]Mackenzie reported the weather on Nov. 30 from nearby New York City as "rain all night, and most part of this day, attended during the night, with a strong wind at N.E. The transports here cannot move until the wind and weather are more favorable." Mackenzie, *Diary*, I: 117.

leave women to guard the spoils until they could return to help carry them off.[1]

The morning of November 30, Ewald's Jaeger company was reinforced by thirty troops from the 16th Dragoons, and skirmished with some rebel militia. They were certain that Lee's corps was somewhere in the area. The night of November 30, Ewald linked up with the 2nd Battalion of Light Infantry, commanded by Major Maitland, at the village of Connecticut Farms Meeting (modern Union). Maitland's light infantry had been protecting Cornwallis' right flank for the past couple of days; now they did the same with Ewald's company as Cornwallis advanced. Ewald stopped in the Rahway area for the night, kept his men under arms, posted sentries and would not permit any campfires. Cornwallis spent the night of November 30 with his main army at Rahway while Maitland and Ewald protected his right flank from a surprise attack.

Various elements of Cornwallis' army were spread out along the Upper Road between Newark and Woodbridge. It appeared to be a dangerous situation for the Crown forces, partially caused by Cornwallis's now-determined pursuit of Washington's army. However, unknown to Cornwallis and his army, there was no strong body of American troops to attack their isolated columns. The next morning, December 1, Cornwallis resumed his advance towards New Brunswick. At the same time, Ewald and Maitland entered Rahway around noon and followed the Upper Road to join the main British army, which was approaching the Raritan River.[2]

---

[1]This scene is based on an eyewitness description of the looting of a house by Crown soldiers in Piscataway. Lundin, *Cockpit of the Revolution*, 174. For a fuller discussion of women in the army, see Evan Cornog, *Come all you Gallant Heroes* [exhibition catalog] (New York: Fraunces Tavern Museum, 1991), 17.

[2]Baurmeister, *Revolution in America*, 73; Ewald, *Diary*, 22-24; "Glyn Diary," Nov. 28, 1776. New Jersey historian Cornelius Vermeule made the intriguing statement that the Crown forces advanced in two divisions to the Raritan River. Vermeule said, "They had come down in two divisions; one by way of Elizabeth and Rahway , its progress marked by burning buildings and ravished homes; the other by way of Springfield and Scotch Plains, which did less damage, possibly because it was more exposed to attack by the militia." Vermeule, "Some Revolutionary Incidents in the Raritan Valley," *Proceedings of the New Jersey Historical Society*, New Series, VI (1921), 76. Vermeule did not give his sources for this information. However, there is evidence that Colonel Carl Emilius von Donop's brigade of Hesse Cassel grenadiers advanced from Newark or Elizabethtown to the Raritan River via Springfield, Scotch Plains, and Quibbletown (part of modern Piscataway) at the same time that Cornwallis was advancing along the Upper Road. There are a few clues to indicate that von Donop marched to the Raritan via Springfield and Scotch Plains. One is a comment by Ensign Glyn, dated Newark, November 28: "Col. Donop will stop at Lord Cornwallis's Quarters where he will

Washington had a very different set of concerns during those days. He was up early on November 30, which some have called the worst day of the American Revolution. He faced a host of problems at his hastily-established headquarters in Cochrane's Tavern in New Brunswick.[1] To his mortification, the only reinforcements found at New Brunswick were some stragglers from the Flying Camp. Washington now confronted the reality that on December 1, the next day, the enlistments of two thousand soldiers representing almost half his army would expire. And the enemy was just hours away.

The Commander-in-Chief wrote Congress that day to explain his dreadful situation. He asked for help from the Pennsylvania militia, "the situation of our Affairs being truly alarming." His force was now very small, he warned, and the British were only four or five miles away and were reportedly landing fresh troops at Perth Amboy. He had also learned that a second enemy column of Hessians was moving against his right flank, having arrived at Springfield the night before. "I do not know how far their views extend, but I doubt not they mean to push every advantage resulting from the small number and State of our Troops." Stopping the enemy was unlikely, as his army was dwindling. The general wrote of the failure of the New Jersey militia to turn out in the face of the invasion, a circumstance he found vexing in the extreme. That was not all. "Added to this," he wrote, "I have no assurances, that more than a very few of the Troops composing the flying Camp will remain after the time of their engagement is out; so far from it, I am

---

receive his instructions." *Glyn Diary*. Perhaps von Donop was given a special assignment. Another is a reference by Washington to a second column of Hessian troops advancing towards the Raritan River via Springfield. Fitzpatrick, ed., *Writings of Washington*, VI: 315.

There is one piece of solid evidence that the Crown forces advanced from Newark to New Brunswick in a single column along the Upper Road. The evidence is from the diary of Archibald Robertson, a British engineer who marched with Cornwallis from Newark to New Brunswick. Robertson said that von Donop's corps was at Elizabethtown on November 29. His entry for November 30 includes "Donop's Corps to Woodbridge." Robertson, *His Diaries and Sketches*, 114. Looking at the military situation, it seems unlikely that a Crown forces column would have been ordered to march to the Raritan River through the rebel-held area around Springfield and Plainfield--especially since Cornwallis was convinced that General Charles Lee was somewhere in the area with his corps.

[1]Douglas Southall Freeman called Nov. 30, 1776 "that most miserable of his wretched days." *George Washington* (New York: Charles Scribner's Sons, 1951), IV: 271; Richard Durnin, *George Washington in Middlesex County, New Jersey* (North Brunswick: Middlesex County Cultural and Heritage Commission, 1989). Cochrane's Tavern was located at the southwest corner of present Neilson and Albany Streets.

told, that some of Genl Ewing's Brigade, who stand engaged to the lst of January, are now going away." As a rule, Washington's communications with Congress were circumspect, but he had pulled no punches in this letter.[1]

The general still had no idea where Lee was. He wrote Lee soon after arriving at New Brunswick on the 29th, patiently urging him to move, but, as in the past, failing to issue a direct order.[2] Washington felt compelled to downplay his anger at the sensitive Lee to preserve harmony and keep the Continental Congress from finding new reasons to meddle in army affairs. Amid all that, a courier arrived from Lee's camp with a letter addressed to Washington's aide, Reed. With Reed away on assignment, Washington eagerly took the sealed dispatch and tore it open, believing it contained public business and, he hoped, good news. Washington quickly realized that it was a personal communication, a reply to the letter Reed had sent Lee from Hackensack. In disbelief, Washington read:

> My Dr. Reed:
> I receiv'd your most obliging, flattering letter -- lament with you that fatal indecision of mind which in war is a much greater disqualification than stupidity or even want of personal courage -- Accident may put a decisive Blunderer in the right -- but eternal defeat and miscarriage must attend the man of the best parts if curs'd with indecision."[3]

Washington was stunned to discover that his dearest friend and confidant had engaged in a secret correspondence with his imperious senior lieutenant. Worse, Reed and Lee seemed to share a low opinion of Washington's leadership.[4] It was a harsh blow, but Washington had to overlook it, in the interest of unity, rather than confront Reed. He refolded the letter, put it back in its envelope and sent Reed an apologetic note. "The inclosed was

---

[1]Twohig, ed., *Papers of Washington*, VII: 232-233.

[2]Fitzpatrick, ed., *Writings of Washington*, VI: 311-312.

[3]*Lee Papers*, II: 305-306.

[4]Washington's high opinion of Joseph Reed is revealed in a letter Washington wrote Reed from New York City, dated Apr. 15, 1776. Reed had resigned his post as a temporary staff officer and Washington wrote him, "When, my good Sir, will you be with me? I fear I shall have a difficult card to play in this Government and could wish for your assistance and advice to manage it." Fitzpatrick, ed., *Writings of Washington*, IV: 483.

put into my hands by an Express from the White Plains," he wrote. "Having no Idea of its being a Private Letter, much less suspecting the tendency of the correspondence, I opened it, as I had done all other Letters to you, from the same place and Peekskill, upon the business of your Office, as I conceived and found them to be." This was the only reason, he assured Reed, that he had seen the contents of the letter. He then thanked the younger officer for his efforts on his recent mission, for which he wished success, and closed with a greeting for Mrs. Reed.[1] Washington, personally wounded, had reacted with stoic self-restraint.

The next day, the general paraded the troops whose enlistments were expiring and pleaded with them to stay. They were badly trained and equipped, but he needed every man. Washington and his senior officers exhorted and appealed in vain; on Sunday, December 1, some 2,060 troops gathered their belongings and walked off without an apology or backward glance. This was not the worst. The remaining soldiers of the Flying Camp, whose enlistments expired on January 1, also began deserting. Washington had to order units to patrol the roads leading towards Pennsylvania and the ferries across the Delaware River to apprehend them. Despite these efforts, losses to desertion were serious. No amount of patrolling could stop all of the men determined

---

[1]Force,ed., *American Archives*, Fifth Series, III: 921. Joseph Reed survived this nasty episode and his friendship with Washington continued until Reed's death (1785) at the age of 44. Politically savvy, Reed realized his bad judgment in befriending the busybody Charles Lee. Reed apologized for his secret correspondence with Lee in a letter to Washington of Mar. 8, 1777. "My pressing him most earnestly to join you as soon as possible," he wrote, "led to expressions and an answer which must have been disapproved by you, and which I was far from expecting....No man in America, my dear General, more truly and ardently wishes your honour, happiness, and success, or would more exert himself to promote them." William Reed, *Life and Correspondence of Joseph Reed* (Philadelphia: Lindsay and Blakiston, 1847), I: 259. Reed mentioned the incident in another letter to Washington (June 4, 1777). He said that he understood "how difficult it is to regain lost friendship; but the consciousness of never having justly forteited yours, and the hope that it may be in my power fully to convince you of it, are some consolation for an event which I never think of but with the greatest concern." Reed asked that Washington "judge of me by realities, not by appearances, and believe that I never entertained or expressed a sentiment incompatible with that regard I professed for your person and character, and which, whether I shall be so happy as to possess your future good opinion, or not, I shall carry to my grave with me." *Ibid.*, 259-260. This time Washington replied cooly (June 14, 1777). "I was hurt," he wrote, "not because I thought my judgement wronged by the expressions contain'd in it, but because the same sentiments were not communicated immediately to myself. The favorable manner in which your opinion, upon all occasions, had been received...entitled me, I thought, to your advice upon any point in which I appeared to be wanting." Fitzpatrick, ed., *Writings of Washington*, VIII: 247.

to go home. The rebel chief was left with only 3,400 effectives as scouts came into New Brunswick with the news that Crown forces were less than two hours away.[1] Rumors persisted that additional British reinforcements had landed at Perth Amboy. The shallow Raritan River, with numerous fords, would not delay the enemy long.

Washington resorted to minor trickery: He kept his little army in constant motion at New Brunswick to make the enemy believe he had a much bigger force. On December 1, he also wrote Lee again, this time practically begging him to bring his corps into New Jersey: "I must entreat you to hasten your march as much as possible, or your arrival may be too late to answer any valuable purpose."[2]

The Commander-in-Chief had no options except to retreat further into the New Jersey interior; the same logic then dictated that he might have to cross the Delaware River into Pennsylvania in the hope of forming a new defensive line. This, of course, required boats that he did not have.[3] Thus, even before abandoning New Brunswick, he took steps to assure his ability to reach Pennsylvania. He ordered Colonel Richard Humpton of the 11th Pennsylvania Regiment to go to the two Delaware ferries at Trenton and secure all the boats. Humpton also was ordered to gather all other boats he could find on the Delaware River and bring them to the Trenton ferries. Boats were not the only problem; there were also the army's supplies and equipment to worry about. In addition to finding all available watercraft, the rebel general

---

[1]Force, *American Archives*, Fifth Series, III: 822. A Newark return dated November 23 notes that the enlistments of the following brigades were to expire on December 1: General Beall's Maryland Brigade (1,200 men); General Heard's Brigade of Flying Camp men from New Jersey (800); and Colonel Bradly's (60). Fitzpatrick, ed., *Writings of Washington*, VI: 312. In a letter to Governor Livingston, Washington mentioned the names of the two large brigades that departed on December 1 and candidly admitted that he expected other losses to expired enlistments and desertions. Congressman George Read of Delaware wrote his wife on Dec. 6, 1776, that some of the members of the Flying Camp had arrived in Philadelphia, although he hoped that urgent appeals would induce some of them to reenlist, if only briefly. Read to Gertrude Read, Dec. 6, 1776, Smith, ed., *Letters of Delegates*, V: 582. John Marshall, *The Life of George Washington* (London: Printed for Richard Philips by J. Adlard, 1804) II: 597.

[2]*Ibid.*, 599; Fitzpatrick, ed., *Writings of Washington*, VI: 318.

[3]Washington had failed to make any preparations to get the garrison of Fort Washington across the Hudson River and he was determined not to repeat this mistake; he made sure that there were boats waiting to take his army across the Delaware River.

further instructed Humpton to get the army's baggage across the Delaware and to secure it in some safe place just beyond the river on the Pennsylvania side.[1] Humpton was a reliable officer whom Washington had already entrusted with important missions. A former British captain who had emigrated to Pennsylvania at the end of the French and Indian War, Humpton quit his 600-acre farm when the Revolution broke out and joined the rebellion. His military experience was welcomed. Washington sent General William Maxwell to join in Humpton's mission, and ordered General Israel Putnam to have rafts made from timber available at Trenton.[2]

Once Washington was satisfied with the Pennsylvania arrangements, he turned his attention to his problems in New Brunswick. At about 1:30 p.m. on December 1, the first British troops reached the banks of the Raritan River. They quickly brought up two field pieces and began an intense artillery duel with the few rebel batteries across the river. Two Americans were killed. The

---

[1]Twohig, ed., *The Papers of George Washington*, VII: 248. On Dec. 1, Washington ordered Colonel Richard Humpton to proceed to the Trenton area and "to see all the boats there put in the best Order with a sufficiency of Oars and poles and at the same time to Collect all the Additional Boats you [can] from both above and below and have them brought to those ferry's and Secured for the purpose of Carrying over the Troops and Baggage in most expeditious Manner." Quartermaster and other personnel were to render all possible assistance, and Humpton was to take special care to secure Durham boats. They were large and offered the best means of transporting the army and its baggage and stores. The Durham boat was a shallow-drafted vessel designed to go against the current of the Delaware River; depending upon conditions, could move by oars, poles, or sail, or it could float with the current. It was designed to transport iron made at the Durham furnace, located a little below the Delaware River port of Easton, Pennsylvania, to Philadelphia. It varied in length from 40 to 60 feet and was approximately 8 feet in width. Durham boats carried the bulk of the freight between Philadelphia and the upper Delaware River during the colonial period. They were also used on the Susquehenna and Mohawk Rivers.

[2]Humpton's whereabouts on Dec. 1 have been a matter of speculation; e.g., Stryker, *Battles of Trenton and Princeton*, 15, and Leonard Lundin, *Cockpit of the Revolution* (Princeton: Princeton University Press, 1940), 146. However, the wording in Washington's orders to Humpton and in related correspondence implies that the colonel was in New Brunswick with the Grand Army when he received his orders. Fitzpatrick, ed., *Writings of Washington*, VI: 318-319. Stryker, *Battles of Trenton and Princeton*, 15.

Americans had just five cannons at New Brunswick, all in Captain Alexander Hamilton's company of New York State Artillery.[1] They were lucky to have any artillery at all after the Fort Lee disaster. There is no record of whether Washington took note of young Hamilton, for whom American history had bigger plans. However, George Washington Parke Curtis, Washington's step-grandson, wrote in his *Recollections* that Washington had been "charmed by the brilliant courage and admirable skill" of Hamilton, who directed effective battery fire against the advancing British columns.[2] Surveying his weak position, Washington wrote a second letter to Congress, saying he had to retreat across the Delaware.

Meanwhile, the British were active on the opposite side of the Raritan. No bridge crossed at New Brunswick, but there was a bridge two miles up the river, Landing Bridge, at the village of Raritan Landing. Jaegers, guided by local Tories, hurried north on the Great Road Up Raritan, a roadway following the river on the Piscataway side, passing rich farmland and fine homes.[3] Upon reaching the village, they turned onto a causeway where they could see the bridge a short distance away. Advancing towards the bridge, even the dullest among them realized that its seizure would give the Crown forces an

---

[1]Robertson, *His Diaries and Sketches in America*, 114. Eight companies of artillery were authorized for the Continental army and commanded by Colonel Henry Knox. In addition, several states raised their own artillery companies. New York State raised two companies. In late 1776, one of the units was helping to defend the Hudson Highlands and the other, commanded by Captain Alexander Hamilton, accompanied Washington's army when it crossed the Hudson River to defend New Jersey. During the retreat, Hamilton's company was the only artillery Washington had with him. Robert Wright, Jr., *The Continental Army* (Washington D.C.: Government Printing Office, 1983), 62; and James Flexner, *The Young Hamilton* (Boston-Toronto: Little, Brown and Company, 1978), 122-123.

[2]James Thomas Flexner, *The Young Hamilton* (New York: Little, Brown & Company, 1978), 123.

[3]Burnaby, *Travels Through the Middle Settlements in North America*, 104. Burnaby traveled up the Raritan River from New Brunswick in 1759-1760. In his journal, Burnaby described the countryside along the Raritan River as "exceedingly rich and beautiful; and the banks of the river are covered with gentlemen's houses." The lower Raritan River could be crossed at a point about two miles above Raritan Landing. At this location, the river was shallow and had a firm, rocky bottom. A trail identified as "Vincent's path to Greenland's" crossed the Raritan at this point. C.C. Vermeule, "Raritan Landing That Was," *Proceedings of the New Jersey Historical Society*, 54 (1936): 87. There is no indication that the Crown forces went any further up the Raritan River than Raritan Landing at this point in the Revolution. The probable reason is that they feared operating too far from their main army.

opportunity to bag Washington's army at New Brunswick.

As the jaegers approached the bridge, they found it partially dismantled and defended by rebel riflemen whose marksmanship they had come to respect. The jaegers took cover in buildings on the Piscataway side of the river and started skirmishing with the rebels. Washington went through the motions of appearing to defend New Brunswick, but ordered his army to evacuate at dusk and to march on the Upper Road towards Princeton. The soldiers did not have enough wagons to remove all their baggage; some one hundred tents were burned to prevent the enemy from taking them.[1] As usual, a tenacious rear guard remained behind to delay the enemy.

Captain Fredrich Heinrich Lorey of the jaegers was posted at Raritan Landing. When darkness fell he realized that the rebels had abandoned their positions near the bridge and ordered his men across to form a defense perimeter on the New Brunswick side. He did not advance further for fear that American riflemen still lurked. About the same time, the jaegers captured two sloops below the bridge, loaded with stacks of clothing, shoes and wine.[2]

Any thoughts of advancing into New Brunswick that night were forsaken after a shocking incident at Landing Bridge at dusk. A young Hessian officer of the Block Grenadier Battalion, Captain Von Weitershausen, rode up to Raritan Landing, carrying orders from von Donop. He delivered his dispatch and turned his horse to ride away. Then a rifle shot rang out and Von Weitershausen dropped from his horse, mortally wounded through the breast and spine. That night, the Crown forces sat huddled around their campfires, loaded weapons nearby. They talked about the tragic shooting of Von Weitershausen and of how the rebels were purposely aiming at officers. The sentries were nervous of a surprise attack. Rumors said Lee had crossed the Hudson River from New York with ten thousand rebels and could be near.[3]

Washington stayed with the rear guard at New Brunswick until about 7:30 p.m., then retreated towards Princeton with the last of his comand. His army was already eight miles ahead of him. The next morning, Cornwallis

---

[1]Ewald, *Diary of the American War*, 24.; "Personal Recollections of Captain Enoch Anderson," *Papers of the Historical Society of Delaware*, XVL (1896), 27.

[2]Ewald, *Diary of the American War*, 24.

[3]Letter FZ, Lidgerwood Collection; 42; Letter K, ibid., 42-43. Captain von Weitsershausen died three days later and was buried at New Brunswick.

reconnoitered New Brunswick and occupied it with the Scottish Highlanders. The only rebels the British found were several sick or dead.[1] Cornwallis kept his army in defensive positions in the town and on the alert for a surprise attack, especially from Lee. The specter of Lee, if not the person, was proving an effective deterrent. Cornwallis posted light infantry beyond the town on the road to Princeton, but made no effort to chase Washington. Hessians occupied the houses along the Piscataway side of the Raritan River and British troops occupied the farmhouses further to the rear. On the night of December 1, Colonel Rall was at Newark with his Hessian brigade. He, too, worried about a rebel attack and ordered his pickets doubled when he was warned that rebels commanded by General Matthias Williamson were in the Newark area.[2]

If only Cornwallis had known Washington's actual situation! The American army almost ceased to exist as it retreated south from New Brunswick. Greene wrote shortly afterwards that "when we left Brunswick we had not 3000 men, a very pitiful army to trust the Liberties of America upon."[3] But Washington got his first good news in weeks: through the pleas and influence of General Mifflin, the Philadelphia Associators were en route to Trenton to reinforce the Grand Army.[4] The Commander-in-Chief could only hope that they would arrive in time, and that the addition of these amateur soldiers to the army would make a difference.

[1]Samuel Smith, *The Battle of Trenton* (Monmouth Beach, NJ: Philip Freneau Press, 1965), 5; Stirke, *A British Officer's Revolutionary War Journal*, 166.

[2]Letter K, Lidgerwood Collection, 43; Baurmeister, *Revolution in America*, 74.

[3]Greene to Governor Nicholas Cooke, Dec. 4, 1776; Showman, ed., *The Papers of General Nathanael Greene*, I: 362.

[4]In 1775, the militia of the City of Philadelphia consisted of five battalions and called themselves the "Associators of the City & Liberties of Philadelphia." Boatner, *Encyclopedia of the American Revolution*, 48.

CHAPTER SEVEN

Princeton and Trenton

As we go forward into the country the Rebels fly before us, & when
we come back, they always follow us, 'tis almost impossible to catch
them. They will neither fight, nor totally run away. but they Keep at
such a distance that we are always above a days march from them.
We seem to be playing at Bo peep.
-- Captain William Bamford, 40th Regiment of Foot[1]

News reached Philadelphia on December 2 that the forces of the Crown had crossed the Raritan River and captured New Brunswick; the town was the last American defense line in New Jersey. The road to Philadelphia was now open to the enemy. In days, it was rumored, the British and their Hessian hirelings would reach the city. Philadelphia panicked. Although some patriots strove for calm and worked to prepare a makeshift defense, many shops and schools closed; the roads out of the city were jammed with fleeing people and wagons.

Meanwhile, in New Jersey, Washington's skeleton of an army was in

---

[1]William Bamford, Diary, "The Revolutionary Diary of a British Officer," *Maryland Historical Magazine*, 28 (1933): 17-19.

flight towards the Delaware River. The troops had marched out of New Brunswick after nightfall on December 1, following the Upper Road towards Princeton, Trenton, and the hope of eventual security on the Pennsylvania side of the river. When the army was a safe distance out of New Brunswick, it camped for the night in the woods beside the road. It was a miserable bivouac. Soldiers had no tents or blankets to fight the cold; some suffered without shoes. In the morning, they broke camp and resumed the march towards Princeton through what one traveller had described before the war as "very fine country."[1] A farmer rising at dawn to tend his animals would have met a pitiful sight as the soldiers of the Grand Army passed, organized for fighting in hostile country.[2] First would have come pickets, isolated men on foot or mounted, scouting ahead of the army and alert for trouble. Next would be the advance party, composed of the remnants of Sheldon's Light Horse (Connecticut militia), and Maryland and Virginia riflemen, tough frontiersmen in long hunting shirts of various colors and carrying Pennsylvania rifles. The advance party also would have had some infantrymen, probably reliable veterans detached from the three Continental regiments Washington still had.

After the advance party were infantry regiments, marching according to their place in the order of battle. First was Sterling's brigade, consisting of Isaac Read's 1st Virginia Regiment followed by the remnants of Colonel John Haslet's 1st Delaware Regiment. Better known as "The Delaware Blues," Haslet's corps had formed on the Green in Dover, Delaware, in the summer of 1776, and marched off in high spirits to join Washington's army for the defense of New York City. The Delaware troops had suffered so many battle

---

[1]The details of the encampment of the army on the night of Dec. 1 are from "Personal Recollection of Captain Enoch Anderson," *Papers of the Historical Society of Delaware*, (1896): 27-28. Sergeant McCarty's journal for Monday, Dec. 2, implies that the army stopped for the night between New Brunswick and Princeton. His entry reads, "Day break we march on and came to Princetown," McCarty, 38. M'Robert, *A Tour of the Northern Provinces*, 33.

[2]Lesser, *Sinews of Independence*, 40-44. The order of the Grand Army on the road from New Brunswick to Princeton is based on the "General Return of the Army, December 1, 1776" and "Return of the Forces in the Service of the United States...Under the Command of his Excellency George Washington...December 22, 1776." At the time of the Revolution, the order in which regiments were listed in the returns was the same as the order in which the regiments lined up on a battlefield or their order of march when the army was on the move.

casualties and deaths from disease that by December 1776, they ceased to exist as a fighting unit.[1] Next came the 3rd Virginia (181 officers and men fit for duty) commanded by George Weedon, a former Fredericksburg innkeeper and pre-war acquaintance of Washington. Weedon was followed by the 6th Marylanders (199 officers and men), whose commanding officer, Otho Holland Williams, had been wounded and captured at Fort Washington.

Next came a newly organized brigade. The unit was scratched together from existing battalions, many of which had sustained heavy losses. The commander was General Hugh Mercer, a former Virginia doctor and apothecary shop owner. Mercer's brigade marched with the 232 officers and men of the 27th Massachusetts Continentals in the lead. Following them were 419 men with the 20th Connecticut Continental; then came the "shattered remnants" of Smallwood's Maryland Battalion. The proud Marylanders, after months of hard campaigning, were down to 262 officers and men. Counted among the missing was its commander, William Smallwood, seriously wounded at the Battle of White Plains in October.[2] Next in Mercer's brigade came the Connecticut State Regiment, with only 108 men. Many wore a mix of civilian and military clothing, dirty and threadbare from long campaigning. But no matter how ragged, every soldier had a clean musket and some type of cartridge box, filled with ammunition. At the end of Mercer's Brigade came the 105 remaining officers and men of Moses Rawlings' Maryland and Virginia Rifle Regiment.

Following Mercer on the tense march towards Princeton came the three Virginia regiments of General Adam Stephens. A traveler described one

[1]Blanco, *American Revolution, An Encyclopedia*, I, 452-453; and Dwyer, *The Day Is Ours*, 120. Haslet's Delawares had organized in the summer of 1776 with about 700 men. Some 550 of its men took part in the Battle of Long Island in August 1776. By late 1776, the regiment was down to six men. It was known as the Delaware Blues because its men were smartly dressed in blue coats with red facings. The light infantry company wore distinctive peaked black leather helmets with a tall plate on the front with the inscription, *"Liberty and Independence."* Their commander, Colonel John Haslet, was born in Ireland, where he had studied for the ministry and later medicine. He was a doctor and ardent patriot when the Revolution started. Haslet was killed on Jan. 3, 1777 at the Battle of Princeton.

[2]Fitzpatrick, *Writings of Washington*, VI: 346. Blanco, *American Revolution Encyclopedia*, II, 1538. The regiment was raised by Smallwood and Mordecai Gist in 1776 and was in the heaviest fighting at the Battles of Long Island and White Plains.

1. First Portrait of George Washington as Commander-in-Chief, by Charles Willson Peale. John Hancock was the President of the Continental Congress in the spring of 1776 when George Washington visited Philadelphia to confer with Congress. Hancock used the opportunity of Washington's visit to commission Charles Willson Peale to paint this three-quarter length portrait of the Commander-in-Chief. Washington sat for the portrait twice during his brief stay in Philadelphia. He is shown wearing a light blue silk sash, the badge of rank for the Commander-in-Chief. Peale completed the portrait sometime during the summer of 1776; however, he kept it on display in his studio until early December, 1776. Fearing that the Crown forces would overrun Philadelphia, Peale quickly delivered the portrait to Hancock on December 3rd, 1776 and was paid for his services. A few days later Peale marched off with his militia company to reinforce Washington's army in New Jersey. It is believed that Hancock quickly packed the portrait into a wagon and sent it to his Boston home for safe keeping. Courtesy of the Brooklyn Museum, Dick S. Ramsay Fund.

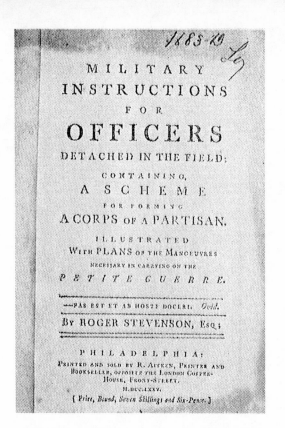

2. Title Page from a 1775 Manual on Partisan Warfare. What we call today guerrilla warfare was known as partisan warfare or petite guerre (small war) at the time of the American Revolution. This is the title page from a military textbook on partisan warfare. The book includes how to stage an ambush and fight using hit-and-run tactics. It was first published in London in 1770 and republished in Philadelphia in 1775.

The publication of *A Manual on Partisan Warfare* in America reflects the colonists interest in possibly fighting a partisan war against the British. Published with permission from The Library Company of Philadelphia.

3. Forcing Hudson River Passage, by Dominic Serres. This painting depicts the action on October 9, 1776 of a British naval squadron running the American defenses on the lower Hudson River. It was painted in 1779 by marine artist Dominic Serres (1722-1793). The large ships depicted are (from left to right) the frigates *Tartar*, *Roebuck*, and *Phoenix*. They are escorted by three smaller vessels (to the left of *Tartar*), which were the schooner *Tryal* and two tenders which cannot be accurately identified. The painting was commissioned by Admiral Sir Hyde Parker, the father of Captain Hyde Parker who commanded the flotilla.

Serres probably executed a total of five copies of this painting. Other than the Hudson River being too narrow in the paintings, they are otherwise accurate. Serres was provided with eye witness descriptions of the action from which he based his work. In the picture, the British warships are sailing north and being briskly cannonaded by Fort Lee on the New Jersey side (left) and Fort Washington on upper Manhattan Island (right). The British warships are sailing close to the Manhattan side of the river. One explanation for this is that the British warships were being guided by an American deserter, described as being the brother of the ferryman at Burdett's Ferry, who knew that the passage through the chevaux-de-frise was close to the Manhattan side. However, it is more likely, that in the 18th Century, the natural channel at this point in the Hudson River was close the Manhattan side.

The flag defiantly flying atop rebel held Fort Washington has thirteen alternating red and white stripes and was referred to as the "Rebel Stripes." It was the first, unofficial American national standard. Courtesy U.S. Naval Academy Museum.

4. A View of the Attack against Fort Washington and Rebel Redoubts near New York on the 16 of November 1776, by Thomas Davies. This eyewitness portrayal of the assault on Fort Washington was made from a vantage point in the Bronx, looking across the Harlem River to upper Manhattan Island. Davies included a hand written note that a battery of twelve-pounders was commanded by, "your humble Servant." Published with permission from the I.N. Phelps Stokes Collection, Miriam and Ira D. Wallach Division of Art, Prints and Photographs, The New York Public Library, Astor, Lenox and Tilden Foundations.

5. Detail of the Map of Northern Manhattan Island. This detail is from a map entitled, *A Topographical Map of the North Part of New York Island,* by Claude Joseph Sauthier (printed in London by William Faden, 1777). It depicts the British assault on Fort Washington on November 16, 1776. The map shows the positions of Fort Washington and Fort Lee. Note that one British frigate, HMS *Pearl*, is shown on the Hudson River, above the Fort Washington-Fort Lee defense line. *Pearl* gave supporting fire to the Hessian assault against the northern defenses of Fort Washington. Author's collection.

Perpendicular Bank of Rock

the Pearl

so dam hard to ascend

B

Landing

East

the Redoubt

Jeffery's Hook

Fort WASHINGTON

Chevaux

HUDSONS or NORTH RIVER

the Shuttell

Va

FORT LEE or Fort Constitution

HAERLEM CREEK

New

Point

Jersey

Hill

Hill

Fort Tryon

Knipps column commanded by

Brigade Islands commanded by

6-7. The Landing of the British Forces in the Jerseys on the morning of the 20th of November 1776, by Captain Thomas Davies. Despite the absence of professional combat artists, the American Revolution produced some outstanding illustrations made mainly by British artillery and engineer officers. These officers were trained to draw and paint, at least in water colors, as part of their curriculum at the Royal Military Academy at Woolwich, England. Among other duties, they were expected to be able to produce rapid and accurate sketches of ground, forts, buildings and landscapes for military evaluation purposes.

A dramatic example of combat art from the American Revolution is this watercolor showing the landing of Cornwallis' army in New Jersey. It was painted by Captain Thomas Davies (1737-1812), a British artillery officer who served in America during the Revolution. Inscribed below the watercolor, in pen and ink, is the caption *The Landing of the British Forces in the Jerseys on the 20th of November 1776 under the Command of the Rt Hon. Lieut Genl Earl Cornwallis.*

Davies illustration of the Crown forces landing in New Jersey was probably begun on the scene. He commanded Cornwallis' artillery and was close to the action during the 1776

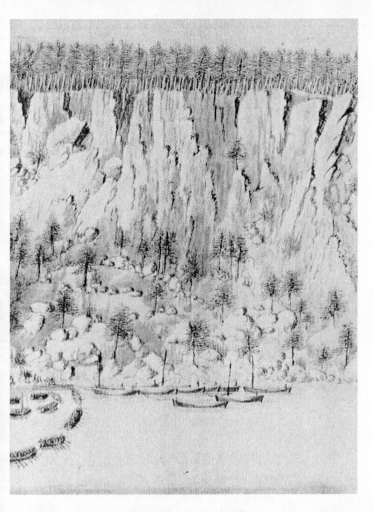

campaign. A close examination of the original watercolor reveals that Davies paid great attention to detail. The exclusion, in the watercolor, of the Blackledge-Keary House (built in 1750 and located at Upper Closter Dock Landing) is further evidence that Cornwallis landed at Lower Closter Dock Landing. See C.P. Stacey, *Thomas Davies* (Ottawa: The National Gallery of Canada, 1972).

This watercolor has sometimes been attributed to Lord Francis Rawdon, later 1st Marquess of Hastings (1754-1826), solely because Rawdon bought the picture from Davies soon after it was made. Most of Davies drawings were done to fulfill his military duties or to be sold to officers who collected, like Lord Rawdon.

Davies was appointed a gentleman cadet at the Royal Military Academy, Woolwich March, 1755. As a student, his natural aptitude for drawing was nurtured by Paul Sandby, Drawing Master at the Academy, who is considered by many today to be the father of English watercolor. Davies was a soldier for most of his adult life and lived in relative obscurity with his artwork hidden in private collections. Published with the permission of the Emmet Collection, Miriam and Ira D. Wallach Division of Art, Prints and Photographs, The New York Public Library, Astor, Lenox and Tilden Foundations.

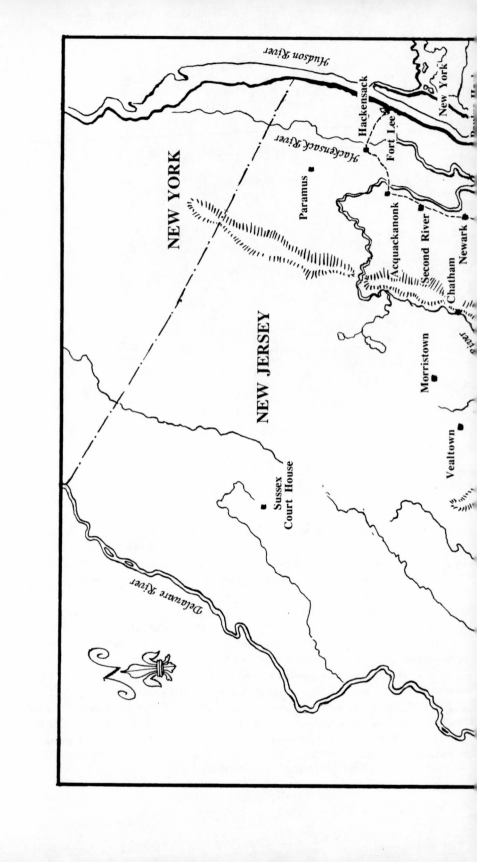

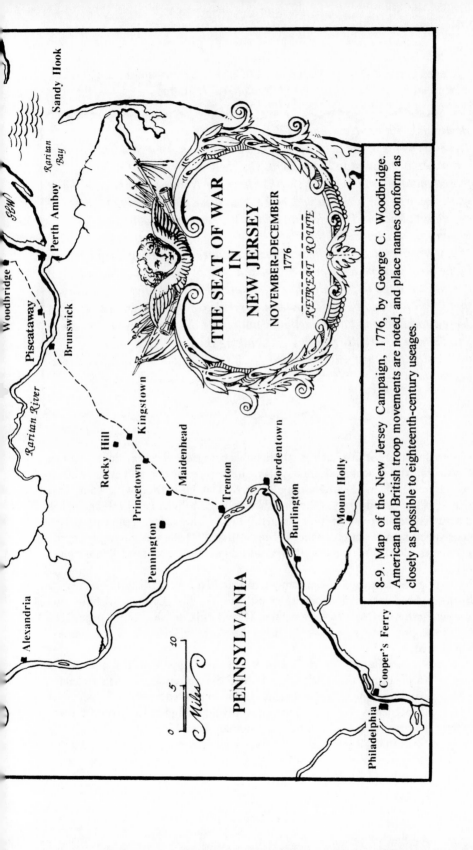

Woodbridge

Sandy Hook

Raritan
Bay

Perth Amboy

Piscataway

Brunswick

Raritan River

Alexandria

Rocky Hill

Kingstown

Princetown

Maidenhead

Pennington

Trenton

THE SEAT OF WAR
IN
NEW JERSEY
NOVEMBER–DECEMBER
1776

RETREAT ROUTE

Bordentown

Burlington

Mount Holly

PENNSYLVANIA

0   5   10
Miles

Philadelphia

Cooper's Ferry

8-9. Map of the New Jersey Campaign, 1776, by George C. Woodbridge. American and British troop movements are noted, and place names conform as closely as possible to eighteenth-century useages.

10. Alleged Letter of George Washington to Charles Lee, November 30, 1776, from William S. Stryker's *The Battle of Trenton and Princeton*

Brunswick, 30th of November, 1776
The movements of the enemy are, since I wrote you from Newark, of such a nature, as things stand at present, sincerely to be wished for. I have feared that they would take Newark, Elizabeth Town and Amboy for their winter quarters in order to undertake from these places early in the spring an attack on Philadelphia and at the same time having a favourable season ahead that they would make a diversion on the Delaware river with their fleet. The advantages they have gained over us in the past have made them so proud and sure of success that they are determined to go to Philadelphia this winter. I have positive information that this a fact and because the term of service of the light troops of Jersey and Maryland are ended they anticipate the weakness of our army. Should they now really risk this undertaking then there is a great probability that they will pay dearly for it for I shall continue to retreat before them so as to lull them into security.

The authenticity of this letter is questionable because it is optimistic, in contrast to Washington's other communications during the New Jersey retreat. On the date this letter was allegedly written, Washington arrived at New Brunswick with what remained of the Grand Army. The British were close behind and Washington was desperate for reinforcements from General Lee. The letter's optimism seems inconceivable under the circumstances. The fact that this letter was intercepted by the Crown forces adds to the suspicion that it was a subterfuge, meant to fall into enemy hands.

The original letter was found among the archives at Marburg, Germany by William Stryker. It was first published in Stryker's, *The Battles of Trenton and Princeton* (Boston and New York: Houghton, Mifflin and Company, 1898), pages 326-327. The original letter supposedly is still in the Marburg Archives, to which access is complicated.

The editors of *The Papers of George Washington* agree that this letter was a forgery. "While I cannot prove that it was a hoax," Senior Associate Editor Philander D. Chase has written, "the language and the content of this letter persuades me that it is not a legitimate letter. I include it in a note in volume 7 in order to warn readers away from it, fearing that some of them will stumble across it in Stryker" or elsewhere "and not realize... that it is fraudulent." Personal communication, Chase to the author, May 18, 1995.

11. General Sir Henry Clinton's Copy of Stedman's *History*. Charles Stedman (1745-1812) was a Philadelphia Loyalist who served as a British army officer. Stedman saw extensive service during the American Revolution. He went into exile in England at the end of the war where he published one of the first histories of the Revolution in London in 1794. Stedman's *The History of the Origin, Progress, and Termination of the American War* was a scathing criticism of General William Howe's management of the war.

General Sir Henry Clinton owned a copy of Stedman's book. This is page 221 of Volume One from Clinton's copy of Stedman. Stedman is describing Clinton's efforts to get the Howe brothers to divert the Rhode Island task force to support Cornwallis by outflanking Washington's retreating army. Clinton added the following note to Stedman's text: "or be landed at Amboy to have Cooperated with L Cornwallis or embarked on board Ld Howes Fleet landed in Delaware and taken possession of Philadeiphia." Published with the permission of the William L. Clements Library.

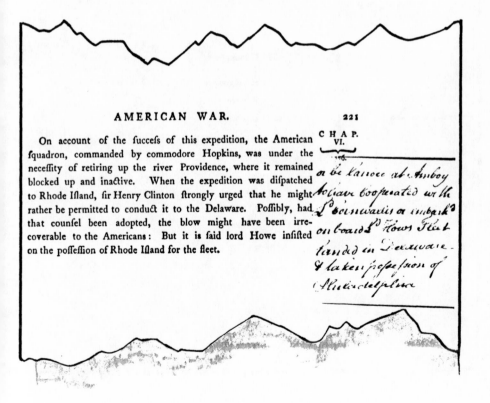

AMERICAN WAR.   221

On account of the fuccefs of this expedition, the American fquadron, commanded by commodore Hopkins, was under the neceffity of retiring up the river Providence, where it remained blocked up and inactive. When the expedition was difpatched to Rhode Ifland, fir Henry Clinton ftrongly urged that he might rather be permitted to conduct it to the Delaware. Poffibly, had that counfel been adopted, the blow might have been irrecoverable to the Americans: But it is faid lord Howe infifted on the poffeffion of Rhode Ifland for the fleet.

C H A P.
VI.

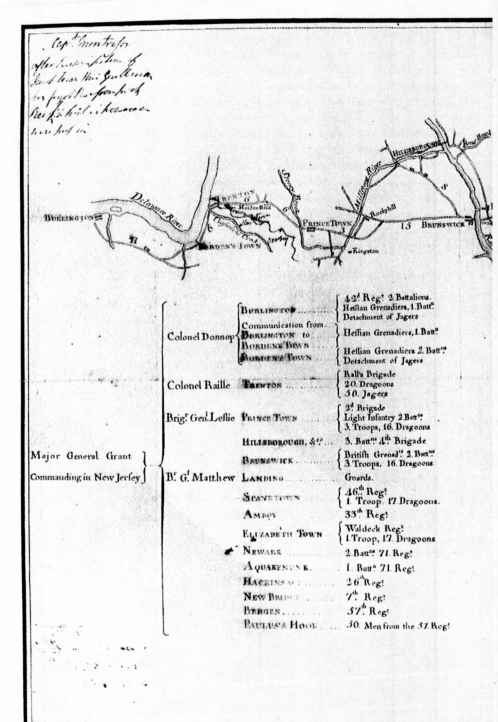

BURLINGTON   Delaware River   TRENTON   Maidenhead   Stony Brook   HILLSBOROUGH   Raretan

Crosswicks Creek   PRINCE TOWN   Rockhill   Millstone River   BRUNSWICK

BORDEN'S TOWN   Kingston

Major General Grant **Commanding in New Jersey**	Colonel Donnop	BURLINGTON	42.ᵈ Reg.ᵗ 2.Battalions. Heſſian Grenadiers, 1.Batt.ⁿ Detachment of Jagers
		Communication from BURLINGTON to BORDENS TOWN	Heſſian Grenadiers, 1.Batt.ⁿ
		BORDEN'S TOWN	Heſſian Grenadiers 2. Batt.ⁿ Detachment of Jagers
	Colonel Raille	TRENTON	Rall's Brigade 20. Dragoons 50. Jagers
	Brig.ʳ Gen.ˡ Leſlie	PRINCE TOWN	2.ᵈ Brigade Light Infantry 2.Batt.ⁿˢ 3. Troops, 16. Dragoons
		HILLSBOROUGH, &c.ᵃ	3. Batt.ⁿˢ 4.ᵗʰ Brigade
		BRUNSWICK	British Grenad.ʳ 2. Batt.ⁿˢ 3. Troops, 16. Dragoons.
	B.ʳ G.ˡ Matthew	LANDING	Guards.
		SPANKTOWN	46.ᵗʰ Reg.ᵗ 1. Troop. 17. Dragoons.
		AMBOY	33.ᵗʰ Reg.ᵗ
		ELIZABETH TOWN	Waldeck Reg.ᵗ 1.Troop, 17. Dragoons
		NEWARK	2. Batt.ⁿ 71. Reg.ᵗ
		AQUAKENUNK.	1. Batt.ⁿ 71. Reg.ᵗ
		HACKINSACK	26.ᵗʰ Reg.ᵗ
		NEW BRIDGE	7.ᵗʰ Reg.ᵗ
		BERGEN	57.ᵗʰ Reg.ᵗ
		PAULUS'S HOOK	50. Men from the 57. Reg.ᵗ

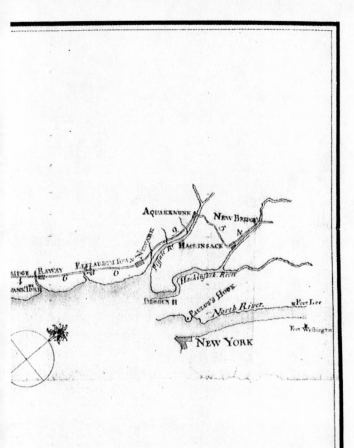

12-13. Projected 1776-1777 Winter Quarters for the Crown forces in New Jersey. This informative manuscript map was drawn by Captain John Montresor (1736-1799) about December 12th, 1776 to indicate projected winter quarters for the army in New Jersey. The map was probably prepared by Montresor for the British high command in America. Montresor was appointed chief engineer in America in December, 1775, and served throughout the New York campaign of 1776. The handwritten note on the upper left corner is in the handwriting of General Henry Clinton and reads, "Capt Montresor after the misfortune of Trenttown this gentlemen has forgot the Assompink [Assumpink] Creek which is however here put in." Assumpink Creek, which runs through Trenton, has been penned into the map. Published with the permission of the William L. Clements Library.

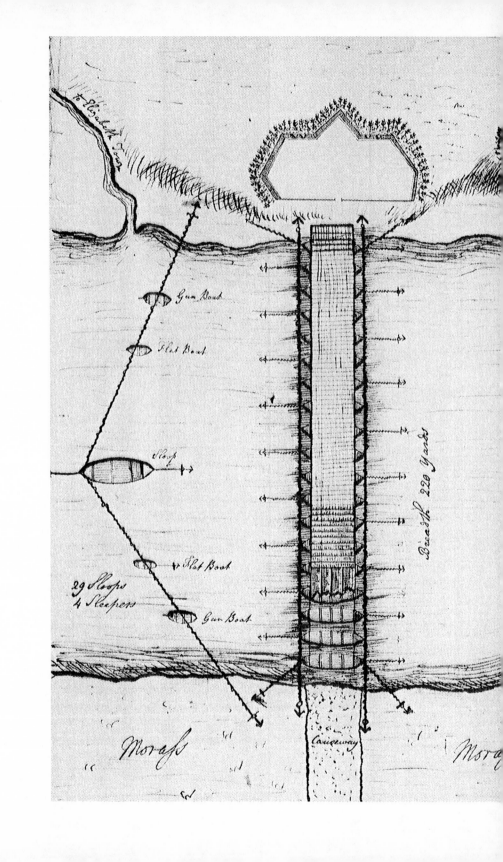

Staten Island
ies, by C'Laid?

14-15. Illustration of a Pontoon Bridge built by British Army Engineers, 1780. Following their retreat across the Delaware River, the Americans expected the Crown forces to bring up pontoons to ford the Delaware River. This pen and ink drawing, from the papers of Sir Henry Clinton, and shows a pontoon bridge that the British built in 1780 across the Arthur Kill, which separates Staten Island from New Jersey. In December 1776, the British had similar boats in New York City and Howe could have transported overland across New Jersey in the special wagons. Once in the water, the boats were fastened together and planking was laid to create a roadway. On the left side of the illustration, the engineers have constructed a barrier to prevent enemy fire ships or fire rafts from reaching the bridge, which also is defended by fortifications (depicted at the top of the illustration). Published with the permission of the William L. Clements Library.

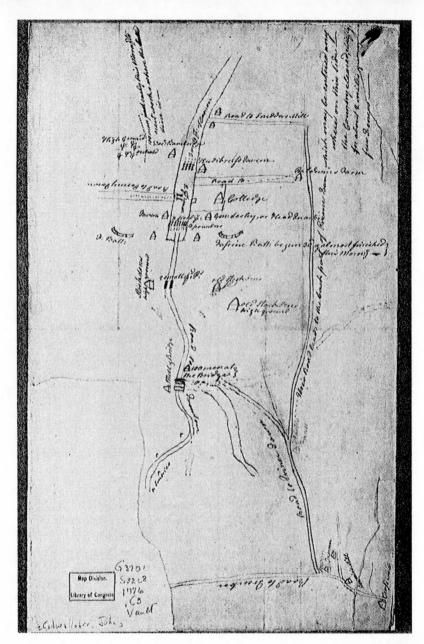

16. The Spy Map of Princeton. On December 31, 1776, Colonel John Cadwalader (1742-1786) wrote General Washington from Crosswicks, New Jersey with information about the enemy garrison at Princeton. Cadwalader included this crude map in his report. The map was probably drawn by the spy whom Cadwalader had sent into Princeton the previous day. Cadwalader only identifies his spy in his letter to Washington as, "A very intelligent young Gentleman." The spy map includes the position of British headquarters and gun batteries at Princeton. Cadwalader apparently sent several spies into Princeton during late December and their information helped Washington execute his successful attack on Princeton on January 3rd, 1777. Library of Congress Collection.

of his regiments as "a set of dirty, ragged people, badly clothed, badly disciplined and badly armed."[1]

Flags probably were dispersed along the line. These were regimental or state flags, probably in tatters.[2] The Americans still had no national flag. Each regiment had a few fifers and drummers.

Moving with the column on horseback were Washington and his official staff. Washington probably wore a blue regimental coat faced with buff and, since it was now December, he also wore a warm black cloak or greatcoat over his regimentals. Even his clothing was somewhat threadbare from hard use. A gold epaulet sat on each shoulder. If Washington went into battle, he would don a distinguishing light-blue sash, symbol of the Commander-in-Chief. Washington's official family included Greene, who was deputy commander, and other high-level functionaries. Typically, these were the acting chief of artillery, Colonel Henry Knox, a quartermaster, a clothier, an adjutant, aides, and secretaries.[3] Washington's aides wore the uniform of their regiments. They rode horses and were armed with sword and, probably, a pair of saddle pistols. Paine, as Greene's secretary, would have ridden on horseback with the official family although he held no military rank and would not be uniformed.

Close to the Commander-in-Chief rode some heavily armed mounted troopers of Washington's Life Guards. Next in the column were the weary men of Ewing's and Hand's Pennsylvania Flying Camp, militia regiments with

---

[1] *Journal of Nicholas Cresswell*, 163-164. Cresswell saw the 6th Virginia as it passed through Leesburg, Virginia, on Oct. 10, 1776. Several months of marching and fighting must have added further to the distress and ragged appearance of the Virginia troops.

[2] Both armies had flags or "colors" at the time of the Revolution. Some colors were quite large in order to assist in unit identification in the field. British Captain George Smith, in his *An Universal Military Dictionary* (London: J. Millan, 1779), 65, specified "the size of the colours to be 6 feet 6 inches flying, and 6 feet deep on the pike." Regiments did not carry national flags and the American army probably never fought with one. It appears that the national flag was used by naval vessels, fortifications, towns, and possibly army headquarters.

[3] Knox's exact whereabouts during late November through early December are a mystery. From his correspondence we know he was with Lee's corps on Nov. 22, 1776. Knox wrote an expense report from Peekskill, New York, on Nov. 23. Sometime in between Knox made his way across northern New Jersey, probably with Lee's corps, because the next reliable information we have to trace his location is a letter he wrote to his wife Kitty dated "Trenton Ferry, December 8th, 1776."

no uniforms. The few cannons left to the army, probably a mix of three-, four- and six-pounders, were dispersed throughout the column, unloaded because of bouncing and jarring on the roadbed but with crews nearby for quick action. The artillery carriage side boxes or lockers, as they were called, carried some ammunition; but the bulk of their shot and powder was in the baggage train at the rear. Flankers were spread out on both sides of the column to warn of a surprise attack.

An early-to-rise New Jersey farmer also might have glimpsed Captain Alexander Hamilton, who commanded the Independent New York Artillery company. A young man, Hamilton already was a veteran with a growing reputation in the army. Long after the war, an officer who had marched on the retreat recalled the New Yorker. He was still "a youth, a mere stripling, small, slender, almost delicate in frame, marching beside a piece of artillery, with a cocked hat pulled down over his eyes, apparently lost in thought, with his hand resting on the cannon, and every now and them patting it as he mused, as if it were a favorite horse, or a pet playing."[1]   Hamilton's company wore dark blue regimental coats with buff facings and breeches. They had seen hard service since the start of the New York campaign.

The army's wagons went behind the marching column, carrying all of the extra ammunition, food and animal fodder, the few tents that the army still possessed, kitchen equipment, bedding and spare clothing belonging to the enlisted men. There may have been a wagon with engineer's tools: shovels, axes, saws and picks and specialized implements. This support train was guarded by a small number of infantry walking alongside, as well as mounted men ready to respond to any alarm.[2]

---

[1]Washington Irving, *Life of Washington* (New York: G. P. Putnam, 1856), III: 88. Washington Irving does not say the incident occurred at Princeton, following the American withdrawal from New Brunswick.   However,   Nathan Schachner, one of Hamilton's biographers, repeats this story, stating that it took place at Princeton: "The Americans made a sorry spectacle as they straggled into Princeton.   But Hamilton's long months of hard driving now showed their effect. His company drew all eyes by the disciplined appearance of its ranks and the brisk, soldierly stride of its men." *Alexander Hamilton* (New York: Appleton-Century Company, 1946), 54.

[2]Knowing the role of the support train of wagons is important to understanding how the American Revolution was fought. For example, the need for many wagon loads of equipment and supplies meant the armies had to stay on or near roads. Therefore, almost all of the fighting of the Revolution was fought near roads. It was impossible for an army to move cross-country. Sometimes, the military wagon trains that saw service in the American Revolution would stretch out for miles.

No matter how destitute the army, it had wagons to carry the officers' personal property. Any officer who could afford the expense also had his own personal wagon or wagons. Washington usually had two, for items such as tents and spare clothing. Following the baggage train came the rear guard riflemen and reliable infantrymen, continually checking behind them for trouble. Further back were a few mounted scouts watching the road from New Brunswick. These experienced men knew the difference between an enemy patrol and an advancing column, and at the first sign of real danger they rode forward to warn the army. Close to the rear of the army were sutler's wagons. These civilians sold necessities and luxuries, including liquor, to those soldiers who could afford them. There were probably few sutlers in the Grand Army at this point, because of the cold weather and the soldiers' poverty. Also at the rear were any women of the army, camp followers and children.

This column filed into Princeton sometime between 8:00 and 9:00 a.m. on the morning of December 2. Princeton was a neat village of only one street formed by the Upper Road. It had somewhere between sixty and eighty houses amid well-cultivated fields, the houses widely separated by gardens and pastures. At its center stood Nassau Hall, housing the College of New Jersey (modern Princeton University). The college building was visible from a considerable distance and dominated the village. A pre-war visitor, Patrick M'Robert, said the village was clean, healthy looking, and had a "fine extensive view of the country round."[1]

The American army found Princeton deserted. Residents had fled when they heard that the British and Hessians were near. The Delaware River ferry crossings to Pennsylvania were choked with frightened civilians, carrying whatever they could on their backs, and sick and wounded soldiers. A girl saw the scene as akin to the Day of Judgment.[2] Residents had to hide whatever belongings they could not carry into the woods or leave them behind; the American vanguard had already taken most of their wagons and horses.

---

[1]This description of Nassau Hall is based in part on the Marquis de Chastellux, who visited Princeton in 1780; *Travels in North America* (London, 1787), I: 160. M'Robert, *A Tour of the Northern Provinces*, 33.

[2]New Jersey had approximately fifty ferries in active use in the middle of the eighteenth century. Among the busiest were those at Lambertville, the two ferries at Trenton, and Cooper's Ferry (Camden). Wheaton Lane, *From Indian Trail to Iron Horse* (Princeton: Princeton University Press, 1939), 44. Lundin, *Cockpit of the Revolution*, 157-158.

The president of the college, John Witherspoon, was known to be "as high a son of liberty as any man in America."[1] Witherspoon, in fact, was one of the New Jersey signers of the Declaration of Independence. When the news came that the American army was retreating, Witherspoon realized the invaders might soon reach Princeton. Calling his students together on November 29, he told them "in a very affecting manner" that he had to disband the college; the students had to leave for their own safety.[2] Some of the students had come to study from as far as Virginia and South Carolina; but all realized they had to flee, and tumult soon filled Nassau Hall as they packed belongings and scoured the village for wagons. Some said goodbyes from room to room. As a signer of the Declaration, Witherspoon was marked as a traitor by the British. He fled Princeton with his family and whatever possessions they could quickly gather.[3]

Like Witherspoon, Princeton landowner and lawyer Richard Stockton had signed the Declaration. He also got away on November 29 after burying the family silver and other treasured objects in the garden of Morven, his large and handsome home. Stockton left his son Richard, 12, at Morven with a trusted servant and took the rest of his family. But instead of heading for the safety of Pennsylvania, Stockton rode south to the home of his friend, John Cowenhoven, in Monmouth County, where he thought he would be safe. However, a band of Tory militia captured Stockton and carried him off to brutal captivity in New York City. The Continental Congress protested his

---

[1]The comment was made by John Adams, who visited Princeton in August 1774. John Maclean, *History of the College of New Jersey* (Philadelphia: J.B. Lippincott & Co., 1877), I: 320.

[2]There is an account by an unknown student of the evacuation. "On the 29th of November, 1776," he wrote, "New Jersey College, long the peaceful seat of science and haunt of the Muses, was visited with the melancholy tidings of the approach of the enemy." Witherspoon, "deeply affected at this solemn scene, entered the [Nassau] Hall where the students were collected, and in a very affecting manner informed us of the improbability of continuing them longer in peace; and after giving us several suitable instructions and much good advice, very affectionately bade us farewell." John Hageman, *History of Princeton* (Philadelphia: J.B. Lippincott & Co., 1879), 124. Lundin, *Cockpit of the Revolution*, 157, also has an account of the closing of the College of New Jersey.

[3]Thomas Wertenbaker, *Princeton 1746-1896* (Princeton: Princeton University Press, 1946), 59. John Witherspoon's country home, "Tusculum," was later pillaged by the Crown forces. Mark Boatner, *Landmarks of the American Revolution* (Harrisburg: Stackpole Books, 1973), 211.

harsh treatment to no avail. Stockton finally succumbed to his tormentors and, to save his life, signed General Howe's pardon. His action marked him as a defector and he was never again active in politics. He died of cancer in 1781.[1]

Washington halted at Princeton only long enough to drop off two brigades under Stirling, then rushed on to Trenton. He told Stirling "to watch the Motions of the Enemy and give notice of their approach."[2] This was a bold move since the troops left at Princeton represented almost half his army.   But Washington made his intentions clear in a letter to Congress, saying he wanted to get his baggage and stores across the river and then "face about with such Troops as are here fit for Service and March back to Princeton and there govern myself by Circumstances and the movements of General Lee." Remarkably, Washington was full of fight and eager to strike some blow.[3] The rebel troops at Princeton promptly made themselves at home in the deserted college building and watched for an enemy advance. American spies continued to filter in and out of New Brunswick. Along the twelve miles from Princeton to Trenton, the troops who pushed on found a good road with many taverns and inns. "The country round about displays variety of agreeable prospects and rural scenes," said one traveller. "I observed many large fields of wheat, barley, and hemp." All around were fertile meadows and pastures. Many of the houses in view were built of rough stone.[4] Large barns with high roofs looked like small churches.

---

[1]Lundin, *Cockpit of the Revolution*, 160-161.

[2]The two brigades left at Princeton consisted of the five Virginia regiments and Haslet's Delawares, about 1,200 men. Fitzpatrick, ed., *Writings of Washington*, VI: 331. Legend has it that Washington stood on the porch of the Olden House, just outside Princeton, to watch his little army march past on their way to Trenton. Boatner, *Landmarks of the Revolution*, 210. Fitzpatrick, ed., *Writings of Washington*, VI: 325.

[3]Fitzpatrick, ed., *Writings of Washington*, VI: 331. On Dec. 5, Washington wrote Congress that "as nothing but necessity obliged me to retire before the Enemy, and leave so much of the Jerseys unprotected, I conceive it to be my duty, and it corresponds with my Inclination, to make head against them, so soon as there shall be the least probability of doing it with propriety." *Ibid.*, 330. Washington also decided to post a strong rear guard at Princeton to protect General Lee's corps if Lee made an attempt to link up with Washington's army in New Jersey.

[4]Wendy Martin, ed., "The Itinerarium of Dr. Alexander Hamilton," in *Colonial American Travel Narratives* (New York: Penguin Books, 1994), 200. Hamilton toured from Annapolis, Maryland, to Portsmouth, New Hampshire, in the summer of 1744.

Washington neared Trenton at noon with his little army. He had heard nothing from Lee for days. Perhaps he hoped that he would find Lee in Trenton, standing in front of his seven thousand veterans and greeting his commander. How splendid it would be to see General Nixon's steady New England brigade, McDougall's combat-tested New Yorkers and General John Glover's 14th Regiment of tough Massachusetts fishermen. It would be a great reunion for the Continental army, and Washington finally could take some offensive action. Instead, in Trenton Washington only found another deserted village, this one on the very edge of New Jersey. But, as Washington entered Trenton from the north, a detachment of twenty-six dragoons moved in from the south. These were the 1st Troop of Philadelphia City Cavalry, the first reinforcements to reach Washington since he left Hackensack. Their commander, Captain Samuel Morris, reported his troop had left Philadelphia on December 1 and brought the heartening news that 1,500 Philadelphia Associators had been mobilized and were marching towards Trenton in order to reinforce Washington.[1]

The boats waiting at Trenton told Washington that Colonel Humpton had done his job well.[2] Washington ordered that they be loaded immediately with all the army's military stores and baggage for ferrying across the Delaware. It took three days of constant crossing and recrossing with every available boat to move everything. Fortunately the enemy had not stirred from New Brunswick, reported Stirling from the rear guard at Princeton. Additional reinforcements from Philadelphia were now trickling into Trenton--410 men,

---

[1]One of the volunteer privates in the 1st Troop was Benjamin Randolph, a master cabinet-maker. The commander-in-chief was happy to see him because the General's wife, Martha, had lived in Randolph's Chestnut Street boarding house for several months. Martha Washington had last seen her husband during the summer when George visited Philadelphia to meet with Congress. When he returned to New York, he left her in the care of the Randolphs. Martha went back to Mount Vernon soon after, but returned to Philadelphia later in the summer in the hopes of joining her husband in New York. The military situation made journeying beyond Philadelphia dangerous, and she remained with Randolph and his family through the late summer and fall of 1776 before returning for a second time to Mount Vernon.

[2]Colonel Humpton cleared the Delaware River and its tributaries of anything that could float in a radius of 40 miles from Trenton. He did the job with the help of the galleys of the Pennsylvania Navy and the Hunterdon County, New Jersey militia. See John W. Jackson, *The Pennsylvania Navy* (New Brunswick: Rutgers University Press, 1974), 74-76.

part of the recently recruited regiment of Pennsylvania and Maryland Germans commanded by Colonel Nicholas Haussegger.[1] The Philadelphia Associators, roused in part through General Mifflin's efforts, were still on the way.

The troops arriving at Trenton were welcome but they were inexperienced. What Washington wanted was Lee with his veterans. He was desperate for news when a post rider finally galloped into Trenton on December 3 with a dispatch from Lee. It was dated November 30 and written at Peekskill, New York. The letter began, "Dear General: I received yours last night, dated the 27th, from New-ark. You complain of my not being in motion sooner, I do assure you that I have done all in my power, and shall explain my difficulties when we have both leisure." Lee wrote that he would enter the Province of Jersey "with four thousand firm and willing troops, who will make a very important diversion. Had I stirred sooner, I should have only led an inferior number of unwilling."[2]

Lee promised to cross the Hudson "the day after tomorrow" (December 2). Intially, Washington was relieved. Finally, he thought, Lee was on the move toward the main part of the army. But Lee quickly dashed his commander's hopes. He closed his letter by asking that Washington "bind me as little as possible, not from any opinion, I do assure you, of my own

---

[1] On Nov. 25, the Continental Congress called out the Associators of Philadelphia and the surrounding counties to serve for six weeks. The Congress also directed that the German Battalion (commanded by Colonel Haussegger) was to march immediately. Worthington Ford, *et al.*, eds.., *Journals of the Continental Congress, 1774-1789* (Washington D.C.: Government Printing Office, 1904-1937).

[2] *The Lee Papers* (New York: New York Historical Society, 1873), II: 322. Heath recalled that Lee arrived at his headquarters on Nov. 30, en route to New Jersey., and asked for a cup of tea. Lee's second request was for 2,000 men from Heath's command to march with him to New Jersey. Heath refused. Lee reduced his request to 1,000 men. Heath again refused, stating that not a single man would march because Heath had positive written instructions from Washington not to remove any of his troops from the defense of the Hudson River. The argument continued, with Lee claiming he was Heath's superior and would detach two of Heath's regiments. But Lee left Peekskill the following morning without taking anyone from Heath's command and crossed the Hudson on Dec. 2 and 3. Heath thought that Lee's men were as good as any in the army, but noted that "many of them were so destitute of shoes, that the blood left on the rugged frozen ground, in many places, marked the route they had taken; and a considerable number, unable to march, were left at Peekskill." William Heath, *Memoirs of Major-General Heath* (Boston: I. Thomas and E.T. Andrews, 1798), 94-96.

parts, but from a persuasion that detached Generals cannot have too great latitude, unless they are very incompetent indeed."[1] Washington read Lee's letter in disbelief. The commander-in-chief did not want Lee operating independently, but to reinforce the Grand Army. Surely, Washington reasoned, Lee had misinterpreted his instructions, and he dashed off a letter that same day imploring Lee to come: "You will readily agree that I have sufficient cause for my anxiety, and to wish for your arrival as early as possible."[2] Greene saw the situation differently, and politely warned Washington about Lee in a letter dated December 7. He stated bluntly that he did not think that Lee could be trusted with discretionary orders: "I think General Lee must be confined within the Lines of some General Plan, or else his operations will be independant of yours."[3]

Lee now had to move. He had run out of excuses for inaction, and he feared that continued recalcitrance would provoke the Continental Congress; thus he prepared to move his division across the Hudson River and into the New Jersey theater of operations.[4] But Lee's immense ego would not let him put himself under Washington's command any longer. Lee had decided he was a better soldier than Washington, and determined to maintain a separate command as long as possible. He began crossing the Hudson at Peekskill on December 2 with about 2,500 men.[5] He kept up his new game in a letter to

---

[1]*Lee Papers*, II: 322.

[2]Fitzpatrick, ed., *Writings of Washington*, VI: 326.

[3]Showman, ed., *The Papers of General Nathanael Greene*, I: 366.

[4]Whatever his opinion of Washington, Lee had to maintain the good will of Congress if he wanted to replace Washington. Congress wanted to know Lee's situation, and on Dec. 2 directed Washington "to send Colonel Stewart, or any other officer express to General Lee, to know where and in what situation he and the army with him are." Ford, ed., *Journals of the Continental Congress*, VI: 1000. Washington admitted that he had lost touch with Lee, although he had tried to contact him. He feared that his letters had failed to get through. Fitzpatrick, ed., *Writings of Washington*, VI: 324-325. The "Colonel Stewart" mentioned by Congress was Lt. Colonel Walter Stewart, an' aide-de-camp to General Gates. Francis Heitman, *Historical Register of Officers of the Continental Army* (Washington D.C.: Rare Book Shop Publishing Company, 1914) , 520-521; Fitzpatrick, ed., *Writings of Washington*, VI: 325n.

[5]When Lee crossed the Hudson on Dec. 2, he commanded a force of between 2,500 and 3,000. This small number seems implausible given the 7,500 men in Lee's division in early November. However, the numbers are correct and show the serious

Washington from Haverstraw, New York, on December 4, stating that the retreat from New Brunswick made it impossible for him to know where to rejoin the main army. Instead, Lee wanted to add the troops from the Northern Army, which were nearing Morristown, to his own force. This would give him a total of 5,000 men to startle the enemy, "hanging on their flanks or rear."[1]

Washington sent personal emissaries to apprise Lee of his situation. The first was the dependable Humpton, whom he dispatched on December 5 to find Lee and report back concerning his strength, condition, and route of march. In addition, Washington told Humpton to find out about the eight regiments under General Gates, as well as the militia attached to General Williamson. Two days later, without waiting for news from Humpton, Washington sent Major Robert Hoops to find Lee. Hoops carried a letter telling Lee that he could safely cross the Delaware at Alexandria (modern Frenchtown, New Jersey). Washington had secretly ordered boats and troops to wait for Lee at this point on the river, far above the enemy's positions.[2]

Lee, however, advanced through New Jersey at the proverbial snail's pace. He seized horses and wagons along his route of march. On December 6, Lee's division was at the Ringwood Iron Works. On December 8, the main column marched through the village of Pompton and the following day they went through Hanover and stopped for the night at Parsippany. Lee's troops were advancing cautiously because there were rumors that 7,000 or 8,000

---

problems which the American cause faced in late 1776. On Nov. 17, Lee lost three Massachusetts militia regiments (2,000 men) when their enlistments expired. Richard Ketchum, *The Winter Soldiers* (Garden City, NY: Doubleday & Company, Inc., 1973), 162; *Lee Papers*, II: 288; Freeman, *George Washington*, IV: 254. The British had accurate information about the strength of Lee's corps, estimating that he had about 2,500 men; Kemble, *Journal*, I: 102. Lee's command consisted of the brigades of Colonels John Glover, Paul Sargent, and Daniel Hitchcock. Hitchcock commanded a consolidated "New England Brigade" composed of units from Rhode Island, Massachusetts, and New Hampshire. Hitchcock, a Rhode Islander, was in the last stages of consumption, but insisted upon marching with Lee. He died at Morristown on Jan. 13, 1777. Herbert Wade and Robert Lively, *This Glorious Cause* (Princeton: Princeton University Press, 1958), 92-93. Desertions and sickness drastically reduced Lee's numbers further from mid-November, when he reported 5,589 fit for duty, plus 60 light horse and some artillery. Force, ed., *American Archives*, Series Five, III: 831-832.

[1] *Lee Papers*, II: 329-330.

[2] Fitzpatrick, ed., *Writings of George Washington*, VI: 329, 335-336; *Lee Papers*, II: 336-338. For information about the gathering of boats to take Lee's corps across the Delaware River, see Fitzpatrick, ed., *Writings of Washington*, VI: 337, 341.

Hessians and Tories had marched from New Brunswick to intercept them. Lee and his suite advanced ahead of his main column. He stopped at Morristown on December 8 and reached the village of Chatham, a few miles east of Morristown, later that day. He remained at Chatham to await his corps, which arrived on December 10.[1]

It was at Morristown on December 8 that Humpton, Washington's first emissary, found Lee. Although Humpton was sent to gather information, he also was to encourage Lee to quickly move to join Washington on the Delaware. Lee sent Humpton back to Washington with a letter stating that 1,000 New Jersey militia were expected to join his own corps of 2,700 at Morristown. Still secretly determined to maintain his independent command, Lee found reasons to remain in northern New Jersey. "If I was not taught to think that your army was considerably reinforced," he wrote, "I should immediately join you; but as I am assured you are very strong, I should imagine we can make a better impression by hanging on their rear." Lee said he would use Chatham as his base of operations. "It is at a happy distance from Newark, Elizabethtown, Woodbridge, and Boundbrook."[2]

Having sent Humpton off with this disingenuous missive, Lee moved his corps east from Morristown to Chatham on December 8 to get closer to the enemy while still having the protection of the rugged terrain of Morris County. Chatham was the gateway to Morris County. It sat on the west bank of the Passaic River, a strategic location, and astride an important road that ran from Elizabethtown to Morristown. Chatham had a bridge over the Passaic, which was fordable at only a few places as it snaked through central New Jersey. Lee probably made Day's Tavern his headquarters.[3] On the afternoon of December 8, Major Hoops arrived in the village. Responding to Hoops' dispatch, which reiterated Washington's pleas for Lee to hurry to the Delaware, Lee remained evasive. "I cannot persuade myself that Philadelphia is their

---

[1]Hay to Heath, Dec. 15, 1776, in Force, ed., *American Archives*, Fifth Series, III: 1236. Lee to Colonel Chester, Dec. 7, 1776, in Henry Johnson, *The Campaign of 1776 Around New York and Brooklyn* (Brooklyn: The Long Island Historical Society, 1878), 145. Louise Rau, ed., "Sergeant John Smith's Diary of 1776," *Mississippi Valley Historical Review*, 20: 263.

[2]Lee to Washington, Dec. 8, 1776, *Lee Papers*, II: 337.

[3]Donald White, *A Village at War* (Rutherford. NJ: Fairleigh Dickinson University Press, 1979), 73. Day's tavern was ideally located by the main road and the bridge; it soon after appeared on an American army map.

object at present," he wrote the commander-in-chief, adding that "it will be difficult, I am afraid, to join you; but cannot I do you more service by attacking their rear? I shall look about me tomorrow, and inform you further."[1]

This communication hardly reassured Washington of Lee's intentions, and dispatches between the two generals now flew back and forth at a frantic pace. Humpton returned to Washington's Delaware River headquarters on the night of December 9 with Lee's letter, and Washington shot back another reply the following day. The general almost begged Lee to move: "I cannot but request and entreat you and this too, by the advice of all the Genl. Officers with me, to march and join me with all your whole force, with all possible expedition."[2] On December 11, a worried and perplexed Washington wrote again. He wanted Lee to come on with all speed and warned "that Philadelphia, beyond all question," was the British objective. Loss of the *de facto* captial city, he was sure, would have "fatal consequences" for the embattled rebel cause.[3] (The recalcitrant Lee probably never got the chance to read this letter, but that comes later in the story.)

Yet Washington did much more in his first days at Trenton than try to communicate with the elusive Lee. From the moment the Continental commander reached Trenton, he knew that ultimately he would have to deal with the British on or near the Delaware. Thus he busily shipped his supplies across the Delaware and counted his reinforcements. He used every minute, while Cornwallis sat motionless with his impressive army in New Brunswick. Washington and his officers were baffled by the British army's inertia; the only explanation Washington could offer was the heavy rain.[4] Whatever the reason, the patriot general was glad of the respite.

At New Brunswick, Loyalists were arriving with reports that

---

[1]*Lee Papers*, II: 337.

[2]Washington to Lee, Dec. 10, 1776, Fitzpatrick, ed., *Writings of George Washington*, VI: 341-342. It is surprising that Washington never gave Lee a direct order to bring his corps to Pennsylvania. The commander-in-chief may have doubted himself after the loss of Fort Washington, or he may have wanted to avoid an open controversy within the officer corps in order to discourage any intervention by Congress. Certainly Washington never forcefully complained to Congress about Lee's dilatory march; e.g., Fitzpatrick, ed., *Writings of George Washington*, VI: 336.

[3]Fitzpatrick, ed., *Writings of Washington*, IV: 348.

[4]Washington to the President of Congress, Dec. 4, 1776, Force, ed., *American Archives*, Fifth Series, III: 1070.

Washington's army was in wretched shape. Cornwallis knew that an assault now would destroy or scatter Washington's army and open the road to Philadelphia, but Howe's orders pinned him at the Raritan River.[1] Cornwallis raced an aide back to Howe's headquarters in New York to seek permission to press the pursuit.[2] Howe replied that he would come to New Brunswick and make a decision on the spot. However, Howe and his older brother, Admiral Lord Richard Howe, were preparing a different kind of assault, which they hoped would end the American rebellion; Cornwallis would have to wait.

In accepting command of British forces in America, the Howe brothers also were named "the King's Commissioners for restoring peace to his Majesty's Colonies and Plantations in North America." They took this role seriously, and already had made several peace overtures to the Americans, notably a meeting with a delegation from the Continental Congress after their thrashing of Washington's army on Long Island in August, 1776. The Howes chose their moments well for conciliatory gestures.

On November 30, with British forces advancing unchecked across New Jersey and Washington's army seemingly in ruins, the Howes felt the time was right for another peace initiative. They announced a decision to offer a pardon to "all persons whatsoever, who are assembled together in arms against his Majesty's government, to disband themselves, and return to their dwellings, there to remain in a peaceable and quiet manner." The offer was comprehensive, and extended to rebels active in government and politics, including those in Congress. Anyone who appeared within sixty days before a representative of the British government, including a military officer, could receive a pardon by signing an oath of allegiance. They would then be free to go about their business. In the view of the Howes, the offer was not only

---

[1]A Parliamentary inquiry later asked Cornwallis if Howe had ordered him to halt at New Brunswick. "I understood it to be the General's directions," Cornwallis responded, "that I should halt at Brunswick, but had I seen that I could have struck a material stroke, by moving forward, I certainly should have taken it upon me to have done it." Cornwallis also claimed, rather improbably, that his men were worn out from their march and in no real condition to strike a quick blow at Washington. In part, he may have been covering for Howe, whose conduct of the New Jersey campaign had come in for serious criticism. Troyer Steele Anderson, *The Command of the Howe Brothers During the American Revolution* (New York: Oxford University Press, 1936), 201-203. Cornwallis would have pushed on against Washington immediately if he had not been ordered by Howe to halt at the Raritan River.

[2]Thomas Fleming, *1776, Year of Illusions* (New York: W.W. Norton & Company, Inc., 1975), 419-420.

politic, but generous, coming as it did in the wake of the dramatic British successes in the field.[1]

An immediate taker was Joseph Galloway (1731-1803). Galloway was a leading lawyer, former speaker of the Pennsylvania Assembly and a confidant of Benjamin Franklin. Prior to the Revolution, Galloway and Franklin had shared a vision of an imperial union between America and England. But, once the war began, Franklin abandoned the idea and warmed to the rebel cause. Not Galloway, who remained adamant in his beliefs. He was particularly unhappy with the democratic constitution that Pennsylvania adopted in September, 1776. Galloway became an outcast and sought refuge in his country home, Trevose. By late 1776 he was convinced that the rebellion would collapse. Galloway also feared for his life, left his wife to guard their home, and headed for the British army in New Jersey. He got to New Brunswick with a wagon-load of belongings and several British sympathizers from his neighborhood and swore an oath of loyalty to the King. Galloway was an important rebel defector, but he would quickly prove to be a nuisance to General Howe.[2]

Meanwhile, American spies drifted in and out of New Brunswick in early December, reporting back to Stirling at Princeton that the town was full of British troops. One spy reported that every house in New Brunswick was full of redcoats. He was told that the Hessians were at Bound Brook. Spy Abram Sleight reported about 8,000 enemy troops in and near New Brunswick and another 20,000 between New Brunswick and Elizabethtown. Sleight saw only two field pieces, but other spies saw more cannon across the Raritan in Piscataway. One told Betty Miller that an additional 8,000 British reinforcements were en route to Cornwallis, and the officers talked of winter quarters in Philadelphia.[3] On the morning of December 5, General Howe unexpectedly sailed from New York City to New Jersey. He landed at Elizabethtown Point, where he inspected the fortifications the Americans had built, then continued on to Perth Amboy, distributing copies of his proclamation along the way.

---

[1]Force, ed., *American Archives*, Fifth Series, III: 927-928. According to General Howe, more than 2,700 New Jersey men took the oath during the winter of 1776-1777. Lundin, *Cockpit of the Revolution*, 159.

[2]John Ferling, *The Loyalist Mind, Joseph Galloway and the American Revolution* (University Park: The Pennsylvania State University Press, 1977), 37.

[3]Force, ed., *American Archives*, Fifth Series, III: 892.

Howe cut an impressive figure as he rode through central New Jersey with his entourage. As a privileged aristocrat and commander-in-chief, he had a great many people with him. Howe was dressed for the field in a scarlet, gold-laced uniform coat. A falling collar of dark-blue velvet, and buttonholes set in threes, indicated his rank. Riding with him were his two most important administrators: his adjutant and his quartermaster-general, both in silver epaulets, laced buttonholes set in threes, and crimson waistsashes. Riding close by were Howe's aides-de-camp, representatives who carried out innumerable military and personal duties for the general, including carrying important dispatches and other privileged information. They sported red coats with blue facings, silver embroidery and two gold epaulets.[1]

One of Howe's aides at this time was a young German aristocrat, Captain Levin Friedrich Ernst von Muenchhausen of the Hesse-Kassel Leib Regiment. Von Muenchhausen was fluent in German, French and English. This was essential: Howe spoke only English, and General Leopold Philipp, Freiherr von Heister, commander of the Hesse Kassel forces in America, spoke only German and French. Von Muenchhausen translated British orders into German. He rode at Howe's side through the 1776 campaign.[2] Howe probably had his chief of artillery with him, General Samuel Cleaveland, and one or more engineers whose training as mapmakers was valuable at headquarters. As commander-in-chief, Howe also had at least one military secretary assigned to travel with him (possibly a civilian) who would be privy to everything at headquarters and attend high-level meetings. A military secretary would translate Howe's decisions into orders and draft important correspondence. The general's entourage also would have featured a cook and several servants to attend to his feeding, clothing and other personal needs.

Although the area around Elizabethtown and Perth Amboy was held by the British army, there were still the dangers of rebel skirmishers or, so the British still thought, a surprise attack from Lee's corps. Howe would have had guards, possibly elite Hessian grenadiers, in whom he had great confidence.

---

[1]Charles Lefferts, *Uniforms of the American, British, French, and German Armies* (New York: New York Historical Society, 1926), 148; and Philip Katcher, *Armies of the American Wars* (New York: Hastings House, 1975), 51; John Mollo and Malcolm McGregor, *Uniforms of the American Revolution* (New York: Blandford Press Ltd., 1975), 155.

[2]Ernst Kipping, trans., and Samuel Steele Smith, ed., *At General Howe's Side, 1776-1778* (Monmouth Beach, N.J.: Philip Freneau Press, 1974).

Included in Howe's group of personal bodyguards were probably members of the 16th Light Dragoons.[1] These mounted troops were distinctively dressed and equipped, with white breeches and red coats faced with blue. Their black-painted metal caps bore an elegant red horsehair crest, falling almost to the shoulder. The front plate of their caps bore a ribbon and cipher designating them as "The Queen's Light Dragoons." They were well-armed with a carbine, a pair of pistols in holsters on their saddles, and a sabre. Howe and his military family were on horses or in carriages, but moved along slowly to stay with the infantry assigned to protect them. Armies of the time tended to move slowly anyway because of their cumbersome supply wagons and artillery. Because he was on horseback, Howe could stop for a fine lunch, for example, while the infantry marched. He would catch up later.

Howe spent the night at Perth Amboy as the guest of General Grant, who commanded there. It was a comfortable evening. Grant's house was the largest and best in town, the Governor's Mansion. Perth Amboy sat on a neck of land that faced into New York Bay, and its port had once made it the commercial rival of New York. It was a particularly scenic place. When he first viewed it, William Penn supposedly exclaimed, "I have never seen such before in my life," and another traveler said that Perth Amboy had the best oysters in America. The next morning, Howe left Perth Amboy at 9:00 a.m. for New Brunswick; he took General Grant's 4th Brigade with him and left one regiment behind to guard the town.[2]

Howe and his column passed through a charming landscape, high in places but with valleys, all well-cultivated. The hills afforded views of houses, farms, gardens, cornfields, forests, lakes, islands, roads and pastures in central New Jersey. The weather for the last few days had turned surprisingly warm

---

[1] Kipping and Smith, eds., *At Howe's Side*, 8. On December 26, Captain Friedrich von Muenchhausen noted in his diary that he commanded 20 dragoons, "and deployed them all around the General, about a quarter of an hour's march from him, to search out any harm that might befall him." The light dragoons were the elite cavalry of the time. They prided themselves on their horsemanship and weapons handling. The 16th Light Dragoons, "The Queen's Own," were part of the Crown forces advancing across New Jersey in late 1776.

[2] Benson Lossing, *The Pictorial Field-Book of the Revolution* (New York: Harper & Brothers, 1855), II: 10. Alexander Hamilton, "Itinerarium," in Wendy Martin, ed., *Colonial American Travel Narratives* (New York: Penguin Books, 1994), 204. Grant's 4th Brigade consisted of the 17th, 46th, 55th and 40th regiments.

for early December, which must have added to Cornwallis' frustration as he awaited Howe's arrival in New Brunswick.[1]

At mid-day on December 6, Howe finally arrived in New Brunswick and immediately ordered Cornwallis to advance further into New Jersey. Why, after almost a week of inactivity, had Howe now authorized an advance beyond the Raritan River? Again, Howe had limited goals when he invaded New Jersey: foremost was to take Fort Lee and clear the lower Hudson of rebel fortifications; secondly, he needed New Jersey to provide winter quarters for a portion of his army. Howe had seemed content to halt his offensive at New Brunswick, having conquered much more of New Jersey than he could have hoped when the attack on Fort Lee began.[2] But he changed his mind when all news from New Jersey showed that an advance beyond New Brunswick might disperse the Grand Army and push on to Philadelphia.

In New York, Howe heard that three to four hundred people were coming into New Brunswick each day to take the oath of allegiance.[3] From New Brunswick, Captain Ewald wrote in his diary that "Several distinguished persons arrived from Pennsylvania, who implored the general [Cornwallis] to press General Washington as closely as possible." Such a course, they insisted, would bring the rebels to bay somewhere "in the vicinity of the Delaware, by which his retreat would be cut off. There we could surely destroy or capture his disheartened army." Tempers, Ewald noted, were frayed. One of the civilians, Joseph Galloway, the Hessian reported, was "so enraged over the delay of the English that he exclaimed, 'I see, they don't want to finish the war!'"[4] British spies intercepted a letter from Washington to the Board of War sometime after the Royal army invaded New Jersey, confirming the sorry state of the rebel Grand Army. The stolen letter revealed when the

---

[1]Kalm, *Travels Into North America*, 122; Serle, *Journal*, 155.

[2]*Diary of Frederick Mackenzie*, I: 113; Force, ed., *American Archives*, Fifth Series, III: 926, 1316.

[3]Freeman, *George Washington*, IV: 276n.

[4]Ewald, *Diary of the American War*, 25.

service of all the American troops would expire, and conveyed Washington's apprehensions that the men would not reenlist.[1]

Having taken his time to decide to advance beyond New Brunswick, Howe now moved quickly. He ordered von Donop's Corps and Jaegers to Bound Brook, which lay a few miles further up the Raritan River. Reports told of the rebels taking a strong position on a hill beyond the village, where they also had destroyed a bridge over the Raritan.[2] About 4:00 p.m., Howe advanced his army towards Princeton in two columns. Cornwallis commanded the column on the right, consisting of the Jaegers, Hessian grenadiers, the 42nd Regiment of Scottish Highlanders, and two troops of the 16th Regiment of Light Dragoons. It marched up the south branch of the Raritan to Van Veghten Bridge (in modern Finderne), where it bivouacked for the night. The column on the left, which consisted of the British infantry under General Leslie, made even less progress. They crossed the Raritan at Landing Bridge and bivouacked on the high ground near New Brunswick. Howe dined that evening with Cornwallis.[3]

The advance resumed the next morning. General Howe was with the British infantry on the Upper Road, in the vanguard, which dictated a slow advance because rebel skirmishers prowled the small woods and dense thickets. Howe's column moved steadily in a train with two battalions of light

---

[1]This incident is included in a report from the Committee of Foreign Affairs to the American representatives in France. The report, Dec. 21, 1776, noted that "about this time General Howe became possessed of a letter (by the agency of some wicked person, who contrived to get it from the express) written by General Washington to the Board of War, in which he had given an exact account when the time of service of all our battalions would expire, and his apprehensions that the men would not reenlist without first going home to see their families and friends." Force, ed., *American Archives*, Fifth Series, III: 1326. British spies also managed to steal other letters carried by Army express riders. Serle, *Journal*, 137.

[2]Robertson, *His Diaries and Sketches in America* (New York: New York Public Library, 1930), 115. Carl Emil Kurt von Donop (1740-1777) was a commander of grenadiers and Jaegers. Letter K, Lidgerwood Collection, 43. The hills to which the journal refers probably are the Watchung Mountains, which rise behind Bound Brook.

[3]Ewald, *Diary of the American War*, 25. Ewald's reference to Jaegers and Hessian grenadiers was probably to von Donop's corps, which had advanced to Bound Brook in advance of the Cornwallis column. Kipping and Smith, eds., *At Howe's Side*, 6.

infantry, two battalions of grenadiers, one hundred fifty mounted light dragoons and eight three-pounders marching in battle order.[1]

The pretty countryside was mostly flat. Near almost every farm was a spacious orchard of apple and peach trees. Cherry trees abounded along the road. But the British and Hessian soldiers were too concerned about their safety to enjoy the scenery.[2] Despite their caution, several British scouts were surrounded and killed by rebels in a thicket. Afterward, well over a hundred rebels were seen running away, but the pursuing Crown forces could not catch them. The rebels who harried the British advance probably were detachments from Stirling's two brigades left behind at Princeton.

Early in the morning, a British reconnaissance team commanded by General Erskine left Cornwallis' camp in the direction of Morristown to collect information on the whereabouts of Lee and his corps.[3] The two main British columns continued towards Princeton on their separate routes amid fences and farmhouses, orchards and wheatfields.[4] By this time, Washington had all his army's baggage safely across the Delaware and all the boats standing by on the river at Trenton. With everything ready for a retreat across the Delaware to Pennsylvania, and with no sign that the enemy was stirring at New Brunswick, Washington decided to march back towards Princeton with 1,200 men. Greene preceded Washington and arrived at Princeton on the afternoon of December 6 to assume command of Stirling's brigade. But Greene quickly learned that the British were advancing towards Princeton, and he sent Washington an express to this effect on December 7. When Washington

---

[1]Kipping & Smith, eds., *At Howe's Side*, 6.

[2]This description of the land between Trenton and New Brunswick is from Kalm, *Travels in North America*, 118.

[3]Ewald, *Diary of the American War*, 26-27. According to Ewald, Erskine took the Jaegers, a detachment of Scots and a hundred mounted troops; clearly Erskine considered Lee to be a dangerous enemy.

[4]Most accounts of Howe's advance towards Princeton mention two columns of troops. The exception is the diary of Archibald Robertson, who says there were three columns. Robertson was an army engineer. On Dec. 7, he noted a "Right Column consisting of Donops Corps march'd along the North West Side of the Millstone River By Hillsborough [today's Millstone] and Schencks Bridge, where we were joined by the Centre Column under General Grant consisting of the 4th Brigade. The Reserve and Guards with the General kept the highway." Robertson, *Diaries and Sketches in America*, 115.

received Greene's message, he immediately turned his troops back towards the Delaware.[1]

Howe's troops occupied a nearly deserted Princeton on the evening of December 7. His Hessian aide-de-camp, von Muenchhausen, admired the College of New Jersey. "Its main building," he wrote, "has 36 windows on its length and 24 on its width, and is four stories high. A remarkably excellent library has till now been spared by the war."[2] Howe posted his two Jaeger companies in the woods facing Trenton to prevent a surprise attack.

Stirling's rebel brigade had evacuated Princeton earlier in the day. To slow any pursuit, his troops tore apart the wooden bridge across Stony Brook, a stream a few miles south of the village. As they retreated towards Trenton, the troops skirmished with some of the British advance guards, killing at least one light dragoon. Stirling's brigade arrived at Trenton that night and started crossing the Delaware. However, some of his men must have stayed behind because Ewald wrote in his diary that rebels roamed around Princeton all night, and sporadic fighting continued.[3]

In Princeton, British and Hessian soldiers and their women plundered every building. A big, new house owned by patriot Jonathan Dickinson Sergeant mysteriously burned to the ground that night. Morven, Richard Stockton's magnificent home, was ransacked of everything of value, from furniture and clothing to cattle, horses, hogs, sheep, and grain. The college did not escape either. Valuable books from the library were stolen to be sold later, or thrown into blazing fires to warm the invaders.[4] The lone survivor of the

---

[1]Historian Samuel Smith commented that Washington ordered an immediate retreat back to Trenton when he learned that the enemy was advancing by different roads. Washington thought this might be an attempt by the enemy to get in the rear of his troops at Princeton. *The Battle of Trenton*, (Monmouth Beach, N.J.: Philip Freneau Press, 1965), 6.

[2]Quoted in Smith, *Battle of Trenton*, 6. The college building to which von Muenchhausen refers was Nassau Hall, although his window count was wrong.

[3]Varnum Lansing Collins, *A Brief Narrative of the Ravages of the British and Hessians* (Princeton: The University Library, 1906), 3; Ewald, *Diary of the American War*, 27.

[4]The present site of Sergeant's house is 6 Mercer Street; it was the only Princeton house burned during the Revolution. Boatner, *Landmarks of the American Revolution*, 209. Thomas Wertenbaker, *Princeton 1746-1896* (Princeton: Princeton University Press, 1946), 59. British and Hessian soldiers had plundered libraries in New York City as well;

pillaging at Nassau Hall was the orrery, a complicated scientific instrument built by David Rittenhouse to show the movements and positions of bodies in the solar system. The British intended to ship it back to England. The orrery, an apparatus of balls moved by wheelwork, was a sensation. John Adams saw it during a pre-war tour of the college and recalled that "It exhibits almost every motion in the Astronomical world: the motions of the sun and all the planets, with all their satellites, the eclipses of the moon, sun, &c."[1]

A regiment of soldiers crowded into Nassau Hall and slept in the classrooms, Prayer Hall, and the students' chambers. The basement became a stable. Nassau Hall also was turned into a temporary prison by the British; anyone suspected of being a rebel, or of aiding the rebels, was dragged off to confinement in the college building.[2]

As the Crown forces sacked Princeton, Washington's army was back at Trenton and hurriedly crossing the Delaware. By Sunday morning, December 8, Washington's entire army had been safely transported across the river. Washington had his troops tear down bridges on the New Jersey roads parallelling the Delaware, and every ferry crossing on the Pennsylvania side of the river was guarded.[3]

Among the Philadelphia Associators activated to join Washington at Trenton was a company of eighty-one men. Its second-in-command was a fragile-looking lieutenant named Charles Willson Peale. Peale was an unusual soldier: he was one of America's first professional artists. He studied in London and returned to America to pursue a career as a portrait painter. His clientele was exclusive; in 1772, he painted the earliest known portrait of Washington at Mount Vernon. Peale's militia company departed Philadelphia on the evening of December 5, moving up the Delaware by sailboat. The

---

see Jones, *History of New York During the Revolutionary War*, I: 136.

[1]Mark Boatner, *Landmarks of the American Revolution* (Harrisburg: Stackpole Books, 1973) 208. The Marquis de Chastellux saw the orrery when he visited the college later in the war; it was still a "very beautiful astronomical machine," but not working. Marquis de Chastellux, *Travels in North America* (London, 1787), I: 162-163. A second Rittenhouse orrery was housed at the University of Pennsylvania. The orrery was invented by an English scientific instrument maker named George Graham (1671-1751), who named his invention in honor of his patron, Charles Boyle, 4th Earl of Orrery. Silvio A. Bedini, *Thomas Jefferson: Statesman of Science* (New York: Macmillan Publishing, 1990), 114.

[2]Wertenbaker, *Princeton 1746-1896*, 59.

[3]Marshall, *Life of Washington*, II: 603.

troops linked up with other patriots in Trenton on the afternoon of the 7th, and expected duty in or around the town.[1] But shortly after arriving, they were ordered to join Washington in Pennsylvania. Peale watched the army crossing the Delaware late into the night of December 7. The entire army crossed that night, and the operation, he wrote, "made a grand but dreadful appearance. All the shores were lighted up with large fires," and the boats were jammed with men, equipment, weapons, and horses. "The Hollowing [howling] of hundreds of men in their difficulties of getting Horses and artilery out of the boats, made it rather the appearance of Hell than any earthly scene."[2] As "the sick and half-naked veterans of the long retreat streamed past," Peale thought he saw a familiar face. He looked closely at a ragged and debilitated man wrapped only in an old, dirty blanket. Shocked, Peale recognized his younger brother, James, who had been with Washington since the New York campaign.[3]

General Howe resumed his leisurely advance from Princeton towards the Delaware River the following morning. His vanguard reached the outskirts of Trenton at 2:00 p.m. on December 8.[4] They found Trenton a pleasant town, just off the river on a sandy plain. The houses were mostly two stories high and widely separated, giving Trenton a long, narrow appearance. Most homes had a garden, a well, and a cellar; and while some were stone, most were constructed of wooden planks.[5] Trenton was a busy place before the war. There were some local merchants, but it was mainly a transfer point for goods going between Philadelphia and New York City. Goods arrived at Trenton by boat from Philadelphia, then were loaded onto wagons to complete their

---

[1]Horace Wells Sellers, "Charles Willson Peale, Artist-Soldier," *The Pennsylvania Magazine of History and Biography*, 38 (1914): 271.

[2]Charles Willson Peale, Autobiography, undated manuscript, American Philosophical Society, Philadelphia.

[3]Kenneth Silverman, *A Cultural History of the American Revolution* (New York: Thomas Y. Crowell Company, 1976), 327; Blanco, *American Revolution Encyclopedia*, II: 1284; Charles Sellers, *Charles Willson Peale, Early Life* (Philadelphia: The American Philosophical Society, 1947), 140-141.

[4]Historian Henry Carrington commented on the slow advance of the Crown forces from New Brunswick to Trenton. Carrington calculated that Cornwallis delayed 17 hours at Princeton and took an entire day to march the 12 miles between Princeton and Trenton. Carrington, *Battles of the American Revolution*, 257-258.

[5]Kalm, *Travels in North America*, 117.

journey east. The process was reversed for goods bound from New York to Philadelphia. Travelers had the choice of going between Philadelphia and Trenton by boat on the Delaware, or making the complete Philadelphia-New York City trip by stage wagon or coach. There were two busy ferries. One, located about a mile south of town, was the Old Trenton Ferry, or Trent's Ferry, established in 1726. The second, in operation since 1773, lay a half-mile farther downstream and was known as the New Trenton Ferry. Inns and taverns were plentiful, and included the popular Eagle Tavern.

But Trenton was almost deserted when the Royal army arrived there on the afternoon of December 8. As the troops reached the outskirts of the town, von Muenchhausen recalled, "some inhabitant came running toward us, urging us to march through the town in a hurry so we could capture many of the enemy" who were still crossing the Delaware. But Howe suspected that Washington had artillery on the opposite shore, and did not want to move his main body into range. Instead, he sent only some light troops toward the river. Howe, Cornwallis, and some staff officers accompanied these men, and as they reached open ground near the Delaware, they came under heavy fire. Waiting rebel gunners "opened a terrific fire upon us with all their batteries," von Muenchhausen wrote, and "the light infantry and jaegers were forced to retreat in the greatest hurry to the valley at the left. On their way, in the blink of any eye, they lost 13 men."[1] Washington, the old Indian fighter, had not forgotten how to bait his enemies into an ambush.

While the Crown forces occupied Trenton, Washington deployed his meager force on the Pennsylvania side of the Delaware River, careful to stay away from the riverfront. On December 12 and 13, he divided a seventy-mile riverfront into command sections and spread his forces. Four brigades (Stirling, Mercer, Stephens and de Fermoy) were to guard the Delaware River from Yardley's Ferry (now Yardley, Pennsylvania) to Coryell's Ferry (modern New Hope, Pennsylvania). Individual units were posted within supporting distances.[2] Extending south from Yardley's Ferry to the ferry opposite Bordentown, New Jersey, were the remnants of the Pennsylvania Flying Camp, commanded by Ewing, and some New Jersey militiamen under General Dickinson.

Below them, more Pennsylvania militia extended the line farther south. Their commanding officer was Colonel John Cadwalader, an influential

---

[1]Kipping and Smith, eds., *At Howe's Side*, 6.

[2]Fitzpatrick, ed., *Writings of Washington*, VI: 364.

and active Philadelphia patriot. Cadwalader had established his headquarters at Bristol and his troops occupied positions as far down river as Dunk's Ferry (now Beverly, New Jersey).[1] The third battalion of Philadelphia Associators, under Colonel Nixon, guarded Dunk's Ferry, while galleys of the Pennsylvania Navy patrolled the river. Artillery was apportioned among the brigades, and small redoubts were thrown up at all possible fords. The troops had three days' rations, and every unit was assigned a rendezvous in case the enemy made a successful attack across the river.[2]

Washington's troops were in deplorable shape, and conditions were miserable for the men on the lines. "This night we lay amongst the leaves without tents or blankets, laying down with our feet to the fire," one veteran recalled. "It was very cold. We had meat, but no bread. We had nothing to cook with, but our ramrods, which we run through a piece of meat and roasted it over the fire, and to hungry soldiers, it tasted sweet. The next day we moved up the Delaware. In this way we lived, crouching among the bushes."[3] Times were hard, but the army remained operational.

At Trenton, General Howe was told there were boats at Coryell's Ferry, about fifteen miles up the Delaware. Howe wanted the boats, and ordered Cornwallis to take four regiments halted at Maidenhead (present day Lawrenceville, New Jersey) to go after them. At 1:00 a.m. on December 9, Cornwallis left Maidenhead with the Reserve and the 2nd Battalion of Light Infantry.[4] They passed through the small village of Penny Town (today's

---

[1]One hundred thirty United States Marines were attached to Cadwalader's command and helped to defend the western bank of the Delaware. They were part of four companies of Marines organized in mid-1776 in Philadelphia. There is no evidence that Marines participated earlier in the New Jersey campaign.

[2]Fitzpatrick, ed., *Writings of Washington*, VI: 360-364; Marshall, *Life of Washington*, II: 605; Henry Carrington, *Battles of the American Revolution* (New York: A.S. Barnes & Company, 1877), 264-265.

[3]"Personal Recollection of Captain Enoch Anderson," *Papers of the Historical Society of Delaware*, 16 (1896): 28.

[4]This ferry was also referred to as Corriell's Ferry; it ran between modern Lambertville, New Jersey, and New Hope, Pennsylvania. Sir William Howe to Lord George Germain, Force ed., *American Archives*, Fifth Series, III: 1316-1317. Some sources refer to four regiments being at Maidenhead; others specify that the Reserve and the 2nd Battalion of Light Infantry were there. The references probably confirm each other. The Battalion of Light Infantry equalled roughly one regiment and the Reserve was three

Pennington) and arrived at Coryell's Ferry to find that the rebels had removed or destroyed all the boats in the area. He also found rebel troops behind makeshift fortifications on the Pennsylvania side of the crossing. Taking no further action, Cornwallis returned to Penny Town at 2:00 p.m. that afternoon and bivouacked there.[1] Howe sent additional scouting parties up and down the river, but made no serious attempt to cross the Delaware.

Yet the British commander could have pursued Washington across the Delaware if he had wanted to. Galloway, the Pennsylvania Loyalist with Howe, noted 48,000 feet of boards at Trenton.[2] There were also John Rickey's hardware store and two blacksmith shops in Trenton, from which the British could have procured all the nails and iron necessary to build boats. Failing all else, the invaders could have torn down some of Trenton's one hundred wooden houses for lumber. But nothing was done to construct boats or rafts at Trenton. The British also had the equipment and engineers to quickly bring boats from New York City or New Brunswick to cross the Delaware or use their boats to build a pontoon bridge.

But Howe simply had no intentions of going beyond Trenton. The lack of boats was only later used as an excuse for failure. When Howe reached Trenton, he already had advanced much further into New Jersey than originally planned. In his view, the obstacle of the Delaware River and the approaching winter season were sufficient reasons to order an end to the offensive. Besides, the end of the war seemed almost at hand. On December 13, Howe announced that he was through campaigning for the season. He rode back to New Brunswick on the evening of the 15th and set out for New York on the 16th. It is only in retrospect that not pushing into Pennsylvania stands out as a mistake.

Howe left behind several winter cantonments in New Jersey. Two of the garrisons were placed at Bordentown and Trenton along the banks of the Delaware, eight miles apart. The posts (of greatest honor because they were closest to the enemy) were put under the command of von Donop. Fifteen hundred Hessians would winter at Bordentown under von Donop's immediate

---

regiments.

[1]Washington sent the 400-man regiment of Pennsylvania and Maryland Germans under Col. Nicholas Haussegger to Coryell's Ferry to check any attempt by the British to cross. On Cornwallis' march, see Robertson, *His Diaries and Sketches in America*, 116.

[2]Galloway cited in Stryker, *Battles of Trenton and Princeton*, 37.

command, and fourteen hundred others would stay at Trenton under Colonel Rall. The balance of the "chain of posts" in New Jersey were at Princeton, New Brunswick, Perth Amboy and Elizabethtown. Overall command in New Jersey fell to the tough and capable General James Grant, based at New Brunswick.[1] Howe returned to New York and settled in for the winter with his beautiful mistress and the good company of his fellow officers. A season of theater was already being planned by the talented young Major John Andre.

Rall was given the honor of commanding at Trenton, the most exposed point to the enemy, as a reward for his courage in the assault on Fort Washington. Rall was a good combat leader, but never should have been given command of the brigade assigned to winter at Trenton. His garrison was dangerously isolated, facing rebels across the river with no reinforcements nearby. Rall disdained the rebels. When a subordinate officer asked Rall's permission to erect redoubts to defend the town, he roared, "Lasst sie nur kommen! Keine Schanzen! Mit dem Bajonet wollen wir an sie!" ("Let them come! We want no trenches! We'll at them with the bayonet!")[2] Brave words, but foolish.

Howe adopted a dangerous scheme when he placed his troops in scattered cantonments. It left the individual garrisons isolated and open to rebel assault. But Howe felt he had no choice in the matter. Supplies were short, and spacing out his garrisons would enable the various detachments to live off the countryside.

There was also the question of manpower. The British lacked the strength to augment the size of the garrisons or to increase the number of posts, either of which would have made the entire chain more secure. This was Howe's fault. On November 27, only days after Cornwallis overran Fort Lee, Howe had dispatched some seven thousand troops to invade Rhode Island. The operation, mounted to secure the harbor of Newport for the fleet, succeeded. Howe thought that he could spare the detachment; but many other British officers questioned its wisdom. General Sir Henry Clinton was one of them. Clinton, who commanded the Rhode Island expedition, pointed out that

---

[1]Grant replaced Cornwallis, who had requested leave to winter in England. Grant was one of six general officers serving in America who were members of Parliament. He was famous for a speech he made in the House of Commons in February 1775, proclaiming "that the Americans could not fight, and that he would undertake to march from one end of the continent to the other with five thousand men." Quoted in Stryker, *Battles of Trenton and Princeton*, 48.

[2]*Ibid.*, 107.

a landing at Perth Amboy in late November, in support of a continuing advance by Cornwallis across central New Jersey, might trap Washington's retreating forces in a British pincers. If the redcoat and Hessian columns moved quickly, Clinton thought, the effort could place the rebels in an impossible situation and smash them once and for all.[1] But General and Admiral Howe were adamant, and the fleet sailed with Clinton's men. Their departure not only took pressure off Washington during the retreat, it also allowed Heath to conduct his December operations in New Jersey, and removed thousands of British soldiers from the decisive theater of war at a critical time.[2]

Howe would have to get through the winter with the troops on hand. He was confident that the army could handle any eventuality, but he admitted that his line of posts was thin. "The chain, I own, is rather too extensive," he wrote on December 20, "but I was induced to occupy Burlington to cover the County of Monmouth, in which there are many loyal inhabitants; and trusting to the almost general submission of the County to the southward of this chain, and to the strength of the corps placed in the advanced posts, I conclude the troops will be in perfect security."[3]

If only he had known. From across the Delaware, Washington, still looking for a fight, watched Rall and his Hessians at Trenton like a hungry fox eyeing a chicken coop.

---

[1]William B. Willcox, ed., *The American Rebellion: Sir Henry Clinton's Narrative of His Campaigns, 1775-1782* (New Haven: Yale University Press, 1954), 55.

[2]The decision of the Howe brothers to push ahead with the Rhode Island venture embittered many British and loyalists, who thought that the Howes had thrown away a chance to finish Washington in a link-up between Clinton and Cornwallis somewhere around New Brunswick, or perhaps further toward the Delaware. E.g., *Diary of Frederick Mackenzie* (Cambridge: Harvard University Press, 1930), 105, 113-114; Jones, *History of New York During the Revolutionary War*, I: 130-131. The British garrisoned Newport with about seven thousand men for three years; they gained nothing of strategic importance.

[3]Force, *American Archives*, Fifth Series, III: 1317. The British forces attempted to occupy the Delaware River town of Burlington, New Jersey, on Dec. 11, 1776, but were chased off by the Pennsylvania Navy.

CHAPTER EIGHT

Morristown

*To understand Lee in depth, a psychiatrist instead of a
historian is probably required.*
—Historian John W. Shy (1964)[1]

When General Washington was at Newark, he ordered General Philip
Schuyler to send him reinforcements from the Northern Department. These
reinforcements were commanded by Horatio Gates. Gates was 47 years old,
with the appearance of a kindly grandfather; but behind the soft facade was a
tough, experienced soldier.[2] Gates wasted no time in moving. On December
4, he arrived at Esopus (modern Kingston), New York, where his troops
disembarked from boats and began to march towards New Jersey. Gates
followed the Old Mine Road, which led through lower New York state to the

---

[1]George Athan Billias, ed., *George Washington's Generals* (New York: William
Morrow, 1964), 22.

[2]Gates was born in England in 1728. His parents lacked the means to buy him a
commission, but Gates had the backing of the Duke of Leeds, who employed his parents
and may have been his real father. Leed's bought him a lieutenancy in 1749, when he was
21. He immediately went to America, and eventually served on the ill-fated Braddock
Expedition in 1755 (on which he met Charles Lee, Thomas Gage, and George Washington).
He returned to England after the fighting ended in America, but his humble beginnings
impeded his military career. Returning to America, he purchased 600 acres in western
Virginia. His neighbor and friend was another former British officer, Lieutenant Colonel
Charles Lee. When the Revolution began, Gates offered his services to the rebels and was
quickly appointed a brigadier general. After serving as adjutant-general of the army, Gates
was appointed second-in-command of the Northern Department.

Delaware River near Port Jervis. With Gates, as his second-in-command, was General Benedict Arnold (1741-1801). While passing through the state, Gates appealed to fifteen hundred militiamen with General George Clinton to join him. To Gates' chagrin, they refused, unwilling to leave New York.

On December 11, Gates led the remnants of his force, numbering some six hundred men, along the Old Mine Road into northern New Jersey. [1] They spent the night in the village of Montague, about seven miles from the New York border.[2] The troops had suffered terribly during the journey from Albany. One diarist complained that "what I suffered on the march cannot be described. With no tents to shelter us from the snow and rain, we were obliged to get through it as well as we could."[3] Gates knew little about the military situation when he entered New Jersey. He knew only that Fort Washington had surrendered and Washington's army was retreating toward Pennsylvania. The next day, the column continued south to the hamlet of Walpack, New Jersey, near the Delaware River. It started to snow, which halted the march. Simultaneously, Gates learned that the enemy had occupied Trenton, and he sent an aide-de-camp, Major James Wilkinson, to find Washington and bring back news of the military situation.[4] Gates gave Wilkinson a letter for

---

[1]The Old Mine Road probably was the first wheeled-vehicle road in America. It was an old Indian trail that the early Dutch settlers developed into a wagon road to gain access to the copper and silver mines of northwestern New Jersey. C.G. Hine, *The Old Mine Road* (New Brunswick: Rutgers University Press, 1963, orig. 1909); Boatner, *Landmarks of the American Revolution*, 265; Nelson, *General Horatio Gates*, 74.

[2]Gates arrived in New Jersey with only four regiments from the Northern Department: Stark's, Poor's, Patterson's and Read's. According to the strength report from Fort Ticonderoga dated November 17, 1776, these regiments had 1,653 men. The loss in manpower can be attributed mostly to illness, and the lack of shoes and warm clothing to sustain the troops on their long journey to join Washington's army. "Diary of Chaplain David Avery," microfilm edition of manuscript, Princeton Theological Seminary Library, Princeton, New Jersey.

[3]John Greenwood, *A Young Patriot in the American Revolution, 1775-1783* (Westvaco, 1981), 79; originally published as *The Revolutionary Services of John Greenwood of Boston and New York, 1775-1783*, ed. Isaac J. Greenwood (New York: De Vinne, 1922).

[4]*Avery Diary*, Dec. 12, 1776. Gates occupied the Isaac Van Campen house, near Walpack. Hine, *The Old Mine Road*, opposite p. 147. Wilkinson (1757-1825) was from Maryland, went to Philadelphia in 1773 to study medicine, and enlisted as a private the outbreak of the Revolution. Promoted to captain in 1776, he served as aide-de-camp to Gates and others, and ended the war as a general. Gates' letter to Washington, sent with Wilkinson, is in Twohig, ed., *The Papers of George Washington*, VII: 308.

Washington, explaining Gates' situation and asking the commander-in-chief to give him a safe route to the Grand Army's camp. Then, increasingly anxious about the military situation and without waiting for Wilkinson to return, Gates marched his division away from the river to Sussex Courthouse (modern Newton) on December 13. Sometime during the day, Gates was told that the enemy had three divisions at Princeton, Trenton and Burlington, which further increased his uneasiness.[1] The enemy had obviously moved in force across the center of New Jersey, hardly good news.

Wilkinson's mission was eventful. He reached Sussex Courthouse on the first day of his ride, December 12, where he learned that Washington had crossed the Delaware to Pennsylvania a few days earlier and had removed all boats from the river. He also discovered that General Lee was nearby, at Morristown, with his division. With the enemy reported all along the Delaware, Wilkinson decided it was safer to get information from Lee's corps. The determined major took a guide and followed the muddy road toward Morristown and the camp of the greatly respected Lee.[2]

Lee had arrived at Morristown from Chatham on December 11, the same day that Gates crossed the border into New Jersey. Lee probably was heading for the Delaware to consolidate his force with Washington's Grand Army, per Washington's repeated requests, even though he would have preferred to stay in Chatham, where he was in a good position to cut enemy communications and raid the Crown's outposts at Elizabethtown, Rahway and Newark. On arriving in Morristown, Lee wrote Washington that he had sent out two reconnaissance officers that day, one to tell him where the Delaware could be crossed above Trenton and the other to examine the road to Burlington, a town on the Delaware south of Trenton.[3]

The dispatch of these officers, however, suggests that Lee had much in mind than a march to join Washington. There was no reason for him to

---

[1]See the "Avery Diary," Dec. 13, 1776: "We hear ye Enemy are in three grand divisions, at Princeton, Trenton & Burlington."

[2]James Wilkinson, *Memories of My Own Times,* 4 vols. (Philadelphia, 1816), I: 111.

[3]White, *A Village at War,* 77; Rau, ed., *Sergeant Smith's Diary,* 263. Charles Lee to George Washington, Morristown, December 11, 1776; *Lee Papers,* II: 345.

check where the Delaware could be crossed safely above Trenton, because he already knew from Major Hoops that boats were waiting to take his division across at Alexandria. His mention of sending an officer towards Burlington also is intriguing. If the general planned to ferry the Delaware at Burlington, his force would need to cross the Upper Road (Lee called it "the great Brunswick post road") somewhere along its route through central New Jersey. Lee had wagons with him and had to stay on the roads. This meant he would probably cross the Upper Road at Princeton, where there was a Crown forces garrison. A surprise raid on Princeton, which would have temporarily cut the enemy's communication and supply lines, followed by a successful crossing of the Delaware at Burlington, near Philadelphia, would have been a riveting demonstration of Lee's military skills.[1] Lee also could have been planning an attack on New Brunswick, but this was much less likely.[2] There is no way to tell for certain what was on his mind.

The last lines Lee wrote about his situation in New Jersey give no clue to his plans. "If I stay in this Province" he wrote to Gates, "I risk myself and Army and if I do not stay the Province is lost for ever --I have neither guides Cavalry Medicines Money Shoes or Stockings--I must act with the greatest circumspection."[3] Clearly, though, Lee had his doubts about a quick march out of the state. Lee issued four days' provisions to his troops on December 12 and prepared to move his division out of Morristown early the next morning. A snowfall that night delayed the departure, but by the late morning of the 13th all wagons and carts were loaded, and the division was ready to march to Vealtown (Bernardsville). The sick were left behind. The day became warmer and the melting snow made the road muddy. Many of the soldiers had no shoes and covered their feet with cowhide they had hastily laced together.[4] Sometime during the late afternoon or evening of the 13th, Lee left his division under the charge of his second-in-command, General John

---

[1] There is a second-hand account holding that Lee's secretary had said that "there would be warm Work before they joyned G. Wash." Franklin Dexter, ed., *The Literary Diary of Ezra Stiles* (New York: Charles Scribner's Sons, 1901), II: 105-107.

[2] John Alden, *General Charles Lee* (Baton Rouge: Louisiana State University Press, 1951), 155.

[3] Lee to Gates, Dec. 12/13, 1776, *Lee Papers*, II: 348.

[4] Louise Rau, ed., "Sergeant John Smith's Diary of 1776," *Mississippi Valley Historical Review*, 20 (1933-1934): 264.

Sullivan. Then, accompanied by Major William Bradford, Jr. (an aide-de-camp), two French volunteer officers and a squad of bodyguards, Lee rode to the Widow White's tavern in the village of Basking Ridge to spend the night. The tavern was only three miles from Vealtown, convenient for Lee to rejoin his corps the next morning.

While he could hardly have known it, Lee's decision to leave the security of his camp was one of the most controversial of his explosive career. It remains a mystery, although some historians have speculated that he was seeking the company of a woman.[1] Whatever his intentions (or hopes), events quickly took a dire turn.

At 4:00 a.m. on December 14, Wilkinson caught up with Lee at the tavern in Basking Ridge. The young officer found Lee lying in bed and informed him that his old comrade, Gates, was nearby with six hundred men from the Northern Department. Wilkinson then said he had a letter from Gates to Washington. Lee took the letter, broke the seal, and read it. Nothing more happened that night and the exhausted Wilkinson slept for a few hours.

He awoke later in the morning to find Lee sitting at a table in the tavern in his nightshirt. Lee had just finished breakfast and was completing a letter that he wanted Wilkinson to take back to Gates. Its content was dark. "The ingenious maneuver of Fort Washington," he sarcastically told his former British army comrade, "has unhing'd the goodly fabrick We had been building--there never was so damn'd a stroke--entre nous, a certain great man is most damnably deficient--He has thrown me into a situation where I have my choice of difficulties." While not stating it directly to Gates, Lee also may have wanted to add the Northern regiments to his own forces.[2] Pausing from his writing, Lee invited Wilkinson to have breakfast before returning to Gates' camp. Wilkinson had no need to go on to Washington's command for

---

[1]Historian James Thomas Flexner commented that "Lee had a propensity for sleeping in strange places (and with strange women)." James Flexner, *George Washington in the American Revolution* (Boston: Little, Brown, 1967), 167.

[2]*Lee Papers*, II: 348. Lee's letter to Gates may have been a proposition to encourage Gates to halt his march to Washington's camp and add his regiments to those of Lee. If so, historian Paul David Nelson has insisted that "Gates refused to be shaken from his resolution to obey his orders to join the commander in chief." Paul David Nelson, *General Horatio Gates* (Baton Rouge, 1976), 73-74. Lee mentioned his notion of putting the reinforcements from the Northern army under his command in a letter to Washington dated Dec. 4, 1776; in effect, he also proposed an independent command for himself in the Morristown area. *Lee Papers*, II: 329-330.

information, since Lee and his officers were informed of the Grand Army's situation on the Delaware River.

Breakfast ended dramatically. About 10:00 a.m., Wilkinson got up from the table and looked indifferently out the window. To his horror, he saw a party of British dragoons galloping up the lane towards the tavern with weapons drawn. Wilkinson bellowed a warning to Lee, who jumped up from his chair, saw the charging dragoons, and screamed, "Where is the guard--damn the guard, why don't they fire?" In fact, the surprised guards had fled and the dragoons advanced with virtually no opposition.

How had British dragoons managed to learn Lee's whereabouts so deep in rebel-held territory? Following his occupation of Trenton, Cornwallis became alarmed about the location of Lee and his corps. Cornwallis knew only that Lee was somewhere in New jersey with a force estimated at 7,500 men. Having served with Lee in Portugal during the Seven Years War, Cornwallis knew him to be a clever and enterprising officer. He feared that Lee would launch raids against his isolated garrisons, which were strung out across New Jersey from Fort Lee to Trenton. He had to know where Lee was. On December 12, he dispatched a portion of the 16th Queen's Light Dragoons, consisting of its commander, Colonel William Harcourt (1743-1830), four subalterns, and twenty-five troopers, with orders to find Lee's position.[1]

It was a dangerous mission. Harcourt's party started from Penny Town (modern Pennington) and rode eighteen miles to the village of Hillsborough, where they camped for the night. The village was occupied by a British battalion. Beyond the hamlet lay rebel-held territory. During the night, the house in which the officers slept mysteriously caught fire and burned to the ground. The men escaped and spent the rest of the night in a barn. Next morning, Harcourt and his troopers resumed their mission and crossed the Raritan River on the bridge at Bound Brook. Every additional step took them deeper into enemy territory.

Yet Harcourt was not traveling blindly. At some point north of Bound

---

[1]Worthington Ford, *British Officers Serving in the American Revolution, 1774-1783* (Brooklyn, 1897), 67. Lieutenant Banastre Tarleton was also on the mission and wrote his mother an account of the exploit; Tarleton's letter (of Dec. 18, 1776) is the most reliable account of Lee's capture. Robert Blass, *The Green Dragoon* (New York: Holt, 1957), 20-22.

Brook, a Tory guide evidently joined the scouting party. This was probably Richard V. Stockton.[1] With their guide, the dragoons proceeded north, on what today is King George Road, in the direction of Morristown. Probably from rebels they captured on the way, Harcourt learned that Lee was at a tavern in the remote village of Basking Ridge, protected only by a headquarters guard of thirty soldiers. It was a tempting opportunity, and Harcourt decided to lunge deeper into the interior and capture the rebel general.

Harcourt's dragoons reached Basking Ridge without detection. They found Widow White's tavern with woods on one side and an orchard on the other.[2] The troopers rushed the building from both sides and surprised and scattered the headquarters guards, who had stacked their arms and sought warmth by sunning themselves on the south side of a nearby house. Having chased off the guards, the British horsemen turned to the tavern and their prey. They surrounded the building and began firing into every window and door. Inside were Lee, Major Bradford, Wilkinson, the two French officers and some of Lee's guards. A heated exchange of gunfire went on for several minutes. One of the Frenchmen and some of Lee's guards were wounded.

Harcourt's men then threatened to burn down the building if Lee did not surrender. Several men tried to escape through a back door, but were cut down by the dragoons. The French colonel was captured trying to escape through this door. At almost the same moment Lee emerged from the front door, Wilkinson heard one of the dragoons yell from outside, "Here is the general. He has surrendered."[3] Lee emerged from the tavern dressed in his

---

[1]On the identity of Stockton, see John Alden, *General Charles Lee*, 332, note 21. William Robins, another New Jersey loyalist, also claimed he rode with Harcourt. Patriots always believed that Tories were involved in Lee's capture; one apocryphal account held that a Tory, angered over the loss of a horse to the rebel army, rode all the way to British-held New Brunswick to disclose Lee's location. Joseph Trumbull to Governor Jonathan Trumbull, Dec. 17, 1776. Force, ed., *American Archives*, Series Five, III: 1265.

[2]Dexter, ed., *Diary of Ezra Stiles*, II: 106.

[3]One of the French officers was Lt. Col. Sieur Gaiault de Boisbertrand. He was Lee's adjutant-general and captured along with Lee. Both Frenchmen were volunteers in the American Army. William Bradford, Lee's aide-de-camp at the time, said that a French colonel and a French captain were with Lee at the inn, and that the captain (Jean Louis de Virnejoux) had recently arrived from Paris, by way of Massachusetts, with dispatches for the Continental Congress. Dexter, ed., *Diary of Ezra Stiles*, II: 106; Bass, *The Green Dragoon*, 19.

usual slovenly style, this time in slippers and blanket coat, his collar open, and his shirt soiled from several days' use. There was no time to allow him to put on clothes. Lee was thrown on a horse which the British found saddled and ready. (The horse was Wilkinson's, just made ready to carry him back to Gates' camp.) One of Harcourt's dragoons sounded a trumpet, and the horsemen reassembled and rode off as quickly as they had arrived. It was ten to fifteen minutes from the time the dragoons were spotted racing toward the tavern until they rode off with Lee as their captive. The British horsemen avoided rebel patrols and safely returned to the British outpost at Hillsborough. Lee was sent first to Cornwallis' headquarters at Penny Town and then to New Brunswick.[1]

Bradford, who had narrowly escaped, raced with the news of Lee's capture to Sullivan, the former New Hampshire lawyer who was Lee's second-in-command. He found Sullivan at noon marching with the troops eight miles from Vealtown. Wilkinson, another escapee, also reported to Sullivan before riding back to Gates and delivering Lee's letter.[2] Sullivan tried to intercept Harcourt's dragoons but was too late. They had too great a lead and the rebels had no information on their route.[3]

---

[1]This account of Lee's capture is based on the eyewitness accounts of Banastre Tarleton, a dragoon officer who participated in the raid, and of Wilkinson, who was with Lee but got away. Both accounts are in Commager and Morris, *Spirit of 'Seventy-Six*, 501-504. Lieutenant Colonel William Harcourt received the thanks of Parliament and was made a king's aide-de-camp as a reward for his exploit.

[2]Wilkinson says he rode to Sullivan's column immediately following Lee's capture. He provided some interesting detail in his autobiography: "So soon as Lieutenant-colonel Harcourt retreated with his prize, I repaired to the stable, mounted the first horse I could find, and rode full speed to General Sullivan, whom I found under march toward Pluckamin [a village west of Vealtown]. I had not examined General Lee's letter [the letter Lee had written to Gates just before his capture] but believing a knowledge of the contents might be useful to General Sullivan, who succeeded him in command, I handed it to him, who after perusal, returned it with his thanks, and advised me to rejoin General Gates without delay, which I did the next morning at Sussex court-house, whither he had led the troops from Van Kempt's." James Wilkinson, *Memoirs of My Own Times* (Philadelphia: Abraham Small, 1816), I: 111.

[3]Sullivan had few horse available to attempt a rescue. A "Return of the Forces under the command of General Lee, November 24th, 1776" listed 102 light-horse present and fit for duty. Force, ed., *American Archives*, Fifth Series, III: 831. These troopers were part of the Connecticut Light Horse. Lesser, *Sinews of Independence*, 41. However, these troopers may not have accompanied Lee's division into New Jersey, and Sullivan probably organized a small scratch group of mounted soldiers, whom he sent unsuccessfully after Harcourt's seasoned dragoons.

Now in charge of Lee's brigade, Sullivan immediately ordered the troops to march to the Delaware. Sullivan was in a hurry to reach the relative safety of Pennsylvania as he feared enemy attack as they marched across New Jersey. The column spent the night of December 14 in Germantown, New Jersey (modern Oldwick), and December 15 at Potters Town (Potterstown). There was a scare in the camp the following morning as word circulated of a British attempt to surround the brigade. Sullivan's men quickly loaded up their wagons and marched off. In fact, the command never made contact with the enemy, but the troops were on edge for most of the march.

Moving toward the Delaware, officers knew that boats were waiting for them at Alexandria. But, probably fearing an enemy attack if he moved southwest toward there, Sullivan instead marched due west to the ferry at Philipsburg. His troops crossed the river on the night of December 16.[1]

As Sullivan took his brigade west, Wilkinson returned to Gates' camp and reported Lee's capture. "Major Wilkinson returned from Genl Lee's army," Chaplain David Avery wrote, and brought "tidings that yesterday morning about 70 of the light horse came upon Genl Lee and took him prisoner and a French Colonel."[2] Upon receiving the news, Gates resumed his march to reinforce the Grand Army. On December 15, his exhausted troops crossed the Delaware twenty miles above Easton; they then marched to the Moravian settlement at Bethlehem, Pennsylvania, where a military hospital had been established. There they rested a few days before resuming their trek. They were joined on December 18 at Bethlehem by what was left of Sullivan's division. Gates and his troops pushed on from Bethlehem on December 20 and arrived at Washington's camp on December 22. Elements of Sullivan's division staggered into camp on December 20, 21, and 22.[3] For all concerned, it had been a bitter and difficult trek.

Lieutenant Joseph Hodgkins marched across New Jersey with Lee's division. As he neared Washington's camp, he wrote his wife that "tho we are Very Much fatagued with a long march we have Ben [been] on the march ever since ye 29 of Last month and we are now within 10 or 12 miles of general

---

[1]Rau., ed., *Sergeant Smith's Diary*, 265.

[2]"Avery Diary," Dec. 14, 1776.

[3]Rau, ed., *Sergeant Smith's Diary*, 266; Dexter, ed., *Diary of Ezra Stiles*, 106; Washington to Robert Morris, Dec. 22, 1776, Fitzpatrick, ed., *Writings of Washington*, VI: 420-421.

Washingtons Army we Expect to Be there to night But how long we shall stay there I Cant tell neither Can I tell you much about the Enemy only that they are on one side of the Dilleway River and our army on the other about 20 miles from Philadelphia." He noted the troops crossing the river "Last Sunday 40 or 50 miles above head Quarters on account of the Enemys Trying to intercept our Crosing" and recalled the perilous times of the last several weeks. "We have Marched since we came from Phillips Manner about 200 miles the gratest Part of the way whas Dangrus By Reason of the Enemy being near & not only so But the Contry is full of them Cursed Creatures called Torys." He longed for home, but warned that travel would be difficult. The weather had turned bad, and he could only send his assurance that he remained her "most afectionate Companion Till Death."[1]

Having finished their long march, neither Gates nor Arnold took part in Washington's Christmas night raid on Trenton. Complaining of illness, Gates went to Philadelphia on December 23. Arnold was ordered by Washington to proceed to Rhode Island, to help organize defenses there. The reinforcements that Gates brought from the Northern Department were reorganized under the command of General Arthur St. Clair. Renamed St. Clair's Brigade, they took part in the Christmas night raid on Trenton. The unit had an effective strength of about five hundred men.[2]

What happened to Charles Lee? Following his capture near Basking Ridge, he was held prisoner in New York City. Despite initial threats that he would be tried as a traitor, eventually Lee was well-treated by his captors and exchanged for a British officer in the late spring of 1778. Back with the American army, Lee had few friends among intimates of the commander-in-chief. He also frowned on Washington's efforts to train the Continental Army on the professional European model. Still, Washington allowed Lee to command the American vanguard at the Battle of Monmouth on June 28,

---

[1]Joseph Hodgkins to Sarah Hodgkins, Dec. 20, 1776, in Herbert T. Wade and Robert A. Lively, eds., *This Glorious Cause: The Adventures of Two Company Officers in Washington's Army* (Princeton: Princeton University Press, 1958), 227-228.   Joseph Hodgkins was a company officer in the 12th Continental Regiment (Massachusetts) in late 1776.

[2]St. Clair left Fort Ticonderoga in mid-November with three regiments from the Northern Army whose enlistments had expired. He linked up with Gates somewhere en route, perhaps with some of his soldiers who agreed to stay on. William Smith, *The Life and Public Service of Arthur St. Clair* (Cincinnati: Robert Clarke & Co., 1882), 28, 378. Stryker, *Battle of Trenton*, 354.

1778. Questions over his conduct that day led to a confrontation with Washington and a controversial court-martial, which finally resulted in Lee's dismissal from the army. It was the end of an interesting if tumultuous military career.

Lee died in Philadelphia on October 2, 1782, at the age of fifty-one. Always ascerbic and argumentative, Lee was in good form to the end. "I desire most earnestly," he wrote in his will, "that I may not be buried in any church or churchyard, or within a mile of any Presbyterian or Anabapist meeting-house; for, since I have resided in this country, I have kept so much bad company when living, that I do not choose to continue it when dead."[1]

Who knows what Lee planned if he had escaped capture at the Widow White's tavern in Basking Ridge? Lee was a volatile personality, and fate's stepping in to remove him from the scene is one of the great ironies of American history. Historian James Flexner thought that Lee's conduct on the New Jersey retreat was mutinous.[2] That is too strong a word. The general was less than enthusiastic about abandoning New Jersey, but if he was balky, he was not completely insubordinate. Perhaps he hoped to strike an isolated British outpost on his way out of the state, but no one will ever know. The intrepid Colonel Harcourt saw to that.

---

[1] Alden, *General Charles Lee*, 299.

[2] James Flexner, *George Washington in the American Revolution* (Boston: Little Brown and Company, 1967), 156.

CHAPTER NINE

The Delaware River

The reasons why general Howe did not sooner overtake the distressed fugitives, or why he cantoned his troops, without crossing the river and taking possession of the city of Philadelphia, remains yet to be investigated.
—Mercy Otis Warren (1805)[1]

To the British, the American rebellion seemed on the verge of collapse in mid-December 1776. Crown forces were in possession of New York City, Newport, Rhode Island, and much of New Jersey. Many New Jersey citizens had accepted General Howe's pardon, and hundreds of Loyalists were enlisting in Provincial Regiments. The New Jersey legislature fled before the enemy advance, moving from Princeton to Burlington to Pittstown and finally to Haddonfield. There, on the edge of New Jersey with no where else to go, legislators voted to dissolve on December 2. Members were advised to find someplace to hide. Fearing the capture of Philadelphia, the Continental Congress abandoned the city on the night of December 12. It left behind Generals Israel Putnam and Thomas Mifflin to govern the city under martial law, and granted Washington the power to direct the war on his own.[2] The

---

[1]Mercy Otis Warren, *History of the Rise, Progress and Termination of the American Revolution* (Boston: Manning and Loring, for E. Larkin, 1805), I: 335-336. Warren was the wife of the Governor of Massachusetts during the Revolution.

[2]A good summary of the situation in Philadelphia is in Benson Lossing, *The Pictorial Field-Book of the Revolution* (New York, 1855), II: 18. The Continental Congress granted Washington "full power to order and direct all things relative to the department,

delegates fled to Baltimore, and the news of their departure added to the panic in Philadelphia. Everything seemed to be falling apart.

The military situation remained bleak. General Lee was a prisoner of war and the Northern army, based at Fort Ticonderoga, was in deplorable shape. Some of the eight regiments Washington ordered to join him from Ticonderoga were marching across New Jersey under Gates; but illness and desertions had diminished them. Of the approximately twelve hundred who left Ticonderoga on December 2, only some six hundred stumbled into New Jersey on December 11. Washington privately expressed his desperation in an often-quoted letter to his brother, Lund. "Your imagination can scarce extend to a situation more distressing than mine," he wrote on December 17. "Our only dependence now is upon the speedy enlistment of a new army. If this fails, I think the game will be pretty well up, as, from disaffection and want of spirit and fortitude, the inhabitants, instead of resistance, are offering submission and taking protection from Gen. Howe in Jersey."[1]

Yet there were some encouraging signs. The army still existed. Although the Grand Army lay exhausted and freezing along 70 miles of the Delaware River, it remained in the field and defended Philadelphia. On paper, Washington had a force of 11,500, but more likely he had an effective force of 7,500. This included 1,500 inexperienced Pennsylvania militiamen under Colonel John Cadwalader and 400 soldiers from the newly established German brigade commanded by Colonel Nicholas Haussegger. Thus, if they were considerably the worse for the recent campaign, and if many of their reinforcements were untried, the rebels soldiers were still a force to reckon with; Howe had misjudged their staying power.

There was also an American buildup in northern New Jersey. The village of Morristown, an important agricultural region behind a range of protective hills, had become a gathering place for patriot resistance. It was near the newly established enemy cantonments at New Brunswick, Newark,

---

and to the operations of war." *Journal of the Continental Congress*, VI: 1024-1027; Washington to the President of Congress, Dec. 20, 1776; Fitzpatrick, ed., *Writings of Washington*, VI: 402. Washington was ill at ease with the grant of dictatorial powers, however temporary. Charles Lee, however, may have had fewer doubts. He wrote Congressman Benjamin Rush recommending the need for a military dictator and volunteering for the position, claiming that much could still be done. "Had I the powers I could do you much good," he assured Rush, "might I but dictate one week--but I am sure you will never give any man the necessary power." Lee to Rush, Nov. 20, 1776. *Lee Papers*, II: 288-289.

[1]Fitzpatrick, ed., *Writings of Washington*, VI: 347.

and Elizabeth, all of which were potential targets. By the middle of December, several American forces had passed through the Morristown area. None, however, had stopped long enough to assist or encourage the militia gathering there. On December 11, Lee's corps found a considerable militia force as they arrived in the town. Lee may have directed a few small raids at British parties to the south, but he soon continued his march, leaving the militia on their own.[1] So did General Gates, when he passed nearby with his four skeleton regiments on the way to reinforcing Washington. Worried about a British strike in their direction, yet willing to fight, the lack of Continental leadership was a matter of real concern among local militia officers.

The situation soon improved. On December 14, General Alexander McDougall, one of Lee's brigade commanders, arrived in town. Left at Haverstraw, New York, with severe rheumatism, he recovered sufficiently after eight days and tried to catch up with Lee. Reaching Morristown, he learned of Lee's capture and decided not to continue his journey unescorted. Hearing that three patriot regiments were nearing Morristown en route to Washington, he decided to travel under their protection.[2] The arriving Continental regiments hailed from Massachusetts: Greaton's (designated the 24th Continentals), Bond's (25th Continentals), and Elisha Porter's militia regiment, totaling 520 men. They were commanded by Lt. Colonel Joseph Vose.[3] They marched into Morristown during the evening of December 17.

Meanwhile, a few miles to the east, there had been fierce fighting between rebel militia and British regulars. It started when Howe learned of militia activity at Chatham. He dispatched General Alexander Leslie with eight hundred men from Elizabethtown to rout the Americans; on December 17,

---

[1]Lee informed Washington of finding a strong militia force in Morristown in a letter sent *via* Colonel Humpton, whom Washington had dispatched from Pennsylvania to establish the whereabouts of Lee. Lee reported about a thousand militia around the village. *Lee Papers*, II: 336-337; Billias, ed., *George Washington's Generals*, 38.

[2]McDougall to Washington, Dec. 19, 1776, Force, ed., *American Archives*, Fifth Series, III: 1296-1297; Roger Champagne, *Alexander McDougall and the American Revolution in New York* (Schenectady: Union College Press, 1975), 119-120.

[3]Troop returns for these regiments are in Lesser, ed., *The Sinews of Independence*, 38; and McDougall to General William Heath, Dec. 17, 1776, Force, ed., *American Archives*, Fifth Series, III: 1260. Vose's three regiments departed Fort Ticonderoga on Nov. 18; *ibid.*, 878. For Vose, see Francis Heitman, *Historical Register of Officers of the Continental Army* (Washington D.C.: Rare Book Shop Publishing Company, Inc., 1914), 561.

Leslie's troops clashed with the Eastern Battalion of Morris County Militia, commanded by Colonel Jacob Ford, Jr. The fighting took place near Bryant's Tavern, about three miles east of Chatham. The action broke off at dusk, but renewed battle was expected the following day.[1] During the night of December 17, the militia officers and "principal gentlemen" pleaded with McDougall to order Vose to stay with the militia. Without clear authority, McDougall nevertheless boldly did so. "I have ventured to advise Colonel Vose to remain in this State," he explained to Washington, "and shall post his troops, with the Militia, in the best manner to cover the country not in the hands of the enemy."[2] Vose's troops started marching toward Chatham and the expected fighting early on December 18, but General Leslie broke off and retired towards Spank-Town (between Rahway and Westfield).[3]

Encouraged by the situation, and recognizing McDougall's continued poor health, on December 21 Washington sent Brigadier General William Maxwell to Morristown. Commanding Vose's regiments, plus the militia under Colonel Ford, Maxwell was to open active operations. Washington wanted him to protect the region as best he could while "harassing" the enemy "in their Quarters" and hitting "their Convoys."[4] By the end of December, this series of events had established Morristown as a secure military base for the rebels. It was a development that would soon pay handsome dividends.

Washington also acted on another front. By December 7, he was convinced that Howe would not send part of his army to harass New England. He also knew the British fleet had sailed for Rhode Island. He therefore

---

[1] White, *A Village at War*, 78-79.

[2] McDougall to Washington, Dec. 19, 1776, in Force, ed., *American Archives*, Fifth Series, III: 1296-1297. Washington wrote to approve McDougall's action on Dec. 21. Fitzpatrick, ed., *Writings of Washington*, VI: 419.

[3] McDougall to Washington, Chatham, December 19, 1776, in Force, ed., *American Archives*, Fifth Series, III: 1296-1297.

[4] Fitzpatrick, ed., *Writings of Washington*, VI: 415. Maxwell (1733-1796) was born in Ireland and emigrated to western New Jersey with his parents when he was a teenager. Maxwell was a veteran of the French and Indian War and commanded the 2nd New Jersey Regiment in the Northern Army until that regiment was disbanded in late November 1776.

ordered Heath's Continental troops to leave Peekskill, New York, and march across northern New Jersey to reinforce the Grand Army in Pennsylvania.[1]

Heath crossed the Hudson on December 10 and learned that New Bridge, near Hackensack, was the northernmost Crown garrison. However, much of Bergen County was controlled by the British-armed Loyalist 4th Battalion of New Jersey Volunteers. The Tory troops were plundering local Whigs, and Heath decided to halt his march long enough to restore order. On December 13, Heath sent a reconnaissance party towards Hackensack and raided the town on the 14th. There were only five British soldiers guarding Hackensack, but considerable stores had been collected there for the use of the Loyalists. Heath seized them and carted off the booty to his camp at Paramus. On December 19, Heath was joined by a number of New York militia under General George Clinton. A mixed force of five hundred Continentals and New Yorkers then attacked a Loyalist camp in the vicinity of Bergen Woods (the area between modern Hoboken and Fort Lee) and captured a picket guard of sixteen men from the 4th Battalion of New Jersey Volunteers.

Worried about Heath's activities, the British began maneuvering and reinforcing their eastern New Jersey cantonments. Washington approved of Heath's activities, and he stayed in northern New Jersey until December 23. At that point, under pressure from the New York legislature to defend Westchester County, Heath recrossed the Hudson and returned to Peekskill.[2] The withdrawal forced Clinton to return to New York state with his militia.

Meanwhile, Washington had not been idle on the Delaware. From his headquarters in Newtown, Pennsylvania, he sent raiding parties back into New Jersey and encouraged the local militia. By mid-December, 1776, Washington and other officers were engaging the enemy in New Jersey on a number of fronts. The initial shock of the invasion had worn off, and the rebels were actively probing for weak points along Howe's lines and making life dangerous for small enemy detachments. Yet the significance of this activity seemingly escaped the British commander-in-chief.

Many of Howe's junior officers, however, were concerned at how dangerous the situation had become. "It is now very unsafe for us to travel in Jersey," a Hessian officer noted. "The rascal peasants meet our men alone or

---

[1]Washington to Heath, Dec. 7, 1776, Fitzpatrick, ed., *Writings of Washington*, VI: 335.

[2]There is a detailed account of Heath's activities in New Jersey in *Heath's Memoirs*, 99-103; see also Lundin, *Cockpit of the Revolution*, 182-183.

in small unarmed groups. They have their rifles hidden in the bushes, or ditches, and the like. When they believe they are sure of success and they see one or several men belonging to our army, they shoot them in the head, then quickly hide their rifles and pretend they know nothing."[1]   Colonel Rall, commanding at Trenton, the most exposed and dangerous Crown position in New Jersey, wrote that he needed major forces just to get letters safely from Trenton to Princeton. "Yesterday I sent two dragoons to Princeton with letters," he complained. "They were not gone over an hour when one of them came back and reported that the other soldier had been killed and his own horse had been shot by a concealed enemy." He then "sent immediately one Captain with one hundred men and one piece of artillery to Princeton and asked again of General Leslie to place some troops at Maidenhead."[2] For a supposedly beaten force, the rebels had become troublesome indeed.

Howe had failed to land a knock-out blow, and as December drew to a close, a number of factors worked to restore patriot fortunes. The British failure to advance across the Delaware allowed Washington time not only to gather reinforcements, but to assess intelligence on the enemy. Howe's scattered and isolated posts were obvious attractions. As early as December 14, Washington was looking for an opening for a counter-attack involving Lee, Gates, and Heath. He wanted "to attempt a Stroke upon the Forces of the Enemy, who lay a good deal scattered and to all appearance in a state of Security. A lucky Blow in this Quarter," he wrote to Governor Jonathan Trumbull of Connecticut, "would be fatal to them, and would most certainly raise the Spirits of the People, which are quite sunk by our late misfortunes."[3]

Washington struck the "lucky Blow" on December 25, 1776. The Battle of Trenton resounded through the rest of the war and into legend. He and his troops made their famous Delaware crossing in the cold darkness of Christmas night and then, at dawn on December 26, surprised and routed

---

[1] Kippling and Smith, eds., *At Howe's Side*, 7.

[2] William S. Stryker, *The Battles of Trenton and Princeton* (New York: Houghton, Mifflin & Co., 1898), 331. Rall wrote this letter on December 21.

[3] Fitzpatrick, ed., *Writings of Washington*, VI: 366.   Dec. 14, 1776 is the earliest date that General Washington wrote about a counter-attack on the enemy in New Jersey. He also wrote Major General Horatio Gates on Dec. 14 with the idea of attacking the enemy in New Jersey: "If we can draw our forces together, I trust, under the smiles of providence, we may yet effect an important stroke, or at least prevent Genl. Howe from executing his plans." *Ibid.*, 372.

Colonel Rall and his three Hessian regiments.

News of the affair created a sensation among the British. Captain von Muenchhausen was at headquarters in New York City, and had just finished writing a letter home on December 26 when the first sketchy news of the American attack arrived. He mournfully added a postscript: "I have reopened this letter to report an unhappy affair. Colonel Rall, who was at Trenton with the Knyphausen, Lossberg, and Rall regiments and 50 jaegers, was compelled to surrender at dawn on the 26th, after a fight of one hour, owing partly to the suddenness of the enemy surprise....We know no further details at the moment."[1] Subsequent details were stunning. It appeared that Rall, who had looked with such contempt on the rebels, had failed to take adequate precautions to protect against surprise.[2] He paid the price: Rall, who had shown great bravery in the assault on Fort Washington, was among about 30 Hessians killed in action.[3] An estimated 919 enemy troops were captured, along with six brass cannon and 1,000 muskets. Washington quickly gathered his captives and booty and went back across the Delaware to safety.

But Washington's Christmas-night raid proved only the start of a rebel counter-offensive. Encouraged by the uprising of militia following the raid, Washington returned to Trenton on December 30 as a big enemy force advanced against him under the command of Cornwallis.[4] After several forced marches, Cornwallis arrived at Trenton on the night of January 2, 1777 to find Washington's army in a good defensive position. With his troops exhausted and night approaching, Cornwallis decided to postpone his attack until the next day, proclaiming that he would "bag the fox" in the morning.

During the night, Washington indeed showed the cunning of a fox: he ordered campfires to be kept burning and left a few men behind to march

---

[1]Kipping and Smith, eds., *At General Howe's Side*, 8.

[2]Stephen Kemble, adjutant to General Howe, summed up the problems at Trenton in an entry in his private journal at the end of 1776: "Why Post so small Detachments as to be in danger of Insult, as happened in Rall's Affair, upon the Frontiers of your Line of Communication, or why put Hessians at the advanced Posts, particularly the Man at Trentown, who was Noisy, but not sullen, unacquainted with the Language, and a Drunkard?" *The Kemble Papers*, 105.

[3]Fitzpatrick, ed., *Writings of Washington*, VI: 447.

[4]Cornwallis had planned to winter in England; he was scheduled to sail on HMS *Bristol* from New York on Dec. 27. Upon Rall's defeat at Trenton, Howe ordered Cornwallis to resume command immediately in New Jersey.

constantly in front of the blazes, making plenty of noise. He then had the wheels of his cannons wrapped in rags to muffle noise and silently marched his army on a remote farm road towards Princeton, passing within three miles of twelve hundred British sleeping at Maidenhead. The patriots emerged at Princeton the following morning (January 3, 1777) to surprise three regiments left there by Cornwallis. The Battle of Princeton ended with the surrender of hundreds of British who had barricaded themselves in Nassau Hall.[1]

At Trenton, Cornwallis was readying his assault on the seemingly-bustling rebel camp when he heard the sound of artillery from the direction of Princeton. Realizing he had been tricked, the British general raced back down the high road. But by the time he arrived at Princeton, Washington had retreated into the Millstone Valley towards his stronghold at Morristown.

Sometimes victory and success burst forth with stunning suddenness. Washington's Trenton-Princeton campaign was, simply, one of the most daring in the history of American arms. In ten days (December 25, 1776 to January 3, 1777), Washington reversed the course of the American Revolution and regained his prestige and stature. "This is an important period to America, big with great events," Nathanael Greene wrote to his wife following the Battle of Trenton. "God only knows what will be the issue of this Campaign, but everything wears a much better prospect than they have for some weeks past."[2] Greene wrote from experience. He had seen the worst of the "long retreat," and now he had seen the spirit of the Revolution restored at a stroke.

---

[1] Boatner, *Encyclopedia of the American Revolution*, 617. Washington's celebrated deception did not impress Sir Henry Clinton. Clinton was convinced that the Americans had escaped solely through the negligence of Cornwallis, who had been duped by an elementary ruse. Clinton claimed that he personally tried to cover up Cornwallis' enormous blunder because he did not want to expose "the most consummate ignorance I ever heard of [in] any officer above a corporal." Wilcox, ed., *Sir Henry Clinton's Narrative*, 60n.

The enemy troops surprised at Princeton were the bulk of the British 4th brigade (under Lt. Colonel Charles Mawhood), consisting of three regiments: 17th, 40th and 55th, plus some mounted and dismounted dragoons of the 16th regiment. David Ramsey gave this account of the incident at Nassau Hall: "A party of the British fled into the college and were there attacked with field pieces which were fired into it. The seat of the muses became for some time the scene of action. The party which had taken refuge in the college, after receiving a few discharges from the American field pieces came out and surrendered themselves prisoners of war." Ramsey, *History of the American Revolution*, I: 412.

[2] Greene to Catharine Greene, Dec. 30, 1776, Showman, ed., *The Papers of General Nathanael Greene*, I: 377.

CHAPTER TEN

Assessment and Epilogue

It is great credit to us, that, with an handful of men, we sustained
an orderly retreat for near an hundred miles, brought off our
ammunition, all our field-pieces, the greatest part of our stores,
and had four rivers to pass.
—Thomas Paine, *The American Crisis*[1]

Following the Battle of Princeton, General Howe abandoned his
advance posts and withdrew to the eastern half of central New Jersey. The
British also gave up Elizabethtown and Woodbridge. New Brunswick and
Perth Amboy were their principal cantonments for the balance of the winter of
1776-1777. British and Hessian soldiers often pillaged with a free hand, and
damage to the occupied towns and to the surrounding countryside and villages
was often severe. Then, in early summer of 1777, the fortunes of war changed
and Howe pulled out almost completely; the only posts the British held in the
state for any length of time were small forts at Paulus Hook (modern Jersey
City) and Sandy Hook. New Jersey was redeemed.

Long before Howe's withdrawal, however, and even before
Washington's raid on Trenton, whispers of criticism swirled about the British
commander's generalship in the New Jersey campaign. Captain Johann Ewald,
the Hessian Jaeger officer, had plenty of time to think about it while he

---

[1]Thomas Paine, *The American Crisis--Number One*, in Eric Foner, ed., *Paine,
Collected Writings* (New York: The Library of America, 1995), 98. The four rivers were
the Hackensack, Passaic, Raritan,, and Delaware.

languished at New Brunswick in early December 1776. "Why did we let the corps of five to six thousand men withdraw so quietly from Fort Lee," he asked? "Secondly, why did we tarry so many days until the enemy had peacefully crossed the Second River [Passaic River]? Thirdly, why did we march so slowly that the enemy could cross the Raritan safely?" Finally, he wanted to know "why did we not pursue the enemy at once, instead of lingering here [New Brunswick] for five days?"[1] Ewald was a good soldier, and he was frankly bewildered at Washington's escape.

The explanation was not simple. Part of it involved Howe's intentions when he invaded New Jersey. His objectives, which he had not shared with Ewald or other junior officers, were strictly limited. His first goal was to eliminate Fort Lee to give the Royal Navy unhampered navigation of the lower Hudson River. His second goal was to secure winter quarters for part of his army. Howe never thought of defeating Washington's main army, nor did he ever think seriously about seizing Philadelphia. Howe's best biographer, Troyer Anderson, has emphasized this point. "When everything has been considered," Anderson noted, "it appears that the New Jersey campaign has been somewhat misunderstood." It was not Howe's original intention to bring Washington to a showdown battle or to destroy the rebel army. The effort to catch the patriot army began in earnest only after the initial successes at Fort Lee showed how vulnerable the Continental and militia units actually were.[2]

Even then, Howe pursued within the predictable and deliberate context of eighteen-century warfare. The advance was no *blitzkrieg*. At the time of the American Revolution, logistical problems prevented armies from fighting for extended periods. Howe had been in the field since August, and in action a good deal of the time. Operations had been costly in supplies, food, forage, and equipment; with a supply line that extended 3,000 miles from England, the general required 37 tons of food and 38 tons of fodder each day to feed 35,000 men and 4,000 horses.[3] Howe needed to resupply and reorganize, and the military norms of the day argued for an end to the campaign, not an all-out effort to crush an opponent late in the season. Even Howe's seemingly poor decision to winter the army in dispersed garrisons was

---

[1]Ewald, *Diary of the American War*, 25.

[2]Anderson, *The Command of the Howe Brothers*, 208-209.

[3]Douglas W. Marshall and Howard Peckham, *Campaigns of the American Revolution* (Ann Arbor: University of Michigan Press, 1976), 34.

based largely on the need for the troops to supply themselves from local resources until spring.

Casualties were also a concern. Eighteenth-century battles could be murderous and trained soldiers were valuable. Howe was fighting far from home and soldiers lost to combat, disease, or desertion were not easily replaced. Fearful of serious losses, the general was reluctant to attack strong American positions, such as Harlem Heights or North Castle, especially after the brutal experience at Bunker Hill. Even at Fort Washington, where Howe ordered a frontal assault, he believed the rebels would abandon the fort before he had to attack.[1] An impetuous dash against Washington in New Jersey, or a bold effort to force the Delaware in the face of opposition--and American batteries on the Pennsylvania side had done some nasty work as lead British units had approached the river at Trenton--seemed only to invite needless casualties.

Another problem for Howe was his unusual dual role as warrior and peacemaker. William and Richard Howe may have had instructions, tacit if not written, to bring the Americans to terms by means short of destroying them in the field.[2] While there is no evidence that any such understanding induced General Howe to relinquish any tactical advantage, he understood that the war in America did not enjoy popular support in England. The Howe brothers probably did want to end the war through negotiations; had they done so, they would have sailed home as heroes.

Howe's strategy in 1776 was to soften the rebels by creating the impression of British invincibility and then bringing them to the treaty table. He did not want to harden rebel determination through brutality. He offered peace talks following the Battle of Long Island, and issued the proclamation of pardon after overrunning part of New Jersey. But Howe's velvet-glove failed. Much of the fault lay with his inability to control the behavior of the army. Pillage, wanton destruction, looting, and rape started soon after the British arrived in the state (and in America, for that matter) and bred hostility among the New Jersey population.[3] Atrocities and harassment turned many

---

[1]Henry P. Johnston, *The Campaign of 1776 Around New York and Brooklyn* (Brooklyn: The Long Island Historical Society, 1878), 282n.

[2]Fuller, *Battles of the Revolution*, 21.

[3]Based on their experience in Westchester County, New York prior to their assault on New Jersey, the British knew that there would be problems trying to restrain the enlisted men from looting and rape. Writing in his journal from Westchester on Nov.

neutrals into rebels. By mid-December 1776, the wave of anti-Crown fervor was so strong that some New Jersey partisans may have carried Howe's pardon, crushed in their pockets, as they fought back.

General Howe also failed to comprehend the ability of the Americans to rebuild their army. He beat the rebels in battle, but never destroyed their organization. He captured equipment, but never enough to deprive Washington of sufficient transport or artillery to move his forces and to support them with battery fire. The British drove off thousands of militia and captured General Lee; but they were unable to prevent reinforcements from reaching Washington (albeit in the nick of time), a resurgence of militia activity in December, or the continued march of Lee's troops under Sullivan. Had he remotely suspected the extent of patriot resilience, Howe indeed might have tried to destroy Washington's army when he had the opportunity in New Jersey. As it was, he had enough military skill to create the illusion of success and to hide the opportunities he let slip by in the name of peace or faith that the battered rebel armed forces would fall apart over the winter.

Some patriots were pleased enough with Howe. "It has been said, that we could not have chosen a better adversary than General Howe;" wrote Alexander Graydon, an American officer captured at Fort Washington, "and it is not improbable that one more enterprising and less methodical, might have pushed us harder." Howe was not untalented, Graydon thought, and he often fought skillfully; but he "often treated us with unnecessary respect." A more imaginative officer "might have meant to play us, as an angler plays a fish upon his hook."[1]   Howe was a competent officer in a situation that required an outstanding soldier and statesman.

Under the circumstances, it seems that Washington did a better job than Howe of defining and solving problems. Some historians, however, have disagreed with this assessment, arguing that the patriot Commander-in-Chief grew increasingly unsure of himself over the course of the New Jersey retreat. One of Washington's greatest biographers, Douglas Southall Freemen, thought that the general's judgement became "clouded" and hesitant. John Shy

---

7, 1776, Major Stephen Kemble, a native of New Brunswick, New Jersey, summed up the problem: "8 or 10 of our People taken Marauding; Scandalous behavior for British Troops; and the Hessians Outrageously Licentious, and Cruel to such a degree as to threaten with death all such as dare obstruct them in their depredations. Violence to Officers frequently used, and every Degree of Insolence offered. Shudder for Jersey, the Army being thought to move there Shortly; think it very probable." *Kemble Journal*, 98.

[1]Littell, ed., *Alexander Graydon, Memoirs of His Own Time*, 214-215.

has suggested that Washington was probably plagued with self-doubt during the retreat.[1] Was Washington so exhausted by November 1776 that he was indecisive to the point of incompetence? Certainly he dithered over Fort Washington, and with disastrous consequences, and he was disturbingly lax in his failure to issue Lee a direct order to reinforce the Grand Army after the British invaded New Jersey. Yet these events, however important, were incidents, not the complete picture.

In the final analysis, Washington was a cunning and dangerous adversary. The British army never came close to catching up with him in New Jersey. Washington paced his retreat to match his opponents' advance. Even though Washington was crippled by the loss of the Fort Washington garrison and Lee's recalcitrance, it was extraordinary that when he reached Trenton on December 3, he quickly ferried his baggage to safety in Pennsylvania and started back toward Princeton with three thousand men; he was looking for a fight with an enemy estimated at ten thousand. This daring was combined with prudent planning. As the military situation unfolded in late 1776, Washington diverted Continental regiments to Morristown to encourage the militia and build a strong base of operations. His own units, if thin, were operational. The troops, if hungry, still had food; his cannon had ammunition and his horses had fodder. Washington was able to manage resources in adversity, and that fact alone made him a respectable foe. Desperation made him dangerous. There is some irony in British worries over Lee in late 1776; it was Washington who bore watching.

The New Jersey retreat was one of Washington's most notable military exploits. As Thomas Paine wrote in *The American Crisis*, the events of late 1776 became a trial of Washington's soul. The retreat took Washington not only down the muddy roads of towns such as Newark, New Brunswick, and Princeton, but also through the private thickets of his own fears and self-doubts. It was a trial that led to redemption for Washington and for the fragile hopes of an infant nation. The light of the Revolution's glory shines from many sources, but the road to eventual victory can be traced directly back to the path of Washington's long retreat through New Jersey.

---

[1]Freeman, *George Washington*, IV: 240; John Shy, "Charles Lee: The Soldier as Radical," in George Billias, ed., *George Washington's Generals* (New York: William Morrow and Company, 1964), 38-39.

BIBLIOGRAPHY

Primary Sources: Manuscripts

Avery, David. *Diary of Chaplain David Avery*. Microfilm edition of manuscript. Library, Princeton Theological Seminary, Princeton, New Jersey.

Glyn, Thomas. *Ensign Glyn's Journal on the American Service with the Detachment of 1,000 Men of the Guards Commanded by Brigadier General Mathew in 1776*. Bound original. Manuscript Division, Firestone Library, Special Collections, Princeton University, Princeton, New Jersey.

Hunter, Andrew. *Diary, 1776-1779*. Bound original. Manuscript Division, Firestone Library, Special Collections, Princeton University, Princeton, New Jersey.

William Van Vleek Lidgerwood Collection of Hessian Documents of the American Revolution. Fiche edition of transcripts. Morristown National Historical Park, Morristown, New Jersey.

Peale, Charles Willson. *Autobiography*. Undated manuscript, American Philosophical Society, Philadelphia.

Primary Sources: Books

Anderson, Captain Enoch. *Personal Recollections*. Edited by Henry Hobart Bellas. Wilmington: The Historical Society of Delaware, 1896.

Baurmeister, Carl L. *Revolution in America: Confidential Letters and Journals 1776-1784, of Adjutant General Major Baurmeister of the Hessian Forces*. Translated and edited by Bernhard A. Uhlendorf. New Brunswick, New Jersey: Rutgers University Press, 1957.

Burnaby, Andrew. *Travels Through the Middle Settlements in North America*. London, 1798.

Chastellux, Marquis de. *Travels in North America*. 2 vols. London, 1787.

Clinton, Sir Henry. *The American Rebellion*. Edited by William B. Wilcox. New Haven: Yale University Press, 1954.

Collins, Varnum Lansing, ed., *A Brief Narrative of the Ravages of the British and Hessians at Princeton in 1776-77*. Princeton: The University Library, 1906

Commager, Henry Steele, and Morris, Richard B., eds. *The Spirit of Seventy-Six*. New York: Bobbs- Merrill, 1958.

Cresswell, Nicholas. *The Journal of Nicholas Cresswell, 1774-1777*. New York: Dial Press, 1924.

Ewald, Johann. *Diary of the American War: A Hessian Journal*. Translated from the German, edited, and annotated by Joseph P. Tustin. New Haven: Yale University Press, 1979.

Force, Peter, ed. *American Archives: Fifth Series, Containing a Documentary History of the United States of America from the Declaration of Independence, July 4, 1776, to the Definitive Treaty of Peace with Great Britain, September 3, 1783*. 3 vols. Washington, D.C., 1848-1853.

Graydon, Alexander. *Memoirs of His Own Time*. Edited by John Stockton Littell. Philadelphia: Lindsay & Blakiston, 1846.

Greene, Nathanael. *The Papers of Nathanael Greene*. Edited by Richard K. Showman et al., eds, 8 vols. to date. Chapel Hill, North Carolina.: The University of North Carolina Press, 1976---.

Greenwood, John. *A Young Patriot in the American Revolution, 1775-1783*. Edited by Isaac J. Greenwood. Westvaco, 1981. Originally published as: *The Revolutionary Services of John Greenwood of Boston and New York, 1775-1783*. New York: De Vinne Press, 1922.

Hamilton, Alexander. *The Papers of Alexander Hamilton*. Edited by Harold C. Syrett and Jacob E. Cook, 26 vols. New York: Columbia University Press, 1961-1979.

Hamilton, Alexander. *The Itinerarium of Dr. Alexander Hamilton*, in Colonial *American Travel Narratives*. Edited by Wendy Martin. New York: Penguin Books, 1994.

Jones, Thomas. *History of New York during the Revolutionary War*. 2 vols. New York: New York Historical Society, 1879.

Journals of the Continental Congress 1774-1789. 34 vols. Edited by Worthington Chauncey Ford et al. Washington, D.C.: General Post Office, 1904-1937. Index published in 1976.

Kalm, Peter. *Travels In North America*. (1770; Reprint of the English edition). Edited by Adolph B. Benson. New York: Dover Publications, Inc., 1987.

Kemble, Stephen. *Journals of Lieutenant Colonel Stephen Kemble*. 2 vols. New York: New York Historical Society, 1883.

Lee, Charles. *The Lee Papers*. 4 vols. New York: The New York Historical Society, 1871-1874.

Lesser, Charles H. *The Sinews of Independence*. Chicago: The University of Chicago Press, 1976.

Livingston, William. *The Papers of William Livingston*. Edited by Carl E. Prince, vol. 1. Trenton: The New Jersey Historical Commission, 1979.

M'Robert, Patrick. *A Tour Through Part of the North Provinces of America*. Edinburgh, 1776.

Mackenzie, Frederick. *The Diary of Frederick Mackenzie*. 2 vols. Cambridge, Massachusetts: Harvard University Press, 1930.

Monroe, James. *Autobiography*. Edited by Stuart Gerry Brown with the assistance of Donald G. Baker. Syracuse: Syracuse University Press, 1959.

Muenchhausen, Captain Fredrich von. *At General Howe's Side 1776-1778*. Translated by Ernst Kipping and annotated by Samuel Steele Smith. Monmouth Beach, New Jersey: Philip Freneau Press, 1974.

Paine, Thomas. *Paine, Collected Writings*. Edited by Eric Foner. New York: The Library of America, 1995

Reed, Joseph. *The Life and Correspondence of Joseph Reed*, Edited by William B. Reed. 2 vols. Philadelphia: Lindsay and Blakiston, 1847.

Robertson, Archibald. *Diaries and Sketches in America.* Edited by Harry M. Lydenberg. New York: The New York Public Library, 1930.

Rush, Benjamin. *Autobiography.* Edited by George W. Corner. Princeton: Published for the American Philosophical Society by the Princeton University Press, 1948.

Serle, Ambrose. *The American Journal of Ambrose Serle, Secretary of Lord Howe, 1776-1778.* Edited by Edward H. Tatum, Jr. San Marino, California: Huntington Library, 1940.

Smith, Cap't George. *An Universal Military Dictionary.* London: Printed for J. Millan, 1779

Smith, Paul H. editor. *Letters of Delegates to Congress, 1774-1789.* 21 vols to date. Washington D.C: Library of Congress 1976-.

Stiles, Ezra. *The Literary Diary of Ezra Stiles.* Edited by Franklin Dexter. New York: Charles Scribner's Sons, 1901.

Stedman, Charles. *The History of the Origin, Progress, and Termination of the American War.* 2 vols. London, 1794.

Wade, Nathaniel and Hodgkins, Joseph. *This Glorious Cause..The Adventures of Two Company Officers in Washington's Army* [Diaries]. Edited by Herbert T. Wade and Robert A. Lively. Princeton: Princeton University Press, 1958.

Washington, George. *The Papers of George Washington.* Revolutionary War Series. 7 vols. to date. Edited by W.W. Abbot *et al.* Charlottesville: University Press of Virginia, 1985-.

Washington, George. *The Writings of George Washington from the Original Manuscript Sources 1745- 1799.* 39 vols. Edited by John C. Fitzpatrick. Washington, D.C.: Government Printing Office, 1931-1944.

Webb, Samuel Blachley. *Correspondence and Journals of.. 1772-1806.* Collected and Edited by Worthington Chauncey Ford. 3 vols. New York, 1893-94.

Wilkinson, James. *Memoirs of My Own Times.* 4 vols. Philadelphia: Abraham Small, 1816.

Primary Sources: Periodicals and Monographs

Bradford, William. "The Revolutionary Diary of a British Officer." *Maryland Historical Magazine,* XXVIII (March 1933).

"British and Hessian Accounts of the Invasion of Bergen County 1776." Edited by Major Donald M. Londahl-Smidt USAFR. *Bergen County History,* 1976 Annual.

Judd, Jacob. *Fort Lee on the Palisades: The Battle for the Hudson. A Historical Evaluation of Fort Lee.* Prepared for the Palisades Interstate Park Commission. 1963.

McCarty, Thomas. "The Revolutionary War Journal of Sergeant Thomas McCarty." Edited by Jared C. Lobdell. *Proceedings of the New Jersey Historical Society,* 82 (1964).

McMichael, James. "Diary of Lieutenant James McMichael, of the Pennsylvania Line, 1776-1778." *Pennsylvania Magazine of History and Biography*, XVI, No. 2 (1892).

Smith, John. "Sergeant John Smith's Diary of 1776." Edited by Louise Rau. *Mississippi Valley Historical Review*, 20 (June 1933 to March 1934).

Strike, Henry. "A British Officer's Revolutionary War Journal, 1776-1778." Edited by S. Sydney Bradford. *Maryland Historical Magazine*, 56 (June 1961).

White, Joseph. "An Narrative of Events, As They Occurred from Time to Time in the Revolutionary War; with an Account of the Battles of Trenton, Trenton-Bridge, and Princeton." Charlestown, Mass., 1833. In *American Heritage*, 4 (June 1956). Original in Library of Congress.

Secondary Sources: Books and Dissertations

Alden, John. *General Charles Lee, Traitor or Patriot?* Baton Rouge: Louisiana State University Press, 1951.

Anderson, Troyer Steele. *The Command of the Howe Brothers During the American Revolution*. New York-London: Oxford University Press, 1936.

Bedini, Silvio A. *Thomas Jefferson, Statesman of Science*. New York: Macmillian Publishing Company, 1990.

Benedict, William H., *New Brunswick in History*. New Brunswick: Published by the Author, 1925.

Bernstein, David. *New Jersey in the American Revolution*. Doctor of Philosophy diss., Rutgers University, 1969.

Bill, Alfred Hoyt. *A House Called Morven, Its Role in American History*. Princeton: Princeton University Press, 1954.

Bill, Alfred Hoyt. *New Jersey and the Revolutionary War*. Princeton: D. Van Nostrand Company, Inc., 1964.

Billias, George Athan, editor. *George WashingtonÕs Generals*. New York: William Morrow and Company, 1964

Blanco, Richard L. *The American Revolution-An Encyclopedia*. 2 vols. New York & London: Garland Publishing, Inc., 1993.

Boatner, Mark Mayo, III. *Encyclopedia of the American Revolution*. New York: David McKay Company, Inc., 1966.

Boatner, Mark Mayo, III. *Landmarks of the American Revolution*. Harrisburg, Pa.: Stackpole Books, 1973.

Carrington, Henry. *Battles of the American Revolution*. New York: A.S. Barnes & Company, 1877.

Champagne, Roger. *Alexander McDougall and the American Revolution in New York*. Schenectady: Union College Press, 1975

Fleming, Thomas. *1776 Year of Illusions*. New York: W.W. Norton & Company, Inc., 1975.

Ferling, John E. *The Loyalist Mind, Joseph Galloway and the American Revolution.* University Park, PA: The Pennsylvania State University Press, 1977.

Flexner, James Thomas. *The Young Hamilton.* Boston- Toronto: Little, Brown and Company, 1978.

Flexner, James Thomas. *George Washington in the American Revolution.* Boston-Toronto: Little, Brown and Company, 1967

Freeman, Douglas Southall. *George Washington : A Biography.* 7 vols. New York: Charles Scribner's Sons, 1948-1957.

Godfrey, Carlos E. *The Commander-In-Chief's Guard.* Washington, D.C.: Stevenson-Smith Company, 1904.

Gordon, William. *The History of the Rise, Progress & Establishment of the Independence of the United States of America: Including an Account of the Late War....* 3 vols. New York: Hodge, Allen and Campbell, 1789.

Hageman, John Frelinghuysen. *History of Princeton and its Institutions.* 2 vols. Philadelphia: J.B. Lippincott & Co., 1879

Heitman, Francis B. *Historical Register of the Continental Army.* Rev. ed. Washington, D.C.: The Rate Book Shop Publishing Co., 1914.

Heusser, Albert H. *In the Footsteps of Washington.* Paterson, New Jersey: privately printed, 1921.

Hine, C.G. *The Old Mine Road.* New Brunswick: Rutgers University Press, 1963.

Hull, Joan C. *New Jersey: A description Of Its Military and Supply Assistance to Washington and the Continental Army During the American Revolution.* Thesis, Master of Arts, Montclair State College, 1962.

Irving, Washington. *The Life of George Washington.* 5 vols. New York: G.P. Putnam, 1855-1859.

Jackson, John W. *The Pennsylvania Navy.* New Brunswick: Rutgers University Press, 1974.

Katcher, Philip. *Armies of the American Wars 1775-1815.* New York: Hastings House, 1975.

Ketchum, Richard M. *The Winter Soldiers.* Garden City, New York: Doubleday & Company, Inc., 1973.

Lane, Wheaton. *From Indian Trail to Iron Horse.* Princeton, New Jersey: Princeton University Press, 1939.

Lefferts, Charles. *Uniforms of the American, British, French and German Armies in the War of the American Revolution, 1775-1783.* New York: The New York Historical Society, 1926

Leiby, Adrian C. *The Revolutionary War in the Hackensack Valley.* New Brunswick, New Jersey: Rutgers University Press, 1962.

Lossing, Benson J. *Pictorial Field Book of the Revolution.* 2 vols. New York: Harper & Brothers, 1851-1855.

Lundin, Leonard. *Cockpit of the Revolution, The War for Independence in New Jersey.* Princeton, New Jersey: Princeton University Press, 1940.

Maclean, John. *History of the College of New Jersey*. Philadelphia: J.B. Lippincott & Co., 1877.

Marshall, Douglas W. and Peckham, Howard H. *Campaigns of the American Revolution*. Ann Arbor: University of Michigan Press, 1976.

Marshall, John. *The Life of George Washington*. 5 vols. London: Printed for Richard Philips by T. Gillet, 1804-1807.

Mallo, John & McGregor, Malcolm. *Uniforms of the American Revolution*. New York: Blandford Press Ltd., 1975.

Mintz, Max M. *The Generals of Saratoga*. New Haven: Yale University Press, 1990

Nelson, Paul David. *General Horatio Gates*. Baton Rouge: Louisiana State University Press, 1976.

Neumann, George C. *The History of Weapons of the American Revolution*. New York: Harper & Row, 1967.

Palmer, Dave Richard. *The Way of the Fox, American Strategy in the War for America, 1775-1783*. Westport, Connecticut:. Greenwood Press, 1975.

Ramsay, David. *The History of the American Revolution*. Philadelphia, 1793.

Richardson, Edward W. *Standards and Colors of the American Revolution*. The University of Pennsylvania Press, 1982.

Schachner, Nathan. *Alexander Hamilton*. New York: Appleton-Century Company, 1946.

Sellers, Charles Coleman. *Charles Willson Peale, Early Life*. Philadelphia: The American Philosophical Society, 1947

Sellers, John. *The Virginia Continental Line, 1775-1780*, Ph.D. diss., Tulane University, New Orleans, 1968.

Silverman, Kenneth. *A Cultural History of the American Revolution*. New York: Thomas Y. Crowell Company, 1976.

Smith, William. *The Life and Public Service of Arthur St. Clair*. Cincinnati: Robert Clarke & Co., 1882.

Stryker, William S. *The Battles of Trenton and Princeton*. Boston: The Riverside Press, 1898.

Studlet, Miriam V. *Historic New Jersey Through Visitors' Eyes*. Princeton, New Jersey: D. Van Nostrand Company, Inc., 1964.

UrQuhart, Frank J. *History of the City of Newark*. Newark, New Jersey: Lewis Historical Publishing Company, 1913.

Ward, Christopher L. *The Delaware Continentals 1776-1783*. Wilmington, Delaware, The Historical Society of Delaware, 1941.

Ward, Christopher L. *The War of the Revolution*. Edited by John Richard Alden. 2 vols. New York: The Macmillan Company, 1952.

Warren, Mercy Otis. *History of the Rise, Progress and Termination of the American Revolution*. 3 vols. Boston: Manning and Loring, for E. Larkin, 1805.

Wertenbaker, Thomas Jefferson. *Princeton 1746-1896*. Princeton: Princeton University Press, 1946.

White, Donald Wallace. *A Village at War,Chatham, New Jersey, and the American Revolution*. Rutherford, New Jersey: Fairleigh Dickinson University Press, 1979.

Woodward, Carl Raymond. *Ploughs and Politicks, Charles Read of New Jersey And His Notes on Agriculture, 1715-1774*. New Brunswick: Rutgers University Press, 1941.

Wright, Robert K., Jr. *The Continental Army*. Washington, D.C.: Center of Military History, 1989

Secondary Sources: Periodicals and Brochures

"Major Aldington." *Bergen County History*, 1970 Annual

Durnin, Richard. *George Washington in Middlesex County, New Jersey*. North Brunswick:. Middlesex County Cultural and Heritage Commission, 1989.

Glover, T.N. *The Retreat of 1776 Across Bergen County*. Bergen County Historical Society (1905).

Holst, Donald. *Regimental Colors of the Continental Army*. Military Collector & Historian, Fall, 1968.

Maxwell, Henry Dusenbery. *General William Maxwell*. New Jersey Society of the Cincinnati, 1900

Mosley, Virginia. "The Mystery of Polly Wyckoff." *The North Jersey Suburbanite* [newspaper], November 12, 1975.

Robinson, Walter F. *Old Bergen Township (Now Hudson County) in the American Revolution*. Bayonne, NJ: Bayonne Bicentennial Committee, 1978.

Sellers, Horace Wells. "Charles Willson Peale, Artist-Soldier." *Pennsylvania Magazine of History and Biography*, XXXVIII, No. 3 (1914).

Spring, John. "The 1776 British Landing at Closter." *Bergen County History*, 1975 Annual.

Vermeule, Cornelius. *Proceedings of the New Jersey Historical Society*, New Series, VI, No. 2 (1921); XIII (1928); LIV, No. 2 (1936).

INDEX

Printed in the United States
5316